COACHING
AND
MENTORING
FOR BUSINESS

To Tim, Fiona and Seán for their love, for the wonderful times we spend together, for listening and asking great questions.

GRACE McCARTHY

COACHING AND MENTORING FOR BUSINESS

⑤SAGE

Los Angeles | London | New Delhi
Singapore | Washington DC

Los Angeles | London | New Delhi
Singapore | Washington DC

SAGE Publications Ltd
1 Oliver's Yard
55 City Road
London EC1Y 1SP

SAGE Publications Inc.
2455 Teller Road
Thousand Oaks, California 91320

SAGE Publications India Pvt Ltd
B 1/I 1 Mohan Cooperative Industrial Area
Mathura Road
New Delhi 110 044

SAGE Publications Asia-Pacific Pte Ltd
3 Church Street
#10-04 Samsung Hub
Singapore 049483

Editor: Kirsty Smy
Editorial assistant: Nina Smith
Production editor: Katherine Haw
Copyeditor: Kate Harrison
Proofreader: Jill Birch
Indexer: Anne Fencott
Marketing manager: Alison Borg
Cover design: Francis Kenney
Typeset by: C&M Digitals (P) Ltd, Chennai, India
Printed in Great Britain by
CPI Group (UK) Ltd, Croydon, CR0 4YY

© Grace McCarthy 2014

First published 2014

Library of Congress Control Number: 2013947797

British Library Cataloguing in Publication data

A catalogue record for this book is available from
the British Library

ISBN 978-0-85702-335-3
ISBN 978-0-85702-336-0 (pbk)

CONTENTS

ABOUT THE AUTHOR

Dr Grace McCarthy is Associate Dean (Education) in the Faculty of Business, University of Wollongong, New South Wales, Australia. Following many years in industry, Grace now specialises in coaching, mentoring and education. Grace developed the Master of Business Coaching at the University of Wollongong, combining inputs from industry with academic research and the requirements of professional associations. Launched in 2008, the course attracts experienced internal and external coaches, human resource and other professionals from around Australia, each passionate about coaching and seeking to enhance their skills and understand the theoretical underpinnings of their practice. Grace is on the Editorial Board of the *International Journal of Evidence-Based Coaching and Mentoring* and reviews for this and other journals and conferences. In 2012, Grace was awarded an Australian Government Office of Learning and Teaching citation for 'Using a coaching approach to inspire a love of learning among students and colleagues'.

ACKNOWLEDGEMENTS

I wish to acknowledge my heart-felt gratitude to the students of the Master of Business Coaching at the University of Wollongong, whose passion for coaching inspired me to write this book. I am also delighted to acknowledge the vision of Professor John Glynn, Executive Dean of the Faculty of Business, University of Wollongong, who encouraged and helped me to develop the Master of Business Coaching in conjunction with industry practitioners. I acknowledge sincerely how much I have learned from my colleagues, Gordon, Julia, Pádraig, and Vanessa. I am also grateful to colleagues in other universities, in particular Deusto in Spain, and Oxford–Brookes, Sheffield–Hallam and York St. John in the UK. I have also enjoyed learning from those I have mentored over the years. Thank you to all of you for your generosity in sharing what you do, how you do it and how you think about life. I look forward to continuing to learn with you.

ABOUT THE COMPANION WEBSITE

Coaching and Mentoring for Business by Grace McCarthy is supported by a companion website.

Visit **www.sagepub.co.uk/mccarthy** to take advantage of the learning resources for students and lecturers.

For Lecturers

- PowerPoint slides for each chapter for use in class
- Lecturer's guide to in class activities and notes on self assessment

For Students

- Links to relevant websites
- Skills and Knowledge self assessments and quizzes

1

INTRODUCTION

Introduction

In today's business world, faced with the challenges of globalisation and the opportunities afforded by information and communication technology, there is an urgent need for organisations to be flexible, innovative and sustainable. To implement well-designed strategies and to cope with constant change require an engaged workforce, committed to the organisation for which they work. Coaching and mentoring offer practical ways to inspire employees to achieve both their personal goals and the goals of their organisations.

Research supports the effectiveness of coaching and mentoring in a wide range of contexts. Coaching and mentoring lead to improved performance and productivity, goal attainment, smoother transitions for new or recently promoted employees, gains in employee engagement and high returns on investment (Leimon et al. 2005; Parker-Wilkins 2006; Catling 2008; Grant et al. 2009; McCarthy and Milner 2013). Coaching and mentoring help clients to learn, to transfer their learning to the workplace, and to sustain changed behaviour (Olivero et al. 1997; Alred and Garvey 2000; Spencer 2011). A recent survey placed coaching and mentoring among the most effective talent management activities, with both coaching and mentoring increasingly integrated with organisational development and performance management activities to drive organisational change (CIPD 2012). These findings mirror those of a range of international reports. In the US, a report by the American Management Association (AMA 2008) identified a range of benefits relating to leadership development, individual and organisational performance improvements, addressing workplace problems and improving recruitment and retention, while a European report (EFMD 2009) also found improved performance and motivation.

Given these benefits, it is not surprising that many organisations are keen to implement coaching and mentoring, whether as interventions with individuals, as a program across all or parts of an organisation, or as a leadership style and way of working within an organisation. Even where organisations do not implement a specific program, many individual managers are keen to develop their coaching and mentoring skills. However, there continues to be confusion about the nature of coaching and mentoring, neither of which is subject to regulation. Many practitioners are self-taught or have only attended short training programs (McCarthy and Ahrens 2012).

The intention of this book is to focus on applications of coaching and mentoring in business, drawing on a rapidly increasing evidence base, and integrating coaching and mentoring theory and practice with business practices such as strategy, innovation and change management. Both coaching and mentoring are seen here as collaborative processes, in which one person works with others through dialogue to help them to enhance their self-awareness, to grow, to improve their performance, and to understand whether and how their personal goals and values align with those of the organisation for which they work. In coaching and mentoring for business, the focus is not only on the individual but also on the achievement of business objectives.

In this book, the term 'coach mentor' is used where the concept being discussed is common to both coaching and mentoring. Where the discussion relates to differences or specific research relating to one or the other, 'coach' or 'mentor' is used. 'Coachee' is a person being coached and a 'mentee' is a person being mentored. The term 'client' refers to any person being helped through coaching or mentoring, whether that person is within the same organisation or in a different organisation. 'Employee' is a person being coached or mentored by their manager.

This chapter explores similarities and differences between coaching and mentoring; summarises the commonly used purposes for coaching and mentoring; and looks at differences between internal and external forms of coaching and mentoring. It concludes with an outline of the organisation of the book.

Similarities and differences between coaching and mentoring

The terms 'coaching' and 'mentoring' are often used interchangeably (Hamlin and Sage 2011). Gray et al. (2011) confirmed previous research showing that coaching and mentoring are broadly similar. Although researchers and practitioners argue about distinctions in both purpose and application, coaching and mentoring use many of the same skills and are often used in similar contexts, overlapping in their shared purpose of development and/or performance improvement, achieved through dialogue in a trusting, collaborative relationship. Both coaching and mentoring are based on the fundamental belief that people can change, and that people make the best choices available to them (Connor and Pokora 2012). Eby and Lockwood (2005) reported that formal mentors provided coaching, advice, and help with career planning, but did not find evidence of the deep and long-lasting relationship characteristic of informal mentoring (Kram 1985). This suggests that formal mentoring and coaching may be more alike than formal and informal mentoring.

Common skills

Skills used by both coaches and mentors include listening, questioning, goal setting and feedback. Coach mentors establish a positive relationship to create an environment in which coaching or mentoring conversations can succeed. Success in coaching and mentoring is discussed in Chapter 12. Active listening is used by both coaches and mentors. Questions may be used by both coaches and mentors to clarify, challenge or re-frame. Feedback is often used by both coach and mentor to heighten the client's self-awareness. Skills are discussed in more detail in Chapter 3.

Differences

Despite the similarities, there are also differences. Gray et al. (2011) found that role modelling and career counselling were more important in mentoring, while business knowledge was more important in coaching. Some differences may only be seen in the case of some coaches or mentors, not all. For example, some mentors spend more time talking and share more of their own experience and knowledge than coaches. On the other hand, some coaches also share knowledge (Cavanagh and Grant 2010). Mentors may focus less than coaches on feedback for performance enhancement and more on development, but this again varies with individual coaches and mentors.

Directive versus non-directive

Whether mentoring is more or less directive than coaching is debatable. Directive versus non-directive form a continuum rather than a pair of polar opposites (Clutterbuck 2008). The purpose of the conversation and the needs of the client alter how directive the coach mentor is. For example, if a mentor is advising a protégé on how to progress within their organisation or if a coaching manager is sharing organisational goals, both coach and mentor may act more at the directive end of the spectrum. On the other hand, if a mentor is helping someone become aware of a wide range of options open to them or if a coach is helping someone identify options to address a work-related issue, the coach mentor is likely to be less directive. Authors such as Clutterbuck (2008) have drawn back from the strict non-directive approach advocated in earlier coaching literature. For example, Cunningham (2008) suggests that being totally non-directive can waste a client's time, if, for example, the coach is aware that relevant best practice has been identified elsewhere and could help the client if the information were shared with them. It is up to the client to decide whether to adapt and adopt the practice in his/her context. Coaching managers alternate between coaching and mentoring, and between being non-directive and directive in the same conversation, as shown in Vignette 1.1.

Vignette 1.1   He won't take advice

'David just won't take advice', complained David's manager Leo, to his own manager Tom.
'Oh', said Tom, 'what's the problem?'
'He never tells me he has a problem until he has to'.
'And what impact does that have?

(Continued)

(Continued)

'Mostly it's okay because he has it sorted by the time he tells me, but I feel like I'm not in control, when he tells me afterwards'.

'So you trust him to get things sorted, you just want to know about it sooner?'

'Yeah, I suppose that's what it's really about, it's my department and I should know what's happening.'

'And what have you tried to do about it?'

'The last time it happened, I lost my temper, and I don't want that to happen again.'

'Have you any other ideas about how to tackle it?'

'No, I don't know what else to try.'

'And what do you want me to do about it?'

'I don't know', said Leo. 'Maybe he'll listen to you.'

'Maybe we can try something else first', said Tom. 'Would you like my advice on something to try?'

'I can't very well say no, can I,' said Leo with a wry smile, 'not when I'm complaining about someone not taking my advice.'

'Well, how about you and David sit down and share how you both see the process of problem resolution working, and explore options for how you would both like it to work? That way instead of me or you telling him what to do, you come up with something together. How does that sound?'

'It's worth a shot, I guess', said Leo.

'Oh, and I've got a project I'd like the two of you to work on together, so when you and David have had your chat, come to see me together and I'll tell you more.'

In Vignette 1.1, Tom begins with a non-directive approach, asking about the issue, checking he has understood correctly, and asking about Leo's ideas. When it becomes clear that Leo is at a loss, Tom offers advice, after checking that Leo is willing to receive it. He finishes up in directive mode, noting that he has a project for Leo and David to work on together.

Purposes of coaching and mentoring

Awareness

A common purpose of coaching and mentoring is to help clients develop insights and self-awareness, and to understand the impact of their behaviour on others. This is a vital first step. It may be a reaction to a 360° or other form of appraisal or feedback or a proactive step to help employees at any level of an organisation to develop and enhance their performance. Only when clients accept and are willing to learn from feedback, will they choose to consider how to address either the perception, or the behaviour prompting the perception, or both. Whereas previous applications of coaching were often remedial in nature, aiming to 'fix problem employees', applications of both coaching and mentoring are now more likely to be focused on enhancing good performance, just as star athletes continue to receive coaching to help them understand how to improve their performance (Coutu and Kauffman 2009).

Options and consequences

A further purpose of coaching and mentoring is to help people identify options and understand the consequences of their decisions so that they make an informed choice and commit to it. A thinking partner (Kline 1999): helps articulate and clarify our thoughts; prompts us to think broadly when we restrict our options unnecessarily, ignore other perspectives or possible consequences; and challenges us, if we choose options to which we are not fully committed. For example, if a client is offered a new job, a coach mentor helps explore the options of choosing the new job or staying with their existing job, thinking through the consequences of both options from a variety of perspectives. Few of us have such accurate self-awareness that we do not benefit from a mentor acting as critical friend who challenges assumptions, tests the logic of decisions and prompts us to question our own behaviour and motivation (Clutterbuck and Megginson 1999; Garvey 2004). This is very different from the role of a consultant, who recommends solutions, or a therapist helping someone understand problems whose roots may lie in the past.

Goal setting

Another purpose of coaching and mentoring is to help with goal setting. While not all coaching and mentoring sessions are concerned with goal setting, there is considerable evidence to support the positive impact of goals, if set appropriately and at the right time, as discussed in Chapter 3. A mentor often has more freedom than a coach in exploring possibilities, depending on the nature of the contract with the sponsoring organisation. However, even where confined to a focus on organisational goals, coach mentors still help clients to articulate their personal values and understand whether and how their goals and the organisation's goals align. Without such alignment, the client's well-being will suffer and their engagement and productivity will decline (Rostron 2009). Alred and Garvey argue in favour of using mentoring '*to facilitate and accelerate movement towards achieving the organisation's vision and goals*' (2000: 270). If the individual's own goals are in conflict with those of their organisation, a positive outcome of coaching or mentoring might be for the person to find another organisation with which they feel more aligned.

Tacit knowledge and learning

Coaching and mentoring help make tacit knowledge explicit, encouraging the client to articulate ideas, assumptions, and practices which they have previously taken for granted – a knowledge engineering role, as described by Nonaka (1991). Mentoring has been described as a form of passing on organisational knowledge – ensuring valuable knowledge is not lost when the mentor leaves (Geisler 2007). Indeed, Swap et al. (2001) say that mentoring and storytelling do more than any other mechanism to promote the transfer of tacit knowledge within organisations. When people join an organisation, coaching and mentoring help them understand how to get things done in their new organisation (Barnes et al. 1989, Berman and Bradt 2006).

Coaching and mentoring also help with the application of what has been learned in training. The sustained application of learning in the workplace requires persistence and effort. A mentor, according to Alred and Garvey, can help the mentee *'discover the motivation to discard old habits, practices and attitudes'* and offers *'support and encouragement as the mentee grapples with their new understanding'* (2000: 270). The increase in the application of what was learned in training can be dramatic. Olivero et al. (1997) for example, found an 88% improvement in productivity when coaching was combined with training, compared with a 22% increase when training was used on its own.

It is important to be clear on the purpose of coaching and mentoring so that the effectiveness of coaching or mentoring can be assessed in relation to its purpose, rather than by some generic calculation of 'Return on Investment' as will be explored in Chapter 12.

Internal and external coaching and mentoring

Coaches

Coaching and mentoring can be carried out by people internal or external to an organisation. There are advantages and disadvantages to both. Compared to an internal coach, an external coach offers relative independence, although as he or she is being paid by the organisation, the focus of the conversation will relate to whatever has been contractually agreed with the organisation, and is not a totally free-ranging discussion of whatever the client may find of benefit or interest. In fact, Garvey warns that because the coach holds delegated organisational power, *'deep and meaningful conversations may not occur in this context'* (Garvey 2004: 7).

An internal coach may have a long-standing relationship of mutual trust and respect, providing a solid foundation for a coaching interaction. Internal coaches may either have full- or part-time roles, e.g. in Human Resource Development, providing coaching to employees with whom they do not have a line management relationship. The internal coach understands the organisation and the industry, which may be an advantage in terms of credibility. However, such familiarity should not lead them to jump to solutions based on previous experience. A European report (EFMD 2009) notes a sizeable shift towards the use of internal resources, both in the form of internal coaches and coaching managers. On the other hand, the fact that external coaches are independent of the organisation may lead to them being seen as more trustworthy than an internal person. In many organisations, external coaches are used for executives and for sensitive areas, while internal coaches are used with managers and other employees (AMA 2008).

Mentors

Internal mentors are common in large organisations where they help an employee take responsibility for their own development, and help them progress in their careers, opening doors and introducing them to new contacts and networks. This sponsorship mentoring approach is particularly common in North America (Clutterbuck 2008). Alternatively, a mentor's focus may be more on the development of employees, exploring with them their goals, dreams or ambitions and ways to achieve them, such as undertaking a range of learning and development activities – a form of mentoring common in Europe and becoming more common in North America. It is rare for a line manager to be formally appointed as a mentor. However, a line manager will often act as mentor in terms of an employee's career progression. Unfortunately, line management responsibilities take precedence over mentoring and so the employee may not get the full benefit of mentoring from their line manager, in particular in relation to the psycho-social aspects of mentoring (Garvey 2010).

An external mentor performs the same functions as an internal mentor but may also help the client develop external rather than internal networks. Small companies may not have enough people to mentor new or junior employees or may want to provide mentors as sounding boards for their CEO or senior managers. In large companies, external mentors may be offered to high-fliers to accelerate their growth and development. Some universities now also train community members and alumni to provide mentoring to current students or participants in leadership development programs. Such mentoring is generally unpaid but the mentors benefit from the training and support they receive, which they can then use in their own organisations.

Coaching managers

A coaching manager uses many of the skills of the coach mentor in the way they engage with their employees: listening to them; asking questions to prompt their employees to think rather than providing answers; providing constructive feedback; and helping their employees to develop and improve performance. As discussed further in Chapter 6, coaching managers also face a number of challenges, but the rewards are considerable, especially where a coaching approach is deployed consistently throughout an organisation. Table 1.1 summarises some of the dimensions which may vary between external and internal coach mentors and coaching managers.

Where the coach mentor is external, both parties need to get to know each other and agree that there is a good fit. The first meeting may be enough to put the relationship on a good footing. However, if a coach or mentor is assigned by the organisation with no choice on the part of the individual client, or with the individual client not seeing any value in taking part in the process, or indeed if managers are required to adopt a coaching approach rather than choosing to do so, then the relationship may not be successful. Where both coach mentor and employee are in the same organisation, they will probably already have a relationship. If this is not a good relationship, it will be difficult for coaching or mentoring to succeed, as coaching and mentoring rely on what Rogers (1957) termed 'unconditional positive regard'. Even where there is a good relationship, both parties, as well as the Human Resources (HR) manager or coaching sponsor, need to address in advance such issues as what to do if a problem arises, and where the interests of the organisations are in conflict with the interests of the individual (Connor and Pokora 2012). Such dilemmas are discussed further in Chapter 11.

Table 1.1 External and internal coach mentors and coaching managers

	External	Internal	Coaching Manager
Independence	Independent of organisation	Independent of line management	Not independent
Familiarity with organisation	Unfamiliar. May be familiar with industry	Familiar with organisation and industry	Familiar with organisation and industry
Credibility	Needs to develop	Has credibility within organisation	Has credibility with own team
Rapport	Needs to develop	May need to develop with individuals	Has rapport with own team
Trust	Needs to develop – independence may be seen as trustworthy	May need to develop with individuals	Trusted by own team
Ethical issues	Confidentiality between organisations	Confidentiality within organisation	Dual role and confidentiality within organisation
Cost	Fees vary	Less by hour than external coach mentor	No additional cost
Feedback	Based on third party assessments and/or brief snapshots	Based on third party assessments and/or brief snapshots and/or additional sources of internal feedback	Has ongoing opportunity to observe and give feedback
Development	Identifies external possibilities	Identifies internal possibilities	Identifies internal possibilities
Networks	Helps develop external networks	Helps develop internal networks	Helps develop internal networks
Power	Has no power over client	Has no power over employee	Has power to fire someone or withhold training and development opportunities
Reward	Does not provide rewards or negative consequences	Does not provide reward or negative consequences	May affect recognition and reward

Organisation of this book

The book begins with an overview of coaching and mentoring theory and practice. Chapter 1 introduces coaching and mentoring in an organisational context. Chapter 2 examines the coaching and mentoring process and theories with particular relevance to business are discussed. Chapter 3 considers skills common to both coaching and mentoring in a business context, in particular, observation, listening, questioning, goal setting and feedback.

The next part of the book looks at applications of coaching and mentoring with individuals in organisations. Chapter 4 explores how coaching and mentoring relates to individual change. Chapter 5 focuses on coaching and mentoring for leaders, while Chapter 6 refers to coaching and mentoring by leaders, including coaching of their teams.

Next, the book discusses applications of coaching and mentoring for business. Chapter 7 discusses coaching and mentoring for strategy development and implementation. Chapter 8 considers how coaching and mentoring can be used to foster innovation in organisations, while Chapter 9 looks at how coaching and mentoring support organisational change.

Finally, the book explores challenges in coaching and mentoring. Chapter 10 examines cross-cultural coaching and mentoring, and coaching and mentoring at a distance. Chapter 11 focuses on ethical issues in coaching and mentoring. Chapter 12 concludes with a discussion of critical success factors in coaching and mentoring, ways of evaluating success, and briefly considers developments in coaching and mentoring.

Some readers may choose to go directly to chapters which they find of particular interest, while others may prefer to work through the book chapter by chapter.

Each chapter includes links to online resources. As online resources sometimes change their addresses, if a link no longer works, you may be able to find its new location by searching for the organisation name. Whether a resource specifically targets coaches or mentors, or both, the sites are likely to be of use to both.

Useful links

This chapter highlights organisations which promote good practice in coaching and mentoring.

Association for Coaching – http://www.associationforcoaching.com/pages/home

UK-based organisation with its own accreditation system and resources for coaching.

European Mentoring and Coaching Council – http://www.emccouncil.org/

European association for coaches and mentors with its own accreditation system and resources.

International Coach Federation (ICF) – http://www.coachfederation.org/

Organisation founded in US, now accrediting coaches worldwide.

International Institute of Coaching (IIC) – http://internationalinstituteofcoaching.org/

Originally European, now international, offers its own accreditation system.

International Mentoring Association – http://mentoring-association.org/

Originally US, now international. Focus on mentoring.

Worldwide Association of Business Coaches – http://www.wabccoaches.com/

Founded in the US, focused on internal and external coaches in an organisational context. Has its own accreditation system.

References

'New ethos transforms attitudes and approaches at RS Components: Key role of coaching in customer services', *Human Resource Management International Digest*, 18: 33–6.

Alred, G. and R. Garvey (2000) 'Learning to produce knowledge – the contribution of mentoring', *Mentoring & Tutoring: Partnership in Learning*, 8: 261–72.

AMA (2008) *Coaching a global study of successful practices*, American Management Association.

Barnes, A. K., J. L. Mendleson and G. T. Horn (1989) 'Structured mentorship for new employees: a case study', *Journal of Applied Business Research*, 5: 74–7.

Berman, W. and G. Bradt (2006) 'Executive coaching and consulting: "Different Strokes for Different Folks"', *Professional Psychology – Research & Practice*, 37: 244–53.

Catling, T. (2008) 'Mentoring – the objective support that managers need', *The British Journal of Administrative Management*, January, 22–23.

Cavanagh, M. J. and A. M. Grant (2010) 'The solution-focused approach to coaching', in E. Cox, T. Bachkirova and D. Clutterbuck (eds) *Complete handbook of coaching*. London, Sage, pp. 54–67.

Chartered Institute of Personnel Development (CIPD) (2012) 'Learning and Talent Development Annual Survey'. CIPD, London.

Clutterbuck, D. (2008) 'What's happening in coaching and mentoring? And what is the difference between them?' *Development and Learning in Organizations*, 22: 8–10.

Clutterbuck, D. and D. Megginson (1999) *Mentoring executives and directors*. Oxford, Butterworth-Heinemann.

Connor, J. and J. Pokora (2012) *Coaching and mentoring at work*. Maidenhead, Open University Press.

Coutu, D. and C. Kauffman (2009) 'What can coaches do for you?', *Harvard Business Review*, 87: 91–7.

Cunningham, I. (2008) 'Coaching shouldn't be non-directive – or even directive: really responding to needs', *Development and Learning in Organizations*, 22: 5–7.

Eby, L. T. and A. Lockwood (2005) 'Protégés' and mentors' reactions to participating in formal mentoring programs: A qualitative investigation', *Journal of Vocational Behavior*, 67(3): 441–58.

EFMD (2009) 'Issue 3 Special Supplement: The role of corporate coaching in business', *Global Focus: Magazine of the European Foundation for Management Development*.

Garvey, B. (2010) 'Mentoring in a coaching world', in E. Cox, T. Bachkirova and D. Clutterbuck (eds) *Complete handbook of coaching*. London, Sage, pp. 341–54.

Garvey, R. (2004) 'The mentoring/counselling/coaching debate: call a rose by any other name and perhaps it's a bramble?', *Development and Learning in Organizations*, 18: 6–8.

Geisler, E. (2007) 'The metrics of knowledge: mechanisms for preserving the value of managerial knowledge', *Business Horizons*, 50: 467–77.

Grant, A. M., L. Curtayne and G. Burton (2009) 'Executive coaching enhances goal attainment, resilience and workplace well-being: a randomised controlled study', *The Journal of Positive Psychology*, 4: 396–407.

Gray, D. E., Y. Ekiknci and H. Goregaokar (2011) 'A five-dimensional model of attributes: Some precursors of executive coach selection', *International Journal of Selection and Assessment*, 19: 415–28.

Hamlin, R. G. and L. Sage (2011) 'Behavioural criteria of perceived mentoring effectiveness: An empirical study of effective and ineffective mentor and mentee behaviour within formal mentoring relationships', *Journal of European Industrial Training*, 35: 752–78.

Kline, N. (1999) *Time To think, listening to ignite the human mind*. London, Ward, Lock, Cassell.

Kram, K. E. (1985) *Mentoring at work*. Glenview, IL., Scott, Foresman and Company.

Leimon, A., F. Moscovici and G. McMahon (2005) *Essential business coaching*. Hove, Routledge.

McCarthy, G. and J. Ahrens (2012) 'How and why do managers use coaching skills?', *Irish Academy of Management Annual Conference*. Maynooth, Ireland, Irish Academy of Management.

McCarthy, G. and J. Milner (2013) 'Managerial coaching: challenges, opportunities & training', *Journal of Management Development*, 32(7): 768–79.

Nonaka, I. (1991) 'The knowledge-creating company', *Harvard Business Review*, 69 (11–12): 162–71.

Olivero, G., K. D. Bane and R. E. Kopelmann (1997) 'Executive coaching as a transfer of training tool: effects on productivity in a public agency', *Public Personnel Management*, 26(4): 461–9.

Parker-Wilkins, V. (2006) 'Business impact of executive coaching: demonstrating monetary value', *Industrial and Commercial Training*, 38(3): 122–7.

Rogers, C. R. (1957) 'The necessary and sufficient conditions of therapeutic personality change', *Journal of Consulting Psychology*, 21(2): 95.

Rostron, S. S. (2009) *Business coaching international*. London, Karnac.

Spencer, L. (2011) 'Coaching and training transfer: a phenomenological inquiry into combined training-coaching programmes', *International Journal of Evidence-Based Coaching and Mentoring*, Special issue 5: 1–18.

Swap, W., D. Leonard, M. Shields and L. Abrams (2001) 'Using mentoring and storytelling to transfer knowledge in the workplace', *Journal of Management Information Systems*, 18: 95.

2

COACHING AND MENTORING THEORY AND MODELS

Introduction

There are many approaches to coaching and mentoring, some of which have come from psychology and psychotherapy, while others have evolved from education, human potential, sociology, philosophy and sport. Regardless of their origin, all coaching shares a common theoretical underpinning in adult learning, according to Cox et al. (2010) and Lennard (2010). The same can be said of mentoring (Zachary 2011). When people change in some way, it is because of something they have learned. This could be, for example, something about themselves and their impact on others, a better appreciation of what is needed to succeed in their organisations, or a way to dispute negative thoughts. Adult learning shares common principles with coaching and mentoring. Adults are internally motivated and self-directed. They learn best when their learning is at the right time, is relevant and addresses a need they have identified (Knowles, Holton III et al. 2005). The same is true of coaching and mentoring. If someone is forced to participate in coaching or mentoring, they do not get the same benefit as if they have acknowledged the need themselves, see it as relevant and are self-motivated.

Adults learn through experience and make sense of their experience through reflection (Schöen 1983; Kolb 1984). Learning is transformative when people's long-held beliefs are challenged and, through reflection, they arrive at a new understanding, which impacts their behaviour (Mezirow 1990; Mezirow 1991). The type of disorientating dilemma which Mezirow describes as leading to transformation is often experienced by clients when feedback from others differs greatly from their self-perception. An understanding of adult learning theory helps coach mentors to understand the motivation and learning preferences of their clients.

Despite its long history, much of what is known about mentoring is still *'anecdotal, prescriptive, and based on "best practice opinion"'*, according to Hamlin and Sage (2011: 755). There are also continuing calls for more research into coaching, e.g. Joo, Sushko et al. (2012) and McGurk (2012). A number of journals dedicated to coaching and mentoring have appeared such as the *International Journal of Evidence-Based Coaching and Mentoring*, and *Coaching: An International Journal of Theory, Research and Practice*. Coaching and mentoring research appears in a wide range of journals, particularly those focusing on management, human resource development, training, psychology and education. Part of the challenge for coach mentors and coaching managers is simply to locate the research that exists so that they can ensure their practice is evidence-based and effective. Practitioners too can contribute to the growing research base (McCarthy 2011b).

This chapter outlines some key themes emerging from coaching and mentoring research, focusing on the mentoring and coaching relationship and process, before highlighting a range of models. It then summarises different approaches.

Mentoring and coaching theory

Mentoring

Mentoring has a longer history than coaching, with many authors citing the origin of the word as the character Mentor who advised Telemachus, son of Odysseus in ancient Greece, with the legend stating that the goddess Athena disguised herself as Mentor when visiting Telemachus (Barry 2012). The story became popular in the 17th century through the writings of French philosopher Fénelon, who highlighted the opportunity of learning through observing the ways of the world and discussing with a 'mentor'. However, the notion that leaders could be developed if guided in this way was in opposition to the then prevailing notion of the divine right of kings to rule, leading to Fénelon being banished from the court (Garvey, Stokes et al. 2009).

Barnes, Mendleson et al. (1989) identify mentoring as a helping relationship citing two categorisations – Egan (1975) and Carkhuff (1971). Egan's dimensions are listening, empathy, focusing, challenging, and developing preferred scenarios and action, while Carkhuff lists the helping dimensions as empathy, respect, concreteness, genuineness, initiation, confrontation and immediacy. These categorisations, particularly Egan's, have been applied in coaching as well as to mentoring (Connor and Pokora 2012). Bokeno (Bokeno 2007; Bokeno 2009) categorises both coaching and mentoring as 'learning relationships', i.e. the focus is less on helping people cope with difficulty and more about helping them to learn and grow.

Based on its purpose, there are two broad approaches to mentoring: developmental mentoring which aims to help mentees develop their quality of thinking and help themselves, and sponsorship mentoring which aims to help mentees succeed in their organisation (Bokeno 2007; Clutterbuck 2008; Emelo 2011). A shift in the purpose of mentoring from career advancement towards learning and gaining insight is identified by Zachary (2011) who also identifies a shift from mentor directed to self-directed, with the mentor now seen as a facilitator of learning. Bokeno (2009) describes a split between developmental and relationship mentoring, with the latter focused on helping the mentee develop productive relationships. This shift is also noted by Kram and Higgins (2008) and Chandler, Kram et al. (2011). Haggard, Dougherty et al. (2011) argue that while the focus of mentoring research has shifted over the years, and definitions vary, nevertheless there are some core attributes of mentoring, viz. reciprocity, developmental benefits and regular interaction over time. Zachary (2011) includes learning, development, and mutually defined goals along with reciprocity, relationship, collaboration and partnership in what he describes as the seven critical elements of the learning-centred paradigm.

While reciprocity is not often included in coaching theory, coaching is often described as a helping relationship based on a collaborative approach. Rostron (2009) argues in favour of an assumption of equality in the relationship, with both parties bringing experience, expertise and wisdom, although if both parties benefit equally, one might query why only one party gets paid. However, others see issues of power in all coaching and mentoring relationships, particularly in internal relationships. Welman and Bachkirova (2010) argue that awareness and consent are the two dimensions which most affect whether power is exercised as 'forceful influence' or 'imposition of will'. If the coach mentor is a line manager or a HR manager with the authority to affect the employee's progression or rewards, the coach mentor needs to be particularly careful not to force a client '*to do or be something that is not "them"*' (Hawkins and Smith 2006: 6).

Coaching and mentoring process

Both coaching and mentoring involve a dialogue aimed at helping someone to come to a realisation or a decision about something they may have previously been unaware of, and now wish to change or achieve. The coach mentor listens to the client think out loud, prompts with questions to encourage clarity of thinking, and possibly offers feedback to increase self-awareness. The process includes goal setting if the client decides that they want to set a goal. The coaching process, especially where an organisation is paying for an external coach, is usually shorter term than mentoring, with contracts specifying the number of sessions over a period of months, while mentoring relationships may last for years (CIPD 2011). Coaching managers usually coach their employees on a long-term basis.

Mentoring process

Although the purpose of mentoring varies, the process typically comprises a senior person listening to and advising a junior person in the same or a different organisation. In analysing the process, Kram (1985) distinguished four phases: initiation, cultivation, separation and redefinition. In the initiation phase, mentor and client get to know each other and understand what to expect from each other. In the cultivation stage, the mentor provides support over a period of years, both in terms of career advice and in helping the mentee's personal growth and development. In the separation stage, the mentee becomes more independent, while in the final stage of re-definition, the relationship is reviewed and may evolve into peer support or friendship. The mentoring process is seen as a long-term process, which may not have a definite goal in the early stages, but relies on an understanding that the mentor is there to help the client, whatever this may entail.

Zachary (2011) describes the four stages of the mentoring process as: preparation, negotiation, enabling and closing. He sees goal setting as an essential part of successful mentoring, with goals agreed in the negotiation phase and reviewed in the closing phase. A different model is proposed by Bell and Goldsmith (2013) who use SAGE as their acronym: Surrender (eliminating the power imbalance from the relationship); Accept (creating a safe environment for growth); Gift (advice, feedback or focus, only given after surrendering and accepting); and Extending (enabling the mentee to be a self-directed learner).

Coaching process

Leimon, Moscovici et al. (2005) describe the coaching process as building the relationship, drawing the picture, achieving change, motivating for results and concluding the relationship. The phases of the coaching process have also been identified as a series of checks: an alliance check which defines what will be addressed in coaching; a credibility check of the coach; a likeability check for compatibility between coach and client; a dialogue and skill acquisition stage; and a final action planning stage (Natale and Diamante 2005). Outcomes of the coaching and mentoring process are illustrated in Figure 2.1.

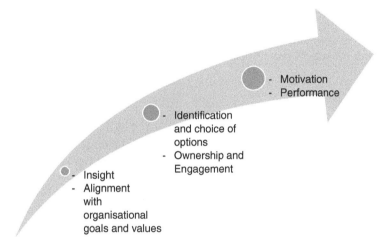

- Motivation
- Performance

- Identification and choice of options
- Ownership and Engagement

- Insight
- Alignment with organisational goals and values

Figure 2.1   Outcomes of coaching and mentoring

Coaching and mentoring relationship

The coaching and mentoring relationship is crucial for both coach mentor and client. Perceived quality of relationship has a strong effect on commitment and taking action based on the advice of the mentor (Son and Kim 2013). The relationship is the most important factor in coaching, according to Bluckert (2005). Similarly Critchley says that:

> *Of all the variables having an effect on outcome, by far the largest impact comes from the relationship itself rather than from any particular method or technique.* (Critchley 2010: 853)

De Haan (2008) states categorically that the coach's approach or techniques make little difference to the clients; it is the relationship which is the greatest predictor of the outcome of coaching. In other words, clients report better outcomes when they see their coach positively. Leimon, Moscovici et al. (2005) also suggest that the perceived attitudes and feelings of the coach have a greater effect on the effectiveness of coaching than the approaches or techniques used by the coach. This is comforting for the new coach mentor, helping him/her to relax rather than worry about skill or technique. Perhaps in relaxing, the coach mentor is be able to be more present and hence more effective in working with the client, thereby making the statement true!

What is needed for the relationship to work? A number of features are commonly suggested, including chemistry between the two parties and willingness to work together. Bluckert (2005) advocates empathy, positive attitude and respect as the basis for the coaching relationship. Advances in understanding emotional intelligence over the past 20 years, e.g. Goleman (1998), Nelis, Quoidbach et al. (2009), show that people can enhance their emotional intelligence, so that they naturally display empathy. Megginson and Clutterbuck (2005) suggest that one way to build rapport is to exchange information on what each person feels passionate about, with the coach mentor modelling attentive listening and self-disclosure. This must be done in a natural way, as the coach mentor must be authentic for the relationship to work. Our body language confirms to the person being listened to that we are there for them. Informal questions and humour may help establish mutual interest, thus contributing to shared bonds (Biswas-Diener 2009). However, this is culturally contingent. In Germany, for example, the relationship is based on respect for the other's professional expertise, and little time is spent on small talk.

Mirroring

People are more likely to listen and accept feedback from coach mentors with whom they have rapport. Coach mentors sometimes try to consciously demonstrate empathy by mirroring the body language of their clients. However, this can lead to loss of trust if the client notices the mirroring and believes it is deliberate or insincere. On the other hand, if the mirroring happens naturally and is perceived as such by the client or not noticed consciously by the client, it may help build rapport. The verbal equivalent is using similar metaphors or figures of speech which indicate that we are 'on the same wavelength' as the other person. Metaphors are discussed further in Chapter 3.

Trust

For both internal and external coaching and mentoring relationships, trust is vital. Son and Kim (2013) found that trust strongly influenced relationships between mentors and their clients, with clients more willing to take the advice of mentors where trust was in place. Morgan, Harkins et al. claim that '*The more trust the coach can generate, the more the coachee can achieve*' (2005: 48). They suggest that coaches build trust through their own self-awareness, empathy, and ability to receive as well as give, and through maintaining strict confidentiality. Bluckert (2005) suggests that the two most important dimensions of trust for coaches are integrity and competence. O'Broin and Palmer (2010) found wide support in the coaching and coaching psychology literature for the importance of trust in coaching. Ladyshewsky (2010) reiterates this in the context of the coaching manager.

A sense of shared values between coach mentor and client is also important. It would be difficult for a coach mentor who values integrity and honesty to mentor a client toward becoming a master criminal. Mertel (2010) advocates that coaches assess their own values so they can hone their effectiveness at identifying their clients' values.

Son and Kim (2013) warn that a client may be reluctant to disagree with a mentor or may feel obliged to follow the mentor's advice, even if they disagree with it, if the mentor is of a higher status than the client. While their study was conducted in Korea, similar issues may be anticipated elsewhere, as mentors are often chosen precisely because they are seen as powerful in the organisation. A bad mentoring relationship will not last, according to Eby, Butts et al. (2010), however, organisational support for mentors and mentees can help reduce the likelihood of a bad experience.

Developing the relationship

Morgan, Harkins et al. (2005) advise coaches to establish ground rules at the beginning of a coaching relationship, covering such items as confidentiality, reporting, monitoring progress and how, why and when the coaching will end. Similarly Megginson and Clutterbuck (2005) highlight the importance of: getting to know one other; establishing the grounds for success; rapport; and setting expectations. Establishing a relationship consists of the two parties getting to know each other and reaching agreement on key parameters such as what information will be shared with whom and how progress will be measured. Machon (2010) describes what he calls the 'container' of the coaching relationship, which includes agreeing expectations, logistics, who is to be involved, and allows the coach to affirm their commitment to the client. Similar steps are found in mentoring.

The relationship between coach mentor and client is not a static one. The coach mentor needs to be sensitive to the changing nature of the relationship and to be present with the client in each session, not assuming the client is still the same person they first met. This is particularly the case with mentoring relationships which are often over a longer period of time than coaching contracts. Starr (2008) identifies certain warning signs which the coach mentor can use to identify that their rapport is waning, for example, feeling separate or detached, not being natural, being unable to make oneself understood or feeling that the other person is not being warm or open.

For both coaching and mentoring, it is advisable for the coach mentor to review with the client (and sponsor where appropriate) whether it is time to conclude the relationship or whether to renew. If it is decided to renew, it is important to spend time reflecting on what has worked well and on what needs to be the focus of any future relationship. If the client has grown through the previous sessions, it is important for the coach mentor to recognise this and consider whether a different thinking partner may now be helpful. If so, it would be unethical to extend the existing contract with the same coach mentor. A coaching manager might find that a team member would benefit from an offline coach mentor. The guiding principle is to do what is in the interest of the client.

For both mentoring and coaching relationships, it is important to plan for a good ending. Mentoring relationships may end for different reasons, for example, the coach mentor may no longer be available, or the client may have grown and developed autonomy to the extent that a different coach mentor may be more helpful. Coaching contracts typically have a finite life span. Hence it is important, as Cox (2010) points out, for the relationship to end well. Where there has been a meaningful personal relationship between coach mentor and client, there may be feelings of loss or grief on either or both sides when the relationship is brought to an end. Cox (2010) suggests that planning for the ending and celebrating it as a rite of passage minimise such feelings and provide recognition of the value both coach mentor and client have received from the relationship.

A range of models is outlined in the next section and can be broadly summarised as helping a client answer three questions: Where am I now? Where do I want to be? How do I get there?

Models

Many coaches find it useful to have a model as a guide in a coaching conversation or across a coaching interaction. A model is simply a way of articulating one's approach in words and/or images. It is, according to Lennard, *'an intellectual device that highlights the key elements of a process and their interrelationships'* (Lennard 2010: 3). Unfortunately, the shorter time frame of the coaching process can lead some coaches to apply models mechanically, keen to get through every step. However, used wisely, models can be a useful prompt for both coaches and mentors of areas that may be useful to explore. This is particularly the case for the 'PERFECT' model advocated by Kauffman (2010), not as stages of a coaching or mentoring session, but as an aide memoire for the various layers of knowledge we can tap into in order to help clients, and as possible areas to explore with them. 'PERFECT' stands for: Physical (biological), Environmental, Relational, Feelings, Effective thinking, Continuity, and Transcendence. This is a useful way to categorise the knowledge coach mentors may wish to draw upon.

The 'GROW' model

The most often cited model is the GROW model, commonly attributed to Sir John Whitmore, although he himself states that he was the first to publicise it, rather than its sole originator (Whitmore 2009). 'GROW' stands for: Goal, Reality, Options and Will or Wrap-up – steps found in many coaching conversations. Others have developed variations such as: IGROW, where the first step is to identify the 'Issue' to be discussed; TGROW, where T is the broad 'Topic'; and RGOW, where the 'Goal' is identified after the current 'Reality' has been explored. The GROW model is easy to remember and its simplicity is appealing. Unfortunately it is often taught in short training courses which offer little time for the aspiring coach to develop their own self-awareness and how to be present with a client. Some attention may be given to active listening, but often new coaches come away with a few questions which they will always ask, and a belief that every coaching client must define a goal at the outset. This was never the intention of those who developed the GROW model, with Whitmore describing it not as a goal-setting framework but a guide to a coaching conversation (Whitmore 2009).

The 'CLEAR' and PRACTICE models

Hawkins and Smith (2006) developed the CLEAR model, where 'CLEAR' stands for: Contract, Listen, Explore, Action, and Review. In other words, this starts before the GROW model in the contracting phase and includes a review at the end. This model is useful for external coach mentors in an organisation. 'PRACTICE' is a similar model developed by Palmer (Palmer 2007; Palmer 2008), where the P stands for problem, but could be used for the topic or issue the client wishes to work on, rather than a problem per se. Like the GROW model, the next steps are R for Realistic goal and A for Alternative solutions (options). The C stands for consideration of the consequences and the T for targeting the most feasible options. The next step is I for implementation (like the W in GROW) followed by E for Evaluation which is like Review in Hawkins and Smith's CLEAR model.

The 'DEEPER' model

Reflecting on how effective an approach is in a particular context helps us to develop our own model (Lennard 2010). There is no right or wrong model, simply models which people find more or less useful. A model I have found helpful in my own practice for both coaching and mentoring is the DEEPER Model of Coaching and Mentoring. 'DEEPER' stands for: Develop relationship, Explore present, Explore future, Prepare, Enact and Renew. Each of these steps is outlined briefly below.

Develop relationship

A sense of shared values develops as rapport and trust build up. It is important to note that a relationship is not merely established when the coach mentor begins to work with a client, but continues to develop through each coaching or mentoring session.

Explore now/Explore future

It is useful to spend time exploring what is currently happening and to explore the client's values and motivation before attempting to define a goal for the future. Conversations at this stage lead to increased self-awareness, which in turn prompts changes in behaviour and improved alignment between the individual and the organisation. A strong focus on articulating values and alignment sets the foundation for sustainable change. These phases are often iterative as the client becomes more self-aware and more trusting of the coach mentor, and the coach mentor becomes more familiar with the client, recognising whether the issues clients are presenting are the real issues or not. The coach mentor can then help the client determine what is most important for them and their organisation.

Prepare

The coach mentor helps the client to get ready to change, whether the client has decided on changing a single behaviour or a more pervasive change. The client may need additional skills, or may need to rehearse their new behaviour, or to increase their motivation to implement the desired change. Self-efficacy (Bandura 1977) is important for change to take place, i.e. the client needs to believe they can implement the change successfully, otherwise they may not even try.

Rehearsal is useful where a new behaviour is involved. For example, someone who has decided not to say 'yes' automatically whenever a director asks them to do something, may need to practise saying 'no' or practise negotiating for more resources, e.g.

> 'I will be delighted to help you with that. I need your help too in demonstrating the need for more resources in this area so that I can provide the level of service you need.'

Practice increases our self-efficacy, our belief in our ability to apply new techniques and to think through other people's possible reactions and the different paths the conversation may take. However, the client should not rehearse to the point where they come across as artificial or unable to respond if the conversation takes an unpredicted turn.

The model could finish here as the client leaves the room. However, DEEPER coaching and mentoring takes the process through to implementation, with the client enacting their chosen actions and reviewing and reflecting on their effectiveness and next steps.

Enact

Here, the client implements the change they have chosen, not just once but on an on-going basis, as their new way of being. While an external coach mentor will not be with clients physically, he/she may be able to support remotely if questions or doubts arise or if the client is tempted to revert to their previous behaviour when they hit a snag such as scepticism among their colleagues. Internal coach mentors and coaching managers have on-going opportunities to observe, support and encourage, as the client makes the change. By expressing their belief in the client's ability to succeed and encouraging the client to persist, coach mentors help clients not only to try to change but to make the change habitual and sustainable.

Renew

Reflecting is taking time out, to consider what has actually happened and what impact it has had. This step allows time for thinking and learning. For example, if the client had decided to be more consistent in holding people to account for their actions, a shared reflection with the coach mentor could look at how this has worked and how the people directly involved responded. The reflection might lead to an exploration of other options while building on the success of what the client has already done. It helps identify patterns in how the client reacts to situations over time and helps the client recognise their successes. Without reflection, we are sometimes unaware of how much our thinking and our behaviour has changed over time and how much we have achieved.

Coach mentors also need to reflect on their own, as well as together with the client. This enables them to consider how the process is working and what other options might be useful. Whether or not coach mentors participate in formal supervision sessions, incorporating a reflection stage allows coach mentors time to think. This forms the basis for coach mentors to learn and to choose changes of their own. Coach mentors sometimes run the risk of discounting events, i.e. ignoring something they or clients said or did, or under-estimating its significance (Hay 2007). Supervision is rare in mentoring and the most appropriate form of supervision for coaching is still under debate, as will be discussed in Chapter 12. Many coach mentors therefore reflect on their own or with peers. Regardless of the format of reflection, they may find it helpful to have some audio or video recordings of some sessions (with clients' permission) or notes taken immediately after each session as an input into their reflection and to help identify patterns and changes over time. Coaching managers also benefit from including some time for reflection in their diaries, as reflection provides a basis for learning and improvement. This reduces the likelihood of 20 years' experience being only one year's experience repeated 20 times!

The usefulness of models

Models are only useful if the people using them find them to be so. The GROW model is attractive because people feel a sense of accomplishment in defining a goal and the steps to achieve it. There is, however, a risk with any model that people may use it unthinkingly, going through each step in a forced and linear fashion, even if the client would benefit from staying longer at a particular stage or from re-visiting previous steps. This appears to be more common with coaches than mentors, perhaps because a goal-driven approach allows the coach to demonstrate a return on investment through the achievement of tangible outcomes. The antidote to this compulsion to 'get to an outcome' is for the coach mentor to be fully present, being there with their clients, often in silence, listening to clients gain clarity and make choices if they wish to do so. Sometimes the right thing for the coach mentor to do will be to challenge or confront, but at other times the client needs to reflect on what is happening rather than decide on an action. A whole session may be about identifying what the issue is, not moving through all the steps of a model.

Models should not be seen as rigid straitjackets, but as a lens through which to view the coaching mentoring session and a prompt about relevant areas to explore. The next section summarises some of the theoretical approaches which can be applied to mentoring and coaching and which may assist coach mentors in defining and developing their own approach.

Theoretical approaches

While mentoring texts, such as Clutterbuck and Lane (2004), explore different aspects of mentoring, they tend not to define different approaches in the same way as coaching texts, for example Cox, Bachkirova et al. (2010) or Passmore (2010a). Perhaps it is because coaching is an industry and companies need to distinguish their offerings, whereas mentoring is often provided without payment. Mentoring is usually not a full-time role and there are far fewer mentoring than coaching companies. Public and private organisations issuing coaching tenders increasingly ask those responding to outline their coaching methodology. For commercial reasons, if for no other, external coaches have to differentiate themselves from the competition.

Some of the approaches described below will appeal to some more than others. Coach mentors should develop an approach that is in keeping with their own philosophy of coaching and mentoring. To apply the approaches outlined here, coach mentors do not need to be psychologists or psychotherapists, although skills in either will enrich their practice. Coach mentors should, however, develop genuine competence in whichever approaches they wish to use with their clients, and not merely pay lip service to an approach they wish to use to sell their services.

As coaching and mentoring use many of the same skills, the same approaches described for coaching may also be applied in mentoring (Connor and Pokora 2012). Coach mentors can enhance their practice by deepening their understanding of the approaches which resonate with them and are effective with their clients. Rather than applying a heterogeneous collection of techniques, coach mentors develop a firm foundation on which to build their model. They can then add techniques which fit within a particular approach.

Cognitive behavioural coaching

Cognitive behavioural coaching derives from cognitive behavioural therapy (Beck 1976) and rational emotive behaviour therapy (Ellis 1994). It aims to help people recognise errors in their thinking patterns such as over-generalisation ('he always does x') and to find constructive ways to handle difficulties (Neenan 2010). Being able to recognise 'cognitive distortions' (McMahon 2009) is helpful to coach mentors as well as their clients, as it prompts them to clarify thinking and dispute automatic negative thoughts. This approach encourages people to understand how their beliefs affect their response to an event and ultimately their performance. It shows that we can dispute those beliefs using logic or data and substitute new beliefs which are both well-founded (i.e. not naïve optimism) and enabling. Grant, Cavanagh et al. (2012) suggest that in a solution-focused approach, the way in which client and coach think and talk about the topics discussed affects the degree to which change is possible. Williams, Edgerton et al. (2010) argue that cognitive behaviour coaching encompasses solution-focused coaching.

Solution- and goal-focused coaching

Solution-focused coaching derives from brief solution-focused therapy (Berg and Szabo 2005; Grant 2010). Rather than focusing on a problem and the causes of the problem, it explores possible solutions and encompasses many widely accepted tenets of coaching, e.g. the client has resources, the client takes responsibility for their actions, and the coach prompts the client to find solutions. Vignette 2.1 illustrates two approaches to a conversation about a business problem.

Vignette 2.1   Focus on the problem or the solution?

a)

'There's a problem, Carlos,' said Jack. 'The metal rods we need for the Daintree order haven't arrived and the order is due tomorrow.'
'Why haven't they arrived?'
'They said their truck broke down just outside their factory, they don't have any other trucks free.'
'This has happened before, hasn't it?' asked Carlos. 'Why are we still using them, if they're so unreliable?'
'Well,' said Jack, 'they're usually okay and their prices are good. What do you want me to do?'
'Better call the customer and let them know the order will be late. Make sure they know it's not our fault.'
'Okay, will do.'

b)

'There's a problem, Carlos,' said Jack. 'The metal rods we need for the Daintree order haven't arrived and the order is due tomorrow. We really need to keep our on-time performance with the customer. That's one of the things they look at when renewing contracts.'
'So what are the options?'

'Well, we could see if some of the local factories have any spares, they're a bit more expensive, but we'd have them soon.'

'Good idea, any other options?' asked Carlos.

'Well,' said Jack, 'one of our other suppliers has a depot near the rod factory – maybe they could help us out and bring the rods on their truck. Or maybe they know someone heading up this way today. Bottom line is, we need to get a supply of rods here by 4pm if we're going to deliver on time tomorrow.'

'Do you want me to do anything?'

'If you can talk to the customer, just to let them know what's happening, I'll start ringing around the suppliers and we'll get something organised.'

In contrast to many descriptions of coaching, solution-focused coaching may be more directive. The coach shares his/her mental models and educates his/her clients (Cavanagh and Grant 2010). The coach is 'openly influential and challenges the coachee to think in a new way' (Grant 2010). Ives and Cox (2012), on the other hand, argue that a non-directive approach to goal-focused coaching is preferable. Goal-focused coaching is defined by Ives and Cox as:

> *A systematic and collaborative helping intervention that is non-directive, goal-oriented and performance-driven, intended to facilitate the more effective creation and pursuit of another's goals.* (Ives and Cox 2012: 26)

These approaches are primarily about raising performance and are action-oriented rather than dealing with emotions. Being able to vary their approach along a continuum from directive to non-directive is helpful for managers who may find a totally non-directive approach difficult to achieve and sometimes in conflict with the demands of their managerial role. In other words, they may need to vary their style between coaching, mentoring and sometimes directing. Managers may also find these approaches easier to apply as they primarily explore cognitive issues rather than emotional issues, which managers may feel ill-equipped to deal with.

Narrative coaching

Narrative coaching emerged from narrative therapy which in turn derived from literary studies and psychology. It recognises that the way people tell their stories or the stories of their organisation affects the way they view themselves and others and the way they act. If, for example, someone describes themselves as a powerless cog in a machine, it will be difficult for them to take advantage of any empowerment offered in their organisations. It is important to respect the existing narrative and to understand what this narrative achieves for the coachee (Drake 2010). The narrative coach does not seek to change the story but, through their listening and questions, encourages the coachee to see their story from different perspectives. People may find new ways to tell their story, rather than feel trapped in a narrative they have told themselves time and again, e.g. instead of a cog in a machine, a client might see themselves as a link between different parts of the organisation. This can help people discover options for acting in a different way. Narrative coaching can also be used to help teams and groups share organisational learning and spread good practices. While most coach mentors are sensitive to the words and images used by clients, the narrative approach heightens the focus on the use of language which can lead to breakthroughs for the client and heightened self-awareness for the coach mentor.

Alignment coaching

In recent years, there has been an increase in interest in spiritual leadership in organisations in western countries – spiritual in the sense of having a sense of meaning or purpose in life, not necessarily related to a religious belief. This is reflected in the alignment coaching approach of Lazar and Bergquist (2003) and Whitmore's transpersonal approach (Whitmore and Einzig 2010). Lazar and Bergquist discuss four types of alignment coaching: spiritual coaching where the coach helps the client discern what is most important in their lives; philosophical coaching which probes underlying assumptions and beliefs; ethics coaching which helps the person clarify their values and ethical beliefs; and personal/ career alignment coaching which focuses on life and career issues and patterns in the work context. Whitmore's transpersonal approach recognises that clients may be going through extremely difficult times, but rather than seeing the client as a problem, instead seizes the opportunity for affirmation and learning, to help the client on their journey to discovery of a sense of purpose and meaning in life, bringing out their creativity through the use of imagery, empathy and intuition (Rowan 2010).

Positive psychology and strengths coaching

Positive psychology and strengths coaching share a common focus on the client's strengths and sense of purpose (Linley 2006; Kauffman, Boniwell et al. 2010; Linley, Nielsen et al. 2010). Derived from positive psychology (Seligman 2002), these approaches encourage clients to use their strengths to identify their goals, to identify options to achieve their goals and to enhance their well-being through fostering positive emotion, engagement, relationships, meaning and achievement (Seligman 2011). Adopting a positive psychology approach does not mean ignoring negative events, but having a balance of more positive than negative in the conversation, with Bjerg (2009) suggesting three positive to one negative sentiments, separating negative events into those that are within and those that are outside the client's control. A related approach is appreciative coaching (Clancy and Blinkert 2010). Derived from appreciative inquiry (Cooperrider and Srivastva 1987) and influenced by positive psychology, appreciative coaching also focuses on strengths and positive emotions, fostering resilience and self-efficacy. Using a collaborative approach, appreciative coaches encourage clients to focus on what is good in the present and what is possible in a desired future, evoking the energy to implement changes to achieve the desired state. In a similar vein, Starcevich (2004) discusses how appreciative inquiry can be applied in mentoring.

Systems coaching

A systems coaching approach is useful in business as it sees the client embedded in the organisations in which they work. It facilitates change because it recognises that changes may also be needed in the wider system in order for the client to be able to implement their change successfully and that support of organisational stakeholders may be necessary (Barner and Higgins 2007). Kiel, Rimmer et al. (1996) note that the data-gathering stage which provides input to a systems oriented approach helps build trust, as the coach establishes their familiarity with the system and the client can recognise their own place in the system more easily. At the same time, Barner and Higgins warn against colluding with the client in accepting lack of change in the system as a reason for the client not to make changes. The coach also needs to take care not to spend too much time understanding the system but to focus on the client, their role in the system and how they can optimise their performance in that system. Chandler, Kram et al.'s (2011) ecological systems perspective on mentoring is broader than systems coaching, considering interactions not only between mentor and mentee and the organisation, but also at the societal level.

A systems approach can be used in combination with other coaching and mentoring approaches, helping coach mentors and their clients to understand the context. It can be combined with narrative coaching to show how clients see themselves in the system, with cognitive behavioural coaching to re-frame the constraints perceived by clients, and with solution-focused coaching to target particular areas for improvement. A systems approach also helps the client think through their impact on their colleagues, and this can be particularly useful with managers who are not naturally empathetic. It is also useful in cross-cultural coaching (Plaister-Ten 2013) as will be discussed in Chapter 10.

Eclectic coaching

While each approach to coaching and mentoring has its own strengths, Passmore (2010b) like Lee (2010) argues in favour of an integrative model, blending elements of behavioural, cognitive, psychodynamic and motivational interviewing, and including a systems focus also. In Passmore's view, most experienced coaches do this already and the integrated model simply describes current practice. While many coaches have been trained in a single model, experienced coach mentors constantly add to their repertoire, choosing what is best in the interest of their clients and in keeping with their own philosophy and values. This 'managed eclectic' approach, as it is termed by Megginson and Clutterbuck (2009), is not simply a pick-and-mix approach, but rather develops through reflection on the approaches that work with particular clients, and combined appropriately in the client's interest (McCarthy 2011a). Examples include combining cognitive behavioural coaching with solutions-focused coaching or combining narrative coaching with systems coaching or appreciative coaching. In contrast, it would be difficult to combine a therapeutic approach based on resolving problems buried in the past with a forward-looking solutions or positive psychology focus.

Coaching managers are even more eclectic in their approach than full-time coaches. They may, for example, adopt a solutions focus, but also adopt techniques from systems coaching or behavioural coaching or appreciative coaching. Furthermore, coaching managers blend tools and techniques from other training they have received such as leadership development or communication skills with their coaching approach (McCarthy and Ahrens 2012). As discussed in Chapters 7 to 9, coaching and mentoring also work very well in combination with theories and techniques of strategy, innovation and change. The blended approach of the coaching manager is guided by pragmatic considerations of what they find effective in their organisations, not by any rigid thinking about what coaching should or should not be.

Coach mentors each develop a unique style, in which they are true to themselves and their own values, deploying approaches which they are competent to deploy and which they believe best serve their clients or employees, drawing on a wide range of tools and techniques to help a particular person in a particular context. This text does not argue that any one approach is superior, and indeed, there is little evidence to support such an assertion. Nevertheless, being aware of a broad range of approaches and continuing to learn more about different approaches will strengthen the coach mentor's ability to meet the needs of their clients and to apply an appropriate approach in an authentic way.

Conclusion

To what extent do coach mentors need to be familiar with theoretical approaches and models? Mentors may be asked to mentor because of their capacity to develop relationships and willingness to help other people develop, not because of any detailed theoretical knowledge of mentoring. On the other hand, Cox, Bachkirova et al. claim that

> *Coaching is no longer seen as an atheoretical enterprise that relies only on common sense and an eclectic combination of tools.* (Cox, Bachkirova et al. 2010: 10)

Coaches selling their services are increasingly asked to define their methodology (Leimon, Moscovici et al. 2005). Understanding theoretical approaches enables coach mentors to enrich their practice by drawing on relevant research to enhance the coaching mentoring experience. Both external and internal coach mentors may need to do this more than mentors or coaching managers. The latter may find that an awareness of principles such as helping people to develop their own solutions is useful within their day-to-day management practices but may not find it necessary to articulate a theoretical position. Moving on from the theoretical approach, the next chapter will explore the key skills of coaching and mentoring in business.

Useful links

These resources support learning about theory and models of coaching and mentoring.

Australian Mentor Centre – http://www.australianmentorcentre.com.au/what+is+mentoring

Introduction and resources for mentoring.

Center for Narrative Coaching – http://narrativecoaching.com/our-story/what-is-narrative-coaching/

David Drake explores narrative coaching.

Chartered Institute of Personnel and Development – http://www.cipd.co.uk/hr-topics/coaching-mentoring.aspx

Resources for coaching and mentoring including research reports and industry surveys.

Coaching: An International Journal of Theory, Research and Practice – http://www.tandfonline.com/action/aboutThisJournal?show=readership&journalCode=rcoa20

Peer-reviewed journal focused on coaching. Published by Routledge in collaboration with the Association for Coaching.

Coaching at Work – http://www.coaching-at-work.com/

Coaching and mentoring research and case studies.

Coaching Psychologist – http://www.sgcp.org.uk/sgcp/publications/the-coaching-psychologist/the-coaching-psychologist_home.cfm

Peer-reviewed journal from the Special Group in Coaching Psychology of the British Psychological Society.

Cognitive Behavioural Coaching – http://www.cognitivebehaviouralcoaching-works.com/

Gladeanna McMahon introduces Cognitive Behavioural Coaching.

GROW Model – http://www.performanceconsultants.com/resources/grow-model

John Whitmore introduces the GROW model.

GROW Model – http://www.bobgriffiths.com/grow_model.htm

Bob Griffiths suggests questions for each step and shares video clips.

International Coaching Psychology Review – http://www.sgcp.org.uk/publications/international-coaching-psychology-review/

Peer-reviewed journal from the Special Group in Coaching Psychology of the British Psychological Society.

International Journal of Coaching in Organizations – http://www.ijco.info/

Focus on coaching in organisations.

International Journal of Mentoring and Coaching – http://www.emccouncil.org/eu/en/journal

Includes research, case studies and reflections.

International Journal of Evidence Based Coaching and Mentoring – http://business.brookes.ac.uk/commercial/work/iccld/ijebcm/

Free peer-reviewed journal on coaching and mentoring from Oxford Brookes University.

Models – http://www.mentoringforchange.co.uk/classic/index.php

Mike the Mentor offers short summaries of a variety of models and other resources.

Solution-Focused   Coaching   –   http://www.solutionsurfers.com/start.php?id= resources/furthermaterial

Peter Szabo shares resources for brief solution-focused coaching.

Solution-Focused Coaching – http://www.sfwork.com

Mark McKergow provides resources for solution-focused coaching.

References

Bandura, A. (1977) 'Self-efficacy: towards a unifying theory of behavioral change', *Psychological Review*, 84(2): 191–215.

Barner, R. and J. Higgins (2007) 'Understanding implicit models that guide the coaching process', *Journal of Management Development*, 26(2): 148–58.

Barnes, A. K., J. L. Mendleson, et al. (1989) 'Structured mentorship for new employees: a case study', *Journal of Applied Business Research*, 5(1): 74–7.

Barry, N. H. (2012) 'The gentle art of mentoring in higher education', *To Improve the Academy: Resources for Faculty, Instructional, and Organizational Development*, 31: 103.

Beck, A. T. (1976) *Cognitive therapy and the emotional disorders*. Madison, CT, International Universities Press.

Bell, C. R. and M. Goldsmith (2013) *Managers as mentors*. San Francisco, Berrett-Koehler.

Berg, I. K. and P. Szabo (2005) *Brief coaching for lasting solutions*. New York, Norton.

Biswas-Diener, R. (2009) 'Personal coaching as a positive intervention', *Journal of Clinical Psychology*, 65(5): 544–53.

Bjerg, H. (2009) 'The practical application of positive psychology in coaching', *The OCM Coach and Mentor Journal*, 9 (Spring): 29–30.

Bluckert, P. (2005) 'Critical factors in executive coaching – the coaching relationship', *Industrial and Commercial Training*, 37(6/7): 336–40.

Bokeno, R. M. (2007) 'Effective (linear) and emergent (nonlinear) mentoring: a practical context for practicing chaos', *Development and Learning in Organizations*, 21(5): 18–20.

Bokeno, R. M. (2009) 'Genus of learning relationships: mentoring and coaching as communicative interaction', *Development and Learning in Organizations*, 23(1): 5.

Carkhuff, R. R. (1971) *The development of human resources*. New York, Holt, Rinehart and Winston.

Cavanagh, M. J. and A. M. Grant (2010) 'The solution-focused approach to coaching', in E. Cox, T. Bachkirova and D. Clutterbuck (eds) *Complete handbook of coaching*. London, Sage, pp. 54–67.

Chandler, D. E., K. E. Kram, et al. (2011) 'An ecological systems perspective on mentoring at work: a review and future prospects', *The Academy of Management Annals*, 5(1): 519–70.

CIPD (2011) *Coaching and mentoring factsheet*. London, CIPD.

Clancy, A. L. and J. Blinkert (2010) 'Appreciative coaching: pathway to flourishing', in J. Passmore (ed.) *Excellence in coaching: the industry guide*. London, Association for Coaching/Kogan Page, pp. 147–56.

Clutterbuck, D. (2008) 'What's happening in coaching and mentoring? And what is the difference between them?', *Development and Learning in Organizations*, 22(4): 8–10.

Clutterbuck, D. and G. Lane (eds) (2004) *The situational mentor: an international review of competencies and capabilities in mentoring*. Aldershot, Gower.

Connor, J. and J. Pokora (2012) *Coaching and mentoring at work*. Maidenhead, Open University Press.

Cooperrider, D. L. and S. Srivastva (1987) 'Appreciative inquiry in organizational life', *Organizational Change and Development*, 1: 129–69.

Cox, E. (2010) 'Last things first: ending well in the coaching relationship', in S. Palmer and A. McDowall (eds) *The coaching relationship: putting people first*. Hove, Routledge, pp. 159–81.

Cox, E., T. Bachkirova and D. Clutterbuck (eds) (2010) *The complete handbook of coaching*. London, Sage.

Critchley, B. (2010) 'Relational coaching: taking the coaching high road', *Journal of Management Development*, 29(10): 851–63.

de Haan, E. (2008) *Relational coaching*. Chichester, Wiley.

Drake, D. B. (2010) 'Narrative coaching', in E. Cox, T. Bachkirova and D. Clutterbuck (eds) *The complete handbook of coaching*. London, Sage, pp. 120–31.

Eby, L. T., M. M. Butts, et al. (2010) 'Are bad experiences stronger than good ones in mentoring relationships? Evidence from the protégé and mentor perspective', *Journal of Vocational Behavior*, 77(1): 81–92.

Egan, G. (1975) *The skilled helper: a model for systematic helping and interpersonal relating*. Monterey, CA, Brooks/Cole-Thomson

Ellis, A. (1994) *Reason and emotion in psychotherapy: comprehensive method of treating human disturbances*. New York, Citadel.

Emelo, R. (2011) 'Creating a new mindset: guidelines for mentorship in today's workplace: mentorship looks very different now than it did 10 years ago. Understanding these changes will help you communicate the value of mentoring in today's workplace', *T+D*, 65: 44+.

Garvey, B., P. Stokes and D. Megginson (2009) *Coaching and mentoring: theory and practice*. London, Sage Publications Ltd.

Goleman, D. (1998) *Working with emotional intelligence*. New York, Bantam.

Grant, A. M. (2010) 'Solution-focused coaching', in J. Passmore (ed.) *Excellence in coaching, the industry guide*. London, Association for Coaching/Kogan Page, pp. 94–109.

Grant, A. M., M. Cavanagh, S. Kleitman, G. Spence, M. Lakota and N. Yu (2012) 'Development and validation of the solution-focused inventory', *Journal of Positive Psychology*, 7(12): 334–48.

Haggard, D. L., T. W. Dougherty, D. B. Turban and J. E. Wilbanks (2011) 'Who is a mentor? A review of evolving definitions and implications for research', *Journal of Management*, 37(1): 280–304.

Hamlin, R. G. and L. Sage (2011) 'Behavioural criteria of perceived mentoring effectiveness: an empirical study of effective and ineffective mentor and mentee behaviour within formal mentoring relationships', *Journal of European Industrial Training*, 35(8): 752–78.

Hawkins, P. and N. Smith (2006) *Coaching, mentoring and organizational consultancy: supervision and development*. Maidenhead, Open University Press.

Hay, J. (2007) *Reflective practice and supervision for coaches*. Maidenhead, McGraw-Hill.

Ives, Y. and E. Cox (2012) *Goal-focused coaching: theory and practice*. Abingdon, Routledge.

Joo, B.-K., J. S. Sushko, and G. N. McClean (2012) 'Multiple faces of coaching: manager-as-coach, executive coaching, and formal mentoring', *Organization Development Journal*, 30(1): 19–38.

Kauffman, C. (2010) 'The last word: how to move from good to great coaching by drawing on the full range of what you know', *Coaching: An International Journal of Theory, Research and Practice*, 3(2): 87–98.

Kauffman, C., I. Boniwell, and J. Silberman (2010) 'The positive psychology approach to coaching', in E. Cox, T. Bachkirova and D. Clutterbuck (eds) *The complete handbook of coaching*. London, Sage, pp. 158–71.

Kiel, F., E. Rimmer, K. Williams and M. Doyle (1996) 'Coaching at the top', *Consulting Psychology Journal: Practice & Research*, 48(2): 67–77.

Knowles, M. S., E. F. Holton III and R. A. Swanson (2005) *The adult learner*. San Diego, CA, Elsevier.

Kolb, D. (1984) *Experiential learning*. New York, Prentice Hall.

Kram, K. E. (1985) *Mentoring at work*. Glenview, IL., Scott, Foresman and Company.

Kram, K. E. and M. C. Higgins (2008) 'A new approach to mentoring', *Wall Street Journal* (22 September).

Ladyshewsky, R.K. (2010) 'The manager as coach as a driver of organizational development', *Leadership & Organization Development Journal*, 31: 292–306.

Lazar, J. and W. Bergquist (2003) 'Alignment coaching: the missing element of business coaching', *International Journal of Coaching in Organizations*, 1(1): 14–27.

Lee, G. (2010) 'The psychodynamic approach to coaching', in E. Cox, T. Bachkirova and D. Clutterbuck (eds) *The complete handbook of coaching*. London, Sage, pp. 23–36.

Leimon, A., G. McMahon and F. Moscovici (2005) *Essential business coaching*. London, Routledge.

Lennard, D. (2010) *Coaching models: a cultural perspective*. New York, Routledge.

Linley, P.A. (2006) 'Strengths coaching: a potential-guided approach to coaching psychology', *International Coaching Psychology Review*, 1(1): 37–46.

Linley, P.A., K. M. Nielsen, R. Gillett and R. Biswas-Diener (2010) 'Using signature strengths in pursuit of goals', *International Coaching Psychology Review*, 5(1): 6–15.

Machon, A. (2010) *The coaching secret: how to be an exceptional coach*. Harlow, Pearson.

McCarthy, G. (2011a) 'Coaching philosophy, eclecticism and positivism: a commentary', *Annual Review of High Performance Coaching and Consulting*, pp. 77–80.

McCarthy, G. (2011b) 'The "how" to of research', *Coachlink* (Aug–Sept): 4–5.

McCarthy, G. and J. Ahrens (2012) *How and why do managers use coaching skills? Irish Academy of Management Annual Conference*. Maynooth, Ireland, Irish Academy of Management.

McGurk, J. (2012) *Coaching: the evidence base*. London, CIPD.

McMahon, G. (2009) 'Cognitive behavioural coaching', in D. Megginson and D. Clutterbuck (eds) *Further techniques for coaching and mentoring*. Oxford, Butterworth-Heinemann, pp. 15–28.

Megginson, D. and D. Clutterbuck (2005) *Techniques for coaching and mentoring*. Oxford, Butterworth-Heinemann.

Megginson, D. and D. Clutterbuck (eds) (2009) *Further techniques for coaching and mentoring*. Oxford, Butterworth.

Mertel, T. (2010) 'Using meaningful coaching for maximum results', *Industrial and Commercial Training*, 42(4): 186–91.

Mezirow, J. (1990) *Fostering critical reflection in adulthood: a guide to transformative and emancipatory learning*. San Francisco, CA, Jossey-Bass.

Mezirow, J. (1991) *Transformative dimensions of adult learning*. San Francisco, CA, Jossey-Bass.

Morgan, H., P. Harkins, et al. (eds) (2005) *The art and practice of leadership coaching*. Hoboken, NJ, Wiley.

Natale, S., M. and T. Diamante (2005) 'The five stages of executive coaching: better process makes better practice', *Journal of Business Ethics*, 59(4): 361.

Neenan, M. (2010) 'Cognitive behavioural coaching', in J. Passmore (ed.) *Excellence in coaching: the industry guide*. London, Association for Coaching, pp. 110–22.

Nelis, D., J. Quoidbach, et al. (2009) 'Increasing emotional intelligence: (how) is it possible?', *Personality and Individual Differences*, 47(1): 36–41.

O'Broin, A. and S. Palmer (2010) 'Exploring key aspects in the formation of coaching relationships: initial indicators from the perspective of the coachee and the coach', *Coaching: An International Journal of Theory, Research and Practice*, 3(2): 124–43.

Palmer, S. (2007) 'Practice: a model suitable for coaching, counselling, psychotherapy and stress management', *The Coaching Psychologist*, 3(2): 71–7.

Palmer, S. (2008) 'The practice model of coaching', *Coaching Psychology International*, 1(1): 4–8.

Passmore, J. (ed.) (2010a) *Excellence in coaching, the industry guide*. London, Association for Coaching.

Passmore, J. (2010b) 'Integrative coaching', in *Excellence in coaching: the industry guide*. London, Kogan Page, pp. 157–71.

Plaister-Ten, J. (2013) 'Raising culturally-derived awareness and building culturally-appropriate responsibility: the development of the Cross-Cultural Kaleidoscope', *International Journal of Evidence-Based Coaching and Mentoring*, 11(2): 54–69.

Rostron, S. S. (2009) *Business coaching international*. London, Karnac.

Rowan, J. (2010) 'The transpersonal approach to coaching', in E. Cox, T. Bachkirova and D. Clutterbuck (eds) *The complete handbook of coaching*. London, Sage, pp. 146–57.

Schöen, D. (1983) *The reflective practitioner: how professionals think in practice*. Aldershot, Ashgate.

Seligman, M. E. P. (2002) *Authentic happiness*. New York, Free Press.

Seligman, M. E. P. (2011) *Flourish*. New York, Free Press.

Son, S. and D.-Y. Kim (2013) 'What makes protégés take mentors' advice in formal mentoring relationships?', *Journal of Career Development*, 40(4): 311–28.

Starcevich, M. M. (2004) *Appreciative mentoring: focusing on talents and strengths*. Mellish & Assoc.

Starr, J. (2008) *Brilliant coaching: how to be a brilliant coach in your workplace*. Harlow, Pearson.

Welman, P. and T. Bachkirova (2010) 'Power in the coaching relationship', in S. Palmer and A. McDowall (eds) *The coaching relationship: putting people first*. Hove, Routledge, pp. 139–58.

Whitmore, J. (2009) 'Business coaching international', *Coaching: An International Journal of Theory, Research and Practice*, 2(2): 176–9.

Whitmore, J. and H. Einzig (2010) 'Transpersonal coaching', in J. Passmore (ed.) *Excellence in coaching: the industry guide*. London, Association for Coaching, pp. 135–46.

Williams, H., N. Edgerton and S. Palmer (2010) 'Cognitive behavioural coaching', in E. Cox, T. Bachkirova and D. Clutterbuck (eds) *The complete handbook of coaching*. London, Sage, pp. 37–53.

Zachary, L. J. (2011) *The mentor's guide: facilitating effective learning relationships*. San Francisco, Jossey-Bass.

3

COACHING AND MENTORING SKILLS

Introduction

Within the theoretical frameworks introduced in Chapter 2, coach mentors deploy various skills in order to help the client achieve the agreed purpose of the coaching mentoring session or program. As noted, the most important success factor is to establish a good relationship between the coach mentor and client. Once this is in place, then the coach mentor can make use of appropriate skills to help their client think, identify options and make choices. In this chapter, we will examine the most important skills of coaching and mentoring, viz. observation, listening, questioning, goal setting and feedback. These skills have been identified in the competency frameworks of coaching and mentoring organisations such as the International Coach Federation and the Worldwide Association of Business Coaches as well as in the Standards Australia Handbook for Coaching in Organizations (SAI 2011).

Observation

Somewhat surprisingly, the skill of observation features in very few coaching and mentoring texts, apart from observing and interpreting body language. Parsloe and Leedham (2009) give examples of key non-verbal signals:

- Empathy – Smiles, open positive gestures, eye contact, nodding/tilting head, being close to the other person.

- Anger or aggression – Rigid posture, staring, clenched/clasped fists, arms folded tightly, tapping feet or pointing fingers.

- Nervousness – Fidgeting, eyes down, touching face.

- Boredom – Yawning, pulling at ear, looking around room.

It should, however, be noted that the meaning of these gestures varies in different cultures. Care needs to be taken not to misinterpret what we see in today's multicultural society and multinational enterprises.

Sometimes, the coach mentor is concentrating so intently on what the client is saying that they miss instances where the client appears to be avoiding discussing a topic, or fail to notice the tone of voice the client used about a colleague, or physical signals such as raised eyebrows or rolling eyes when discussing an employee. Body language indicates the speaker's feelings on the topic, sometimes even contradicting the words used, e.g. a person might claim they have no misgivings about a business decision, but their tight grip on their arm-rests, headshakes or a rapidly beating pulse at their temple might suggest otherwise. Parsloe and Leedham note that observation is not only visual but includes observant listening, commenting that '*It is amazing how much of a person's body language can be detected by actively and deeply listening over the telephone*' (Parsloe and Leedham 2009: 146). Coaching students at the University of Wollongong understood how much they relied on body language in their face-to-face coaching when they undertook an online coaching assignment using text only. One student described not having access to the client's body language as like being amputated, such was the feeling of missing a vital part of the process (McCarthy 2010).

Observation, however, is about much more than body language. It allows us to see how the other person behaves in different circumstances and how they react to different stimuli. According to Bergquist and Mura, external coaches are increasingly invited to observe the coachee in their normal work routines:

> in order for the coach to gain the most unadulterated view of how the person operates in their real life, often stressful, surroundings. The observations are then fed back thoughtfully to the client, allowing the coach and the manager to collaboratively reflect on the meaning and implications of the findings. (Bergquist and Mura 2011: Chapter Three)

Internal coach mentors have ample opportunities to observe. However, each observation is a snapshot open to interpretation. As Hunt and Weintraub (2010) note, there is a need

| I take actions based on my beliefs |
| I adopt beliefs about the world |
| I draw conclusions |
| I make assumptions based on the meaning that I added |
| I add cultural and personal meaning to what I see |
| I select data from what I observe |
| I observe data and events |

Figure 3.1   Ladder of inference (adapted from Ross 1994)

to triangulate observations with other forms of data and to check one's interpretation of what has been observed, citing Ross's Ladder of Inference (Ross 1994), illustrated in Figure 3.1.

Unless we are vigilant, we may jump from observation to inference and action, without checking the validity of our inferences. When a group of people are asked what they observe in a scene, they will often identify different things, although they have all seen the same scene. Some will say they see confusion or lack of engagement, when in fact these cannot be observed directly. People need to slow down their thought processes and identify exactly what they have seen which has made them think they have seen abstract concepts such as confusion or lack of engagement. For example, was it that many people were talking at the same time or was it that some people were not looking at each other or were texting or working on their computers? People then need to consider whether alternative interpretations might be possible for what they have seen and to check their interpretations with participants.

The external coach mentor, who is rarely with the client in the workplace, is at risk of placing too much weight on single observations, of making unwarranted assumptions, and drawing erroneous conclusions. However, if coach mentors are careful, both in their observation and in their interpretation of what they have observed, they will have a useful source of data to compare with the perceptions of both the client and other sources. Each observation helps the coach mentor not by providing a definitive interpretation, but by suggesting possible avenues to discuss so that the client can explain the situation from their perspective.

In interpreting our observations, we are also prone to bias. Biases include the halo effect (where good performance in one area leads us to think positively of the person in other areas) or its opposite, for example where a coach mentee has been described by HR in negative terms. Biases may relate to gender, age, ethnic origin and other stereotypes. The coach mentor also has to guard against over-compensating and being trapped by stereotypes. Rogers' principle of 'unconditional positive regard' (Rogers 1961) offers some defence, as it inspires us to see each individual in a positive light, being fully present with the person in the here and now, rather than seeing a person as a representative of a particular group.

Listening

Listening is the most important skill for coach mentors and one which is used at every stage of the relationship. Indeed, some would argue that if one listens well, questions become, if not redundant, certainly secondary in importance. The listener gives the speaker the rare gift of time and attention, helping develop a positive relationship, authenticity and trust (Scoular 2010; Tyler 2011). In fact, Arnold (2009) states that for many clients, listening is the best part of coaching, as their ideas are being heard and valued at a deep level.

What then are the key elements of listening in the context of coaching and mentoring? The first step is to allow the other person to speak. While this sounds simple, in many everyday conversations, people struggle to be heard. Some people dominate a conversation, keen to expound their views and to ensure that other people have understood them. They are so convinced that they are right, that they assume that others would agree with them, if only they understand their point of view. Each speaker may be simply waiting their turn, mentally rehearsing their argument in order to make their point as soon as they can, regardless of what the other person is saying. By contrast, coach mentors listen in order to understand. They are not waiting to convince the speaker of a different point of view. Through listening, reflecting and paraphrasing, coach mentors help the speaker to come to a new realisation of the situation.

Although managers often attend some form of communication training, which may mention active listening, they may not be given time to practise or given feedback to help them improve their listening skills. Furthermore, Tyler (2011) warns that while communication training may help people develop their listening skill, unless it is accompanied by Rogers' unconditional positive regard, listening is reduced to a manipulative technique.

It is important that the coach mentor demonstrates that they have not only heard the words but understood correctly what is being said. Scharmer (2007) categorises three levels of listening:

- downloading where we listen only to confirm what we know already;

- factual listening where we pay close attention to the facts presented; and

- empathic listening where we connect with the other person and begin to see the world through their eyes.

Coach mentors can check their understanding of what has been said by reflecting, paraphrasing or asking questions. Reflecting and paraphrasing are sometimes lumped together, however, they can be differentiated in that reflecting uses the speaker's own words, whereas paraphrasing uses different words to summarise what has been said. Both reflection and paraphrasing may be stated as questions, however, the coach mentor is not (at this stage) challenging what has been said. Instead, the power of this technique is that when the client hears their own words spoken by someone else, they sometimes realise that what they said is not actually or exactly what they meant. They then clarify their thinking further. If paraphrasing is inaccurate, the client will usually correct the coach mentor and provide further information to explain what they meant.

Examples are given in Table 3.1 of a statement by a client, with examples of different responses used by coach mentors to encourage the client to say more about a particular issue. Some people find reflection feels awkward and are afraid of distorting the facts by paraphrasing. They may find simple encouraging statements more natural. Others use

Table 3.1 Comparison of reflection, paraphrase, encouragement and questions

Client: I am concerned about the way my team refer every decision back to me.			
Reflection	**Paraphrase**	**Encourage**	**Question/Clarify**
So you're concerned about the way your team refers decisions back to you.	You're concerned that your team comes to you even with small decisions which they could take themselves.	Tell me more about the way your team refers decisions back to you.	What is your main concern about your team referring decisions back to you?

questions to understand the specific nature of the client's concern, as different concerns will lead to exploring different options and solutions.

Having reflected, paraphrased, encouraged or clarified, the coach mentor needs to allow time for the client to respond. As noted by Leimon, Moscovici et al., '*communication in business coaching is much more subtle than a stream of Q&A*' (Leimon, Moscovici et al. 2005: 37). True listening does not take place in a conversation which ping pongs relentlessly from one person to another. In silence, a person thinks things through in their own time, while the coach mentor holds the space. Sometimes people will answer their own questions in the silence. Coach mentors should be prepared to enable silence, rather than prompt with their own thoughts or guesses about what the other person is thinking. Their body language should be relaxed and demonstrate that they are comfortable with the silence, not fidgeting or otherwise indicating that they are impatient to move on.

As Bluckert (2006) points out, listening is not the same as agreeing with what the client says. However, he argues that if we show our respect and acknowledge what the client is saying, then the client feels less threatened when challenged. Being defensive limits the client's potential to learn and to change (Hunt and Weintraub 2010). By contrast, when coach mentors focus on the client in a non-judgemental and empathic way, seeking to understand not only the facts but how other people see those facts and feel about them, noticing how things are said, as well as the speaker's body language and what is not said (Zeus and Skiffington 2000), the client feels understood and is less likely to reject feedback.

Coach mentors demonstrate that they are listening through their body language as well as through the words they use. Positive body language may include mirroring the client's body language (in a natural way), keeping an appropriate amount of eye contact, nodding at appropriate intervals and using a warm tone of voice. Exactly how often there is eye contact or how often to nod is determined not by an artificial formula but by what seems natural at the time, varying with different people and in different cultures.

A powerful way to make people feel they have been heard is by using the same metaphors or similar language as clients have used themselves. For example, if the client uses metaphors about being at sea, the coach mentor might ask the client to say more about their image of being at sea, as this may help the client to put some of their uncertainties into words. This may be helpful for senior managers who are not used to describing feelings of uncertainties, seeing it as a sign of weakness.

Where the client's own metaphor is not helpful, the coach mentor may adopt an interventionist approach, using the following steps (Smith 2008):

1. Identify the client's predominant metaphor

2. Map out the value embedded in the metaphor

3. Outline the cognitive and behavioural consequences of living by the metaphor

4. Dispute the image within the metaphor.

For example, where the client is feeling lost at sea, the coach mentor may respond with images of lighthouses or stars shedding light, thereby suggesting that even when at sea, we may not be totally lost or in the dark. This helps the client to identify what might be lighthouses or stars in their context. Disputing the image may be achieved through a range of Rational Emotive Behaviour Therapy techniques (Beal, Kopec et al. 1996) such as reality testing, humour or substituting alternative imagery. Other techniques include asking the person to draw a picture of the situation while they comment on their drawing (Cusack 2010). This may be particularly useful for clients who like to express ideas graphically. In other words, we vary our techniques according to the person we are working with.

The coach mentor also needs to listen to what is not being said. Is there something the client is deliberately or unconsciously keeping back? This may be unintentional in that the client may be so engrossed in spelling out the detail of a situation, he/she may omit some salient features. The coach mentor prompts for relevant details, helping the person adopt a helicopter view. Alternatively the client may not have considered the impact of their behaviour on others, until the coach mentor asks about it. In his discussion of narrative coaching, Drake (2010) highlights the importance of listening carefully to identify how ideas are being expressed, and to identify ideas that want to be expressed. Drake suggests inviting clients to discover new ways of seeing their story or of seeing themselves. While listening carefully, the coach mentor needs to decide whether what has not been said can be left unsaid or whether there is a benefit to bringing it out in the open. This decision needs to be in the best interest of the client, and not to satisfy the coach mentor's curiosity.

True listening is rare in the busy world of business. However when present, it contributes not just to the client's thinking, according to Rostron, '*but also to their ability to make difficult decisions, transitioning through difficult stages of personal learning and development*' (Rostron 2009: 63). In his discussion of mindfulness mentoring and the listening coach, Groom (2009) notes that the most frequent criticism he hears of coaches and coaching programs is that they are too task-oriented and superficial. For him, this happens when we do not listen effectively and move too quickly to the action stage. While he accepts the need to draw on research and proven skills, he advocates moving away from a formula, and instead being fully present and finding a deeper way of listening and being with a person. The importance of listening in coaching and mentoring cannot be over-stated.

Questioning

Questions are important because they invite the client to think for themselves, thus creating more awareness and ownership than if a coach mentor tells a client what to think or do. In a group situation, a general question can help the group to identify different perspectives and to arrive at a shared solution. By contrast, if the coach mentor advises the group what to do, the group may respond defensively and reject the proposed solution.

Far more has been written about asking questions than about any other coaching or mentoring skill. Entire books have been devoted to the art of questions, e.g. Vogt, Brown et al. (2003), Strachan (2007) and Stoltzfus (2008). However, as Leimon, Moscovici et al. point out, sometimes a simple reply of 'And now?' can be just as effective as a cleverly constructed question (Leimon, Moscovici et al. 2005). Brief comments such as this encourage the client to keep talking, allowing them to focus on what they consider important. Sometimes, however, the coach mentor's question shines a light on an area to which the client had not paid attention and this helps unblock the client's thinking.

Open questions, i.e. questions which cannot be answered with a simple yes or no, are mainly used in coaching and mentoring, as they allow the client to articulate their thinking and, in so doing, heighten their awareness. However, coach mentors should not regard this as prescribing that all questions must be non–directive. Directive questions can be used to encourage the client to be more specific. Closed questions, which require a yes or no answer, are useful to choose between alternatives, to commit to a goal or action, or to confirm agreement or understanding. As always, the guiding principle must be the client's best interest.

Questions serve a variety of purposes. Some of these purposes, such as challenging, framing or confronting, are sometimes described as separate skills, but are included here as they are most often phrased by coach mentors as questions. However, many could also be phrased as statements, e.g. 'Tell me how …'. Questions like those listed in Table 3.2 may be used in a more or less directive way. Many coach mentors have preferred formulations that they fall back on because they have found them effective. However, there is a risk of these formulations being used unthinkingly and lacking spontaneity. Instead it is important for the coach mentor to be authentic, natural and fully present with the client. Coach mentors may benefit periodically from some form of refresher education, training or supervision, or from observing other coach mentors, so that they come back to their clients refreshed, in the full sense of the word, being mindful, fully present and ready for new conversations.

Table 3.2   Examples of questions with different purposes

Purpose	Examples	Comment
Establish common ground	When I was involved in a major merger, there were a lot of competing interests. Is anything like that going on here?	Coach mentor is aware of own filter and checks to see if there is a shared experience. May also be used to establish and develop relationship.
Seek information/ determine facts	When did your second in command resign?	Straightforward questions which help the coach mentor to understand the situation as seen by the client and validate information supplied by others.
Clarify/ check for understanding	Would I be correct if I summarised what you just said as feeling that the people who work for you don't want to take responsibility?	Useful to ensure both coach mentor and client are on the same page. May antagonise if coach mentor misinterprets or twists what they have heard.
Raise self-awareness	What do you think about the feedback in your 360 degree survey? When you did x, how did your colleagues react?	Helps people compare their self-perceptions with those of others.
Clarify values/ priorities	What gives you most pleasure in your working day? What would you like to be known for?	Helps people articulate their values and sense of priorities.

Purpose	Examples	Comment
Surface differences	We both agree that it is important to give feedback regularly. How often do you think is appropriate? My assumption here was ... but your assumption seems to be different. Can you say a bit more about how you see the situation?	While some differences may be expressed openly, others may not be noticed. It is important therefore to check that there is a common understanding underpinning agreed 'facts'.
Resolve conflict	How do you feel when ...? How might x feel when ...? Can you tell me more about your concerns (to each group member)? Is there a way to reconcile these concerns?	Helps people understand not only facts but the impact of those facts on themselves and on others. When true concerns are understood, it becomes easier to resolve them.
Challenge generalisations	Are there times when your team meetings do work effectively? Tell me about one of those times.	Used to challenge all or nothing statements, e.g. everyone/no one, always/never. Client gains an insight through processing their own experience that is more powerful than the coach mentor simply providing advice, in this example, on running good meetings.
Challenge assumptions	Can you help me to understand how we know that ... What are we assuming here?	Invites people to articulate their tacit knowledge, which may be valid or which may be based on unwarranted assumptions.
Reframe issue	If we see customers as collaborators, what opportunities might emerge?	Helps people see issue in a different way.
Think through implementation	If you introduce the new process next week, how might your team members react? Can you say more about that idea and what its impact might be? What might happen if we took this approach? Who will be affected by the decision? What are the ethical implications? What else might help this change to succeed?	Helps people to adopt a systems approach, to consider different perspectives and see how their one change may affect the overall system.
Encourage options	What else? How else could we ...? What if ...? What do you like about this option? Is there anything about this option you can't live with?	Encourage people to move beyond the first thoughts that come to mind.

(Continued)

Table 3.2 (Continued)

Purpose	Examples	Comment
Visualise outcome and make goal more precise	If this works/if you woke up in the morning and a miracle had happened … what will it look/feel like? What would I/your co-workers notice you doing differently? If a journalist asked you in 12 months time how you had achieved the turnaround, how would you reply?	Helps the goal become more real and encourages commitment to the goal.
Help people get unstuck	What is happening for you right now?	Helps people articulate their preoccupations and free them to move forward.
Help people get started	What specifically will you do differently this afternoon that will help you toward your goal?	Helps people see how to turn the goal into specific actions.
Establish progress towards goal	On a scale of 1 to 10 (where 10 is you have reached the goal and 1 is you haven't made any progress yet) whereabouts are you now? What makes it a 4 not a 2? What could you do to make it a 5? What would a 10 look like?	Scaling questions can make the goal more attainable as well as challenging over-optimistic views of progress. Client becomes conscious of what they have already achieved and can identify steps to move a little closer. Visualising what the maximum looks like helps people decide if this is really what they want and to commit to it.
Confront	You have committed to doing this three times before. What will you do differently this time?	Client recognises the barriers that have previously prevented them making the change and takes steps to ensure this time is successful – if they really do want to take the step they have identified.

'What?' and 'how?' are the most frequently used questions in coaching and mentoring, allowing the client to open up and talk about what is important to them. 'Who?', 'where?' and 'when?' elicit information. The least favoured question word in coaching and mentoring is the question 'why?'. Although commonly used in quality management to identify root causes of problems, the coaching and mentoring literature suggests that 'why' can arouse defensiveness, with the client becoming more attached to their previous behaviour, and hence it becomes more difficult to create a shift. Rephrasing such questions using 'how' is equally effective in terms of understanding what is happening but does not arouse the same level of defensiveness. However, the occasional use of 'why' questions is very effective, as sometimes clients assume that what they are doing is the only rational thing to do and have never questioned it.

In Grant and O'Connor's (2010) study comparing problem-focused and solution-oriented questions, the use of problem-solving questions increased self-efficacy and participants' sense of being nearer their goal and reduced negative affect. However, problem-solving questions did not influence positive affect or participants' feeling of understanding the problem. Solution-focused questions in contrast resulted in greater insights into the problem, enhancing positive as well as reducing negative affect, and increasing participants' sense of being nearer their goal. This supports a focus on the future and on solutions in coaching and mentoring, rather than digging into the past. However, solution-focused questions need not be leading questions, as illustrated in Vignette 3.1.

Vignette 3.1 More than one way to solve a problem

a)

There she was again, thought John, working late. I feel bad that she has to stay late so often.
'Er hello Jane', he said, 'still at it?'
'Well yes', she said. 'The work must get done.'
'You're very good to take it so seriously', said John. 'We should think about getting someone else in to help, shouldn't we?'
'That would be nice', she said, looking a bit surprised.
'Tomorrow, we'll sit down and do the job description together.'
'Great', she said. 'I'm looking forward to it.'
John headed toward the car park, feeling pleased with the conversation and how he had motivated Jane. James, the Finance Manager, wouldn't be too impressed with his commitment to taking on an extra member of staff, but it was clearly needed.

b)

There she was again, thought John, working late. I wonder why she has to stay late so often.
'Er hello Jane', he said, 'still at it?'
'Well yes', she said. 'The work must get done.'
'You're very good to take it so seriously', said John. 'Is there any pattern to it, anything in particular that leads to your having to stay late?'
'There are a couple of things', said Jane thoughtfully. 'It's either when customers return things just before month end. I have to process the returns manually, so if it's just before month end, I have to get them all done so the accounts are right. The other thing is when one of the salespeople wants to know if we've got any of a certain part left, and the data on our system isn't always up to date, so if it's urgent, I go and have a look, and that then holds me up in my other work.'
'So, if everything was working perfectly, what would that look like?'
'Well we'd have an automated returns process and the data on our system would be accurate', she said with a smile. 'Glad you see what the problem is.'

(Continued)

(Continued)

'And have you any ideas about what we could do about it?'
'Lots,' she said, 'and it needn't be too expensive either. The IT department at the university always has students and graduates looking for projects and summer jobs, so we could maybe get a couple of them working on it.'
'Excellent', said John. 'Let's sit down later this week and discuss it in more detail. There might be other things we could address at the same time. Is there anyone else we should bring into the meeting?'
'Oh yes, definitely, Tom from IT and Joe in Operations, and maybe someone from Sales?'
'Okay, are you happy to set up the meeting?'
'Yes', she said. 'It will be great to start working on a solution, instead of just putting up with it. Thanks John.'
John headed toward the car park. It was good, as Jane had said, that they were going to start working on this particular problem, but interesting that Jane had just accepted the situation until now, even though she clearly had ideas about what could be done. He would have to spend some time coaching her to put forward ideas on an on-going basis and would observe whether other people were equally reluctant to put forward ideas unless prompted.

Leading questions are where a coach mentor asks a question which prompts the client towards a solution the coach mentor has already thought of, such as in Vignette 3.1 when John suggests that they should hire an additional person. Although phrased as a question, it is clearly what John thinks should be done, and Jane agrees. Leading questions are sometimes used unintentionally. For example, a coach mentor might ask 'Would it be worthwhile asking your team members to take turns in challenging new proposals?' If coach mentors realise they have just asked a leading question such as 'Do you think it is best to do x?', they may add on alternatives so that the client chooses, e.g. 'Do you think it is best to do x or y or z?'. While not as open as asking 'What do you think is the best thing to do?', it does not completely shut down the client's thinking. Stith, Miller et al. (2012) identify another form of leading question, when the coach mentor defines in detail the top rating in a scaling question, thus losing an opportunity for clients to visualise what they would really like to see happening.

While the words we use are very important, so too is the tone of our own voice and our body language. A coach mentor shouting 'What were you thinking?' at an employee who has just made a mistake, would get a different response to the coach mentor sitting down beside the employee and asking them what they were thinking. The words might be the same but the intention demonstrated by both tone of voice and body language is very different. The same grammatical structure in English can mean quite different things. Compare, for example, a parent asking a child 'Do you want a smack?' with a parent asking a child 'Do you want an ice-cream?' The former is a threat while the latter is an offer of a treat. In email communications, we have to take particular care as emoticons do not compensate for the lack of visual or audio clues as to the speaker's intention.

Coach mentors need to be clear on the purpose of their questions and to word their questions accordingly. Starr (2008) suggests that questions should help the client think through the issues, not help the coach to come up with answers. This can be a difficult discipline to master but an important one. If we are gathering data to help us understand the problem and recommend solutions, we might ask straightforward fact-gathering questions. Questions that help the client think are not as obvious, but include questions such as looking at the issue from different perspectives, using the miracle question to imagine solutions, or questions that help people come up with more options.

As Leimon et al. point out, the coach mentor should not spend all their time thinking up clever questions. To do so, would distract them from being fully present and really listening to their client or group of clients. Starr (2008) stresses the advantage of asking simple questions in meetings if a discussion has become confused or irrelevant. Such simple questions bring clarity and focus to discussion. Summarising and paraphrasing ensure that everyone has the same interpretation of what has been discussed and agreed.

Goals

Goals are a common part of both coaching and mentoring conversations. In fact, as Garvey, Stokes et al. (2009) point out, goal setting is often seen as 'the very essence of coaching', while Zachary and Fischler (2011) advocate that the first step in mentoring should be to define a goal and secondly to track progress toward it. Others, however, suggest that mentoring is more likely to discuss the mentee's dream than a goal, suggesting something more inspirational than a tightly defined work-related goal. A goal is an event or circumstance an individual strives to attain, the difference between the present and the future comprising some form of discrepancy (Latham and Locke 2006). Ives and Cox (2012) define goal setting as a process of discrepancy management, i.e. reducing or removing the gap between where the client is now and some desired state. Goals have been found to be motivational, leading to a higher level of performance than not having a goal, but only if goals are set within certain parameters, i.e. difficult enough to be challenging, but not so difficult as to make people think it is not worth trying to achieve them. Goals should also be specific, according to Latham and Locke, so that we do not fool ourselves into thinking we have achieved a vague goal when we have not yet done so. If we define specific goals, their attainment can be unambiguously confirmed.

Several benefits have been identified for goal attainment, including increases in self-efficacy, resilience, well-being and reducing stress (Latham and Locke 2006; Grant, Curtayne et al. 2009). Achieving one's goals generates a feeling of success and subjective well-being. Having a goal encourages persistence in striving to achieve it and searching for ways to achieve it.

Despite the upsides, there are also potential dangers in goal setting. Goals can be a source of stress (Dubrin 2005). As stress can affect performance negatively, setting goals could then lead to reduced performance. Punishing people for failure to meet a goal can encourage dysfunctional and unethical behaviour in order to achieve a goal or a tendency to define a non-challenging goal in future, thus losing the positive impact on performance (Ordonez, Schweitzer et al. 2009). Managers who associate goal attainment with success and with their own self-esteem may be tempted to try anything that ensures they achieve their goals, regardless of the impact on others (Latham and Locke 2006).

Garvey, Stokes et al. (2009) warn that goals allow external coaches to limit conversations to issues acceptable to the organisation paying for the coaching, noting that internal coaches are even more controlled by the organisation. Dubrin (2005) suggests that goals set in coaching are more likely to be linked to the organisation's mission, while goals set in mentoring may be more focused on personal or career goals. Individual clients benefit from setting a broad goal and having a sense of purpose which may change or be re-shaped as the relationship with their coach mentor develops, rather than having a very narrow focus on a specific goal at the outset (Clutterbuck 2008).

Rostron (2009) argues that goals should be consistent with a person's internal drivers. Similarly, Linley, Nielsen et al. (2010) suggest that impact on well-being is greater when goals are self-concordant, i.e. consistent with a person's values and interests. Although the goal itself may not be freely chosen where the organisation is paying, a coach mentor can help people gain clarity about their motivation, aspirations, and commitment to change (Riddle and Ting 2006). According to Griffiths (2010), alignment between personal and organisational goals fulfils an important human need for meaning and belonging. Hunt and Weintraub (2010) also argue that an employee's development goals should relate in a meaningful way to the needs of the employee as well as the needs of the business. Alred and Garvey argue in favour of the need for mentoring to '*synthesise individual and organisational aspirations as a central condition of organisational success*' (Alred and Garvey 2000: 270).

In managerial coaching, goals may be imposed by the organisation. However, managers can still involve employees in how the goal will be achieved and in shaping what their contribution will be. Employees are often more knowledgeable than their managers in the processes and options for achieving the goal, leading to the identification of stronger solutions. The process of listening to and involving employees makes it more likely that employees will implement the chosen solution. Furthermore, coaching managers help their employees to articulate their own broad development goals and to recognise opportunities to help them achieve their own goals as well as contributing to company goals.

Goals within an organisation need to be defined carefully so that they do not encourage a narrow focus on a specific target to the detriment of the overall or long-term organisational performance, for example, when an organisation sets targets only for new customers, leading to salespeople neglecting existing customers. Even worse, an employee may behave unethically or illegally to generate sales in order to meet targets. To avoid this, executives need to develop their systems thinking ability. Latham and Locke (2006) advise defining an over-arching vision to which the goals of each unit contribute, thus ensuring that people's goals are not in competition with each other. Coach mentors help people think through how the performance of different parts of the organisation impact on each other and the possible consequence of different types of goals.

When people successfully attain their goals, they may be tempted to repeat the same strategies on future occasions, even when circumstances have changed (Latham and Locke 2006). Goal setting can thus encourage inflexibility, according to Dubrin (2005). Too strong a focus on a desired future state can also lead people to ignore problems or opportunities in the present (Garvey, Stokes et al. 2009).

An external coach may be keen to set goals as a way of demonstrating return on investment to the sponsor (Garvey, Stokes et al. 2009). Goals should, however, only be set if they are genuinely in the interest of the client, not if they are only in the interest of the coach. The coach mentor needs to be careful that clients are not buying into goals simply to please their coach mentor (Riddle and Ting 2006). Clutterbuck and Megginson (2009) and Garvey, Stokes et al. (2009) warn of the danger of collusion, where a client goes through the mechanics of goal setting to keep the coach happy, using it to avoid more meaningful or challenging discussions which could hold opportunities for genuine although perhaps temporarily uncomfortable, transformational learning. Warning signs are goals being chosen too quickly or being too easily attainable.

Many people are familiar with SMART goals. Although the words for which the initials stand vary, a common description of a SMART goal is one which is Specific, Measureable, Achievable, Relevant and Time-based. SMART goals are found both in mentoring (Zachary and Fischler 2011) and in coaching literature (Parsloe and Leedham 2009). They can be a useful way to turn a vague goal, a 'starter goal' in Zachary and Fischler's terminology, into something that can be actioned. However, they should not be the first step, as people get engrossed in the mechanics of the process, defining the details of a goal which may not be the most important or fulfilling goal for them to achieve.

Coach mentors should ask themselves whether a goal is the right thing for the client at this point in time. A goal may emerge unforced from an exploration of where the client is and wants to be. However, the client may not yet be ready to commit to change, as is discussed further in Chapter 4. Rather than focusing on a goal, some clients may find it more useful to reflect or take some actions (Connor and Pokora 2012).

If the client is ready to set goals, there are a number of ways in which the coach mentor can help the client identify appropriate goals. Whitmore (2009) distinguishes between end goals and performance goals. End goals are the final goals such as some form of recognition of outstanding achievement, the parallel to a gold medal for an athlete. In business, this might be to become the top salesperson or to win a national award. Whitmore points out that some of the factors affecting attainment of such goals are outside the control of the individual, e.g. the actions of competitors. Performance goals are measures of progress towards the goal and are largely within our own control. They are more achievable than the end goal and help us make progress towards our end goal. Zachary and Fischler (2011) also suggest two types of goals, 'Do' goals which focus on something short term and tangible, and 'Be' goals, which are longer term, less tangible goals, relating for example to personal development and capacity.

Rostron (2009) categorises goals as short-term, medium-term and long-term as a way to help people identify what they can action now, without losing sight of their long-term goals. An example in the 2011 Walker Cup (European–US Golf Trophy for amateur players) was when the captain, Nigel Edwards, told his team to concentrate not on winning the cup but for each individual to play their best (McCarthy 2012). Each player lived up to the challenge and their combined efforts did in fact win the cup.

Articulating end or long-term goals can refresh people's enthusiasm and help motivate them to take steps toward the goal. Linking short-term to long-term goals imbues short-term goals with meaning (Skiffington and Zeus 2003). In turn, achieving short-term goals gives people more confidence and optimism about achieving the related long-term goals. To be motivating, goals should focus on the positive, rather than on addressing deficiencies.

Grant (2012) outlines an integrated model of coach-facilitated goal-attainment, which lists the key steps from perceived need for coaching through goal selection, action plans, goal attainment and outcomes such as goal satisfaction and changes in well-being. Many factors influence the process, such as individual factors, organisational context, coachee's readiness to change and commitment, coach's ability to ensure goal congruence, goal difficulty, persistence and feedback. This complexity highlights that effective goal setting is far from completing a simplistic SMART goals template.

Mentoring often focuses on the mentee's dream (Garvey, Stokes et al. 2009). This notion of a dream or ideal can be explored in coaching also. Although some may find the word 'dream' unbusiness-like, it is dreams which drive entrepreneurs and successful businesspeople, and dreams which are at the heart of appreciative inquiry (Cooperrider and Srivastva 1987), encouraging people to be hopeful about their future. Questions which encourage people to think about dreams and inspirational goals include: Who is your ideal self? What is most important to you? What would you like people to say about you when you retire/die? Of course people's goals change as they go through life. Stopping now and then to think allows people to acknowledge how far they have come and appreciate what they can still achieve.

Visual tools such as mind-mapping can be used to draw on the creative side of the brain. The client may be attracted by many different goals but realistically cannot address all at once. Capturing possible goals in a mind-map or other graphical representation can help the client to identify which goals are related and which are most important. The mind-map can be revisited and updated periodically. Other forms of visualisation are based on the miracle or magic question, where the person imagines the goal having been attained and imagines their own feelings and actions, as well as the reactions of those around them. This helps the goal seem real and attainable. If the feelings on achievement are positive, the exercise can be highly motivating. Megginson and Clutterbuck (2005) suggest the use of visioning helps to define goals or to choose between two different goals, and helps to identify the steps to take in order to achieve the goal.

To identify a goal in a coaching or mentoring context, there are a number of alternatives to SMART, e.g., EXACT (Wilson 2007), OPUS (Stoltzfus 2008), PURE (Whitmore 2009) and CLEAR (Whitmore 2009). Wilson describes EXACT as a goal which is EXciting, as well as Assessable, Challenging and Time-framed, in other words one which requires more than ticking boxes. An exciting and challenging goal motivates people more than one which they complete at their usual pace. Bresser and Wilson (2010) suggest that this is because a goal with these qualities will embed itself in the brain's reticular activation system, the part of the brain that allows us to focus on what is useful amidst all the other things that we register consciously or subconsciously.

Stoltzfus's OPUS model stresses the importance of the client having Ownership of the idea, a Passion to achieve it, a sense of Urgency with a need to do something about it now, and a sense that this goal is Significant and meaningful. McDowall and Millward (2010) warn that coaches should avoid imposing their view of what would be the right goal for the client but instead ensure that the client has ownership, buy-in and commitment. Whitmore (2009) suggests PURE – goals which are Positively stated, Understood, Relevant and Ethical – as well as CLEAR – goals which are Challenging, Legal, Environmentally sound, Appropriate and Recorded. A conversation about goals using these prompts becomes a meaningful conversation which calls on the client to articulate their values and sense of purpose.

Top achievers use a strengths approach for identifying goals, according to Kauffman, Boniwell et al. (2010). They know their capabilities and set goals slightly above their current performance, while low achievers often have less self-awareness and set goals that are 'unrealistically ambitious'. Coach mentors can help the latter heighten their sense of self-awareness and think through the possible consequences of setting such ambitious goals, while working with the former to further build on their strengths.

Hunt and Weintraub (2010) suggest some helpful questions when defining a developmental goal: What are you going to do differently? What should you start doing? What should you stop doing? What should you keep doing? These questions can be used effectively in helping clients decide how to address 360° or other feedback. Goals are categorised by Henderson (2009) citing research by Ford and Nichols (1987) as cognitive, affective, subjective organisation (unity/transcendence), accomplishing tasks, empowering self and supporting others. Coach mentors can use these categories to explore possible goals with a client. Clients may identify many different goals and may need encouragement to choose a small number on which to focus.

Once a meaningful exciting goal has been identified, the SMART goal approach can be used to tie down the details. However, as discussed earlier, getting into the details too soon can result in a simplistic goal which meets the SMART criteria but does not excite or seem meaningful to the client and may not be implemented. Clutterbuck (2007) found that mentoring outcomes were not affected by tying goals down tightly or by commitment as measured early in the relationship. The factor that made a real difference was having and maintaining a shared sense of purpose and alignment.

The term 'goal' is also used in terms of what a client wants to get from a particular coaching session (Starr 2004). Questions such as 'what specifically do you want to achieve in this session?' help the client and coach mentor achieve a shared understanding of the purpose of the conversation. A related question is whether or how this 'session goal' is related to their end goal. If it is not, it may be helpful to understand why it is a priority for the session – perhaps it is in fact the real end goal, rather than what has previously been defined as the end goal.

Team goals may also be appropriate in a goal-focused or systems approach. Team goals provide an interim step between individual goals and organisational goals, enabling individuals to see how they contribute to the shared goal. Ives and Cox (2012) suggest that a variation to the GROW model can help with setting group goals, where the initial steps are similar (Goal, Reality and Options). The next steps help clarify the group goal and ensure that individuals are committed to and competent to achieve the tasks they accept as part of the group goal. While Ives and Cox identify many possible difficulties with group coaching, they argue that it may be the most effective way to attain goals which cannot be achieved by individuals alone.

The client's readiness to commit to the goal is vital. The coach mentor may explore this with simple questions like: 'Is this the right time to start working on this?' Or 'Is there anything else you need in order to make this work?'. Alternatively the coach mentor might use a scaling question, e.g. 'On a scale of 1 to10, how committed are you to achieving this goal?'. While the actual number is irrelevant, what is important is that the client is able to articulate what that number represents. The coach mentor can explore the reasons that make the number less than 10, e.g. is it the goal itself or obstacles within the system or the client's own abilities? Clients may be reluctant to express reservations. Rather than challenging the degree of their commitment, the coach mentor might explore how confident clients feel about achieving the goal and then explore what actions the client could take to increase the number they initially respond with, e.g. from a 5 or 6 to a 7 or 8.

Tools like force field analysis are useful in identifying the forces that are supportive of the client's efforts and those that may make life difficult. Adopting a strengths-based approach, the coach mentor helps the client develop ways to maximise the supportive forces. Sometimes clients give up on the goals they set, just as people give up on New Year's resolutions. Maintaining change is hard, as will be discussed further in Chapter 4. Discussing potential difficulties when setting the goal and strategies to manage them, reduces the likelihood that clients will simply abandon their efforts (Goldsmith and Goldsmith 2006).

Zeus and Skiffington (2000) advocate developing an action plan once the goal has been defined. This helps both coach mentor and client keep track of how and when the goal will be achieved. Having someone else interested in progress helps the client retain focus. The 'measurable' criterion of SMART goals or the 'assessable' criterion of EXACT goals provides a framework against which progress can be measured. In fact, Wilson maintains that: *'A goal without a measure is a dream, not a target'* (Wilson 2007: 45). Dreams are important but may not come to fruition by themselves.

Ulrich (2008) suggests some practical questions to help people strengthen their determination to implement whatever it is that they have decided to do. His technique of 'Four Threes' includes asking the client or employee the questions in Table 3.3:

Table 3.3   Ulrich's 'Four Threes' (adapted from Ulrich 2008)

When?	What?
3 hours	– What specific thing will you do in the next 3 hours?
3 days	– What will you do in the next 3 days to demonstrate sustained commitment?
3 weeks	– What will you put in your diary where you will demonstrate the new behaviour and get feedback on it?
3 months	– What will it look like when the change is embedded?

Achieving interim measures and early successes is highly motivating, boosting the client's self-efficacy and confidence in the coaching mentoring process. Feedback from respected colleagues and/or from a coach mentor can boost this positive effect and heighten the client's awareness and ability to self-regulate.

Despite their best efforts when initially setting goals, life events or organisational changes may mean that clients cannot succeed in their goal at a particular time. This should not be regarded as failure. It may be necessary to change the goal itself, or revise the time or resources needed to achieve it. Clients may need help to reconcile their image of themselves as successful businesspeople with the fact that they have not (yet) achieved their goal. On the other hand, if clients make no genuine attempt to achieve their stated goal and there is no apparent reason for this, the coach mentor and client need to discuss what is happening. Is it perhaps that this was not after all the most important thing for the client to focus on at the time, or alternatively does the client need to further develop skills in prioritisation and time management?

Attention also needs to be paid when clients achieve their goal. As Ives and Cox (2012) point out, while achieving a goal may increase self-efficacy, it can also lead to a sense of aimlessness. They recommend defining a follow up strategy, to track maintenance of the agreed plans and ideally embedding a goal-setting approach in the day-to-day routine of the organisation. A potential pitfall highlighted by Latham and Locke (2006) is that those achieving stretching targets may find even more stretching targets imposed the following year. They advocate instead that high-performing teams and individuals should set their own goals and strategies to attain them.

It is clear from the literature that setting goals should not be a mechanical exercise. If done well, and at the right time, goals can help clients gain clarity and focus. As ever, it is the client's interests which guide the conversation. Setting a goal is an acknowledgement that the client wishes to achieve something. This can be a big step which should not be rushed. There is no point in the client spending a great deal of time defining a goal, then leave the session unsure of whether they really want to take this step or how to tackle potential roadblocks. The follow-up sessions would then be doomed to reviews of lack of progress. How different if instead the client leaves the session feeling prepared and empowered to realise their goals!

Feedback and feedforward

Coaching and mentoring often begin by helping people accept feedback, reconciling a gap between how people see themselves and how other people see their actions (Folkman 2006). Feedback data may be formal based on a 360° assessment, or informal based on conversations between colleagues. It may arise from interviews the coach mentor conducts with other people in the organisation or emerge in relation to progress toward the goal that the client has committed to. The more specific the goal or data, the easier it is to give specific constructive feedback.

Hunt and Weintraub (2010) argue that feedback bridges the gap between performance appraisal and developmental coaching, as the recipient receives on-going inputs to their self-image of how well they are doing and how they can improve. Feedback helps the recipient operationalise their organisation's goals and values, as they receive feedback on what is expected of them in relation to what may sometimes seem quite abstract concepts. Feedback also helps the recipient self-assess as they understand their organisation's expectations better. Feedback recipients improve their self-awareness which can inspire them to learn and to change. There is, however, a risk that recipients may instead focus their attention on impression management (Hunt and Weintraub 2010). However, this is less of a risk where there is genuine trust in the organisation.

Some managers avoid giving feedback, perhaps because they fear a negative or emotional response from their employees. In previous times, an employee could conclude that if the manager did not say anything, then the employee was probably doing a satisfactory job. This completely under-estimated the motivating power of feedback, forgoing the opportunity to reinforce common goals and to develop a shared understanding of what constitutes good practice and where improvement is required. As Hunt and Weintraub (2010) observe, even poorly delivered feedback is better than no feedback. Gen Y employees in particular seek feedback as an input to their future development. Positive feedback is important, but must be genuine to be well received. Line managers do not always do this well or frequently, although they are ideally placed to observe incidents deserving of good feedback, for example, as Brounstein (2000) suggests, meeting team goals, helping other team members or giving good customer service. A conversation at the time (rather than at a periodic performance review) will help both manager and employee understand more about the incident and how to share the good practice observed.

Feedback should be timely and based on the behaviour observed or reported. It is not a criticism of the person but it helps the client become aware of the impact their behaviour has on others. Whether or not the coach mentor has directly observed the incident in question, it is important that coach mentors hear the client's perspective on the incidents which led to the feedback, listening attentively to both what is said and what is left unsaid. Hunt and Weintraub (2010) suggest three useful questions to consider in relation to the content of feedback: What was the person trying to do? What did they do? What was the impact of what they did?

Experienced coach mentors sometimes find it beneficial to go back to being a 'conscious competent', in other words becoming aware again of their application of their skills. For example, one coach said she used to ask for permission before giving feedback when she first began. Then as people usually said yes, she stopped asking. However, she noticed a difference when she started asking for permission again:

> At the very least, it gives people a chance to prepare themselves for the feedback to come, and at other times, it avoids feedback being wasted, if the person isn't ready to receive it.

Self-determination theory suggests that people are motivated when they experience a combination of autonomy, competence and relatedness (Ryan and Deci 2000). Clients are more likely to take feedback on board if they have confidence in their ability and if it is in keeping with the expectations of the people they work with. The notion of autonomy may seem at odds in an organisational setting, but research shows that it makes a huge difference if people positively choose to address the feedback they have received rather than comply with an order. If the issue is serious and must be addressed, the person's autonomy can still be engaged through spending time ensuring both coach mentor and feedback recipient have a shared understanding of the issue and together explore options to address it. The feedback recipient then takes responsibility for the choice and commits to addressing the feedback.

Informal feedback may be given at any time, but formal feedback, particularly about a negative incident, should be given in a quiet confidential setting, where the person can get over the shock which they may experience if the feedback relates to something of which they were unaware of or of which they had a different view. If there is a big disconnect between the views of feedback giver and feedback recipient, it may be better to allow the person time to reflect on their view of the incident, and reconvene later to share perspectives and explore what needs to be done to change either performance or perception.

If the coach mentor has observed a problematic incident, a conversation where they report what they observe and then listen to the employee's view of the incident will help the coach mentor understand how to interpret what they have observed. The employee is more likely to accept constructive feedback if they know the event has been accurately interpreted. The coach mentor may also wish to explore whether the best option for improvement is to focus on a highly specific element of performance or whether a broader discussion of possibilities may be helpful at this time (Hunt and Weintraub 2010). It is said that we judge ourselves by our intentions and others by their actions (Pronin 2008), in other words, we make allowances because we know what we meant to do, whereas we may judge others purely on the basis of what we observe. Coach mentors need to understand the client's intention as well as their actions, before exploring alternatives in a collaborative and non-judgemental partnership.

Coach mentors are themselves sometimes guilty of the thinking errors or cognitive distortions (McMahon 2009) they challenge in their clients. For instance, they may generalise from one incident: 'You always do x' or 'You never do y'. When addressing a specific item with a client or employee, they may throw in all the other items they are aware of. They may label the person rather than the behaviour, blame the person or discount positive behaviour. Coach mentors need to be self-aware and to challenge themselves as they do others.

Some managers and coaches give negative feedback in between two positive pieces of feedback, believing that this feedback 'sandwich' will leave the employee feeling positive. However this can have two unwanted effects. The first is that employees may only focus on the positive and not accept the negative feedback. The other less obvious one is that employees may grow to dread hearing positive feedback, as they expect something negative to follow. Addressing issues separately avoids these effects and ensures a focus on the key issue or issues. The positive element of the conversation emerges in seeking alternatives and the employee's decision on how to address the feedback. An alternative which is driven by the feedback recipient, is cited in Brown (2010). The feedback recipient first asks what the feedback giver likes, then asks if the person has any queries, and finally asks for suggestions for improvement. This approach focuses on the positive and the future and matches well with a coaching and mentoring approach, as it encourages the recipient to take responsibility for seeking and responding to feedback. Generation Y (millennial) employees are known to actively seek feedback and this gives them a useful format to adopt.

As McDowall and Millward (2010) note, research on how much feedback contributes to performance has been mixed. However, the improvement is more marked where feedback is followed up with goal setting through coaching. While feedback is valuable, a future focus or so-called 'feedforward' is a useful way for managers to highlight the strengths of employees and indicate how they might improve in the future (Goldsmith 2006; McDowall and Millward 2010). Feedforward shifts the focus from the past to the future. With feedforward, the coach mentor and client share ideas on how improvements can be made. The client then chooses what to implement. Goldsmith suggests that this approach has several advantages. He argues, for example, that feedforward is taken less personally, and that successful people who may resent what they perceive as criticism in feedback, respond positively to ideas to help them achieve their goals.

Often, the higher people go in an organisation, the less feedback they get and the more difficult it is for them to hear criticism (Ulrich 2008). If, however, they are brave enough to ask for feedback and have created a climate of trust so that people are not afraid to give it, they gain insights that help them to advance in their career and accomplish their goals. Carefully given feedback can lead to the client developing a genuine desire to change. As will be discussed in Chapter 4, awareness of the need to change is required before people decide to change. Goldsmith (2006) suggests that feedforward is more effective than feedback in helping people see that change is possible. Visualisation of the change is an important part of developing self-efficacy. This may explain why feedback combined with coaching or mentoring is more likely to result in change than feedback by itself.

Managers who have themselves been coached develop new mental models of how to give feedback effectively (Steelman et al. 2004). This underscores the need for the coach mentor to role-model a constructive approach to giving feedback, as the client may consciously or unconsciously learn not only from the content of the feedback but also learn good practice in giving feedback.

Conclusion

The coaching and mentoring skills discussed in this chapter can be applied in diverse contexts such as coaching or mentoring for succession in an SME, team-coaching in a large organisation, coaching or mentoring expatriate managers and so on. They can be applied in various models and theoretical frameworks. It is the skill of the coach mentor, applied in the service of the client, which will distinguish a great coach mentor from one who has a fixed number of steps which they work through, without any regard for where the client is at.

It is critically important that the coach mentor is not so attached or reliant on specific models, tools or techniques that it is the model or tool rather than the client which drives the agenda. Instead, the coach mentor needs to be fully present, ignoring both internal (e.g. mind chatter) and external (e.g. traffic or telephone calls) distractions and fully focused on what is happening with the client in that moment (Starr 2008). Tools and techniques should be in the service of the client, not props for the coach mentor who cannot think of anything else to do. The coach mentor aims to develop reflective competence, when they are mindful of the client and relaxed in the use of their skills. Rather than being an 'unconscious competent' such as a good driver who is sometimes unaware of a route they have just driven, the reflective competent can articulate what is happening and look for further ways to support the client and to improve their practice.

Useful links

The links in this chapter highlight resources to support learning about coaching and mentoring skills.

Association for Coaching – http://www.associationforcoaching.com/pages/ac-creditation/ac-accreditation-overview

Competency framework for all coaches plus additional competencies for executive coaches on leadership and working within an organisational context.

Center for Creative Leadership – http://www.ccl.org/leadership/podcast/index.aspx

Series of podcasts on topics such as active listening and feedback.

Coaching Tools Company – http://www.thecoachingtoolscompany.com/free_resources/37-questions-to-liberate-your-clients-from-themselves/

Lists possible questions under categories such as identifying options and taking action.

European Mentoring and Coaching Council – http://www.emccouncil.org/eu/en/15

Describes competencies at four levels: foundation, practitioner, senior practitioner and master practitioner.

Graduate School Alliance for Executive Coaching – http://www.gsaec.org/curriculum.html

List competencies they expect graduates to develop in executive coaching programmes.

Implicit self – http://www.implicitself.com/

Includes assessment tool for goal setting.

International Coach Federation (ICF) – http://www.coachfederation.org/credential/landing.cfm?ItemNumber=2206&navItemNumber=576

Set of 11 competencies including managing the process and accountability.

University of Plymouth – http://www.youtube.com/watch?v=Ss_PO5knpOQ

YouTube clip on qualities and skills of a mentor.

University of Warwick – http://www2.warwick.ac.uk/study/cll/othercourses/wmcett/resources/practitionerarea/mentoring/skills/

Short description of a range of skills including focusing and challenging.

University of Wisconsin – http://www.uwosh.edu/mentoring/faculty/materials.html

Support for mentoring skills including examples of questions.

Worldwide Association of Business Coaches – http://www.wabccoaches.com/includes/popups/competencies.html

In addition to core coaching skills and self-mastery, includes business-related competencies such as systems thinking and organisational development.

References

'New ethos transforms attitudes and approaches at RS Components: key role of coaching in customer services', *Human Resource Management International Digest,* 18(2): 33–36.

Alred, G. and R. Garvey (2000) 'Learning to produce knowledge – the contribution of mentoring', *Mentoring & Tutoring: Partnership in Learning,* 8(3): 261–72.

Arnold, J. (2009) *Coaching skills for leaders in the workplace.* Oxford, How to Books.

Beal, D., A. M. Kopec, et al. (1996) 'Disputing clients' irrational beliefs', *Journal of Rational-Emotive & Cognitive-Behavior Therapy,* 14(4): 215–29.

Bergquist, B. and A. Mura (2011) *Coachbook: a guide to organizational coaching strategies and practices,* Create Space.

Bluckert, P. (2006) *Psychological dimensions of executive coaching.* Maidenhead, Open University Press.

Bresser, F. and C. Wilson (2010) 'What is coaching?', in J. Passmore (ed.) *Excellence in coaching: the industry guide.* London, Association for Coaching, pp. 9–26.

Brounstein, M. (2000) *Coaching and mentoring for dummies.* Hoboken, NJ, Wiley.

Brown, A. F. (2010) *Teaching Feedback Techniques. 26th Annual Conference on Distance Teaching and Learning.* Madison, Wisconsin.

Clutterbuck, D. (2007) *A longitudinal study of the effectiveness of developmental mentoring.* London, King's College London. PhD.

Clutterbuck, D. (2008) 'What's happening in coaching and mentoring? And what is the difference between them?', *Development and Learning in Organizations,* 22(4): 8–10.

Clutterbuck, D. and D. Megginson (2009) 'Client focused techniques', in D. Megginson and D. Clutterbuck, *Further techniques for coaching and mentoring*. Oxford, Butterworth-Heinemann, pp. 129–93.

Connor, J. and J. Pokora (2012) *Coaching and mentoring at work*. Maidenhead, Open University Press.

Cooperrider, D. L. and S. Srivastva (1987) 'Appreciative inquiry in organizational life', *Organizational Change and Development*, 1: 129–69.

Cusack, J. (2010) 'Letting them draw their own conclusions', in G. McMahon and A. Archer (eds) *101 coaching strategies and techniques*. Hove, Routledge, pp. 160–2.

Drake, D. B. (2010) 'Narrative coaching', in E. Cox, T. Bachkirova and D. Clutterbuck (eds) *The complete handbook of coaching*. London, Sage, pp. 120–31.

Dubrin, A. J. (2005) *Coaching and mentoring skills*. Upper Saddle River, NJ, Pearson/Prentice Hall.

Folkman, J.(2006) 'Coaching others to accept feedback', in M. Goldsmith and L. Lyons (eds) *Coaching for leadership*. San Francisco, CA, Pfeiffer, pp. 71–76.

Ford, M. E. and Nichols, C. W. (1987) 'A taxonomy of human goals and some possible applications', in Ford, M. E. and Ford, D. H. (eds) *Humans as self-constructing living systems: putting the framework to work*. Hillsdale, NJ: Erlbaum.

Garvey, R., P. Stokes, et al. (2009) *Coaching and mentoring theory and practice*. London, Sage.

Goldsmith, M. (2006) 'Try feedforward instead of feedback' in M. Goldsmith and L. Lyons (eds) *Coaching for leadership*. San Francisco, CA, Pfeiffer, pp. 45-49.

Goldsmith, M. and K. Goldsmith (2006) 'Why coaching clients give up and how effective goal setting can make a positive difference', in M. Goldsmith and L. Lyons (eds) *Coaching for leadership*. San Francisco, CA, Pfeiffer, pp. 153–9.

Grant, A. M. (2012) 'An integrated model of goal-focused coaching: an evidence-based framework for teaching and practice', *International Coaching Psychology Review*, 7(2): 147.

Grant, A. M., L. Curtayne, et al. (2009) 'Executive coaching enhances goal attainment, resilience and workplace well-being: a randomised controlled study', *The Journal of Positive Psychology: Dedicated to furthering research and promoting good practice*, 4(5): 396–407.

Grant, A. M. and S. A. O'Connor (2010) 'The differential effects of solution-focused and problem-focused coaching questions: a pilot study with implications for practice', *Industrial and Commercial Training*, 42(2): 102–11.

Griffiths, A. (2010) 'Coaching and spiritual values in the workplace: exploring the perspective of coaches', *International Journal of Evidence-Based Coaching and Mentoring* (Special Issue No. 4): 65–82.

Groom, J. (2009) 'Mindfulness listening and the listening coach', in D. Megginson and D. Clutterbuck (eds) *Further techniques of coaching and mentoring*. Oxford, Butterworth-Heinemann, pp. 92–9.

Henderson, S. J. (2009) 'Assessment of personal goals: an online tool for personal counselling, coaching, and business consulting', *Measurement and Evaluation in Counselling and Development*, 41: 244–9.

Hunt, J. M. and J. R. Weintraub (2010) *The coaching manager*. Los Angeles, Sage.

Ives, Y. and E. Cox (2012) *Goal-focused coaching: theory and practice*. Abingdon, Routledge.

Kauffman, C., I. Boniwell, et al. (2010) 'The positive psychology approach to coaching', in E. Cox, T. Bachkirova and D. Clutterbuck (eds) *The complete handbook of coaching*. London, Sage, pp. 158–71.

Latham, G. P. and E. A. Locke (2006) 'Enhancing the benefits and overcoming the pitfalls of goal setting', *Organizational Dynamics*, 35(4): 332–40.

Leimon, A., G. McMahon and F. Moscovici (2005) *Essential business coaching*. Hove, Routledge.

Linley, P. A., K. M. Nielsen, R. Gillet and R. Biswas-Diener (2010) 'Using signature strengths in pursuit of goals', *International Coaching Psychology Review*, 5(1): 6–15.

McCarthy, G. (2010) *Virtual teams, eLearning and developing coaches. 4th Australian Conference on Evidence-Based Coaching.* Sydney.

McCarthy, G. (2012) 'Building self-efficacy in teams – practical examples from the 2011 Walker Cup', *International Journal of Sports Science and Coaching*, 7(Dec.): 89–91.

McDowall, A. and L. Millward (2010) 'Feeding back, feeding forward and setting goals', in S. Palmer and A. McDowall (eds) *The coaching relationship: putting people first.* Hove, Routledge, pp. 55–78.

McMahon, G. (2009) 'Cognitive behavioural coaching', in D. Megginson and D. Clutterbuck, *Further techniques for coachind and mentoring.* Oxford, Butterworth-Heinemann, pp. 15–28.

Megginson, D. and D. Clutterbuck (2005) *Techniques for coaching and mentoring.* Oxford, Butterworth-Heinemann.

Ordonez, L. D., M. E. Schweitzer, et al. (2009) 'On good scholarship, goal setting, and scholars gone wild', *Academy of Management Perspectives for Managers*, 23(1): 82–7.

Parsloe, E. and M. Leedham (2009) *Coaching and mentoring, practical conversations to improve learning.* London, Kogan Page.

Pronin, E. (2008) 'How we see ourselves and how we see others', *Science,* 320(5880): 1177–80.

Riddle, D. and S. Ting (2006) 'Leader coaches: principles and issues for in-house development', *Leadership in Action*, 26: 13–18.

Rogers, C. (1961) *On becoming a person.* Boston, Houghton Mifflin, pp. 283-284.

Ross, R. (1994) 'The ladder of inference', in P. M. Senge, A. Kleiner, R. B. Ross, B. J. Smith and C. Roberts (eds) *The fifth discipline fieldbook.* New York, Currency Doubleday, pp. 242–52.

Rostron, S. S. (2009) *Business coaching international.* London, Karnac.

Ryan, R. M. and E. L. Deci (2000) 'Self-determination theory and the facilitation of intrinsic motivation, social development and well-being', *American Psychologist,* 55(1): 68–78.

SAI (2011) *Coaching in organizations handbook*, SAI Global. HB332–2011.

Scharmer, O. (2007) *Theory U: leading from the future as it emerges.* Cambridge, MA, Society for Organizational Learning.

Scoular, A. (2010) *Business coaching.* London, Financial Times.

Skiffington, S. and P. Zeus (2003) *Behavioral coaching: how to build sustainable personal and organizational strength.* North Ryde, NSW, McGraw-Hill.

Smith, K. (2008) 'Restructuring metaphors: using mental re-mapping in cognitive coaching', *Journal of Rational-Emotive & Cognitive-Behavior Therapy*, 26(1): 16.

Starr, J. (2004) 'The manager's role in coaching. Overcoming barriers to success', *Development and Learning in Organizations*, 18(2): 9–12.

Starr, J. (2008) *Brilliant coaching: how to be a brilliant coach in your workplace.* Harlow, Pearson.

Steelman, L. A., P. E. Levy and A. F. Snell (2004) 'The feedback environment scale: Construct definition, measurement, and validation', *Educational and Psychological Measurement*, 64: 165–84.

Stith, S., M., M.L. Miller, J. Boyle, J. Swinton, G. Ratcliffe and E. McCollum (2012) 'Making a difference in making miracles: Common roadblocks to miracle question effectiveness', *Journal of Marital and Family Therapy*, 38: 380–93.

Stoltzfus, T. (2008) *Coaching questions: a coach's guide to powerful asking skills.* Virginia Beach, VA, Coach 22.

Strachan, D. (2007) *Making questions work.* San Francisco, Jossey-Bass.

Tyler, J. A. (2011) 'Reclaiming rare listening as a means of organizational re-enchantment', *Journal of Organizational Change Management*, 24(1): 143–57.

Ulrich, D. (2008) 'Coaching for results', *Business Strategy Series*, 9(3): 104–14.

Vogt, E. E., J. Brown and D. Isaacs (2003) *The art of powerful questions*. Mill Valley, CA, Whole Systems.

Whitmore, J. (2009) *Coaching for performance*. London, Nicholas Brealey.

Wilson, C. (2007) *Best practice in performance coaching: a handbook for leaders, coaches, HR professionals, and organizations*. London/Philadelphia, Kogan Page.

Zachary, L. J. and L. A. Fischler (2011) 'Begin with the end in mind: the goal-driven mentoring relationship', *T + D*(Jan.): 50–3.

Zeus, P. and S. Skiffington (2000) *Complete guide to coaching at work*. Sydney, McGraw-Hill.

4

COACHING AND MENTORING FOR INDIVIDUAL CHANGE

Introduction to change

Although people often talk about 'resistance to change', there are in fact many positive changes in our lives, such as promotions or holidays, as noted in 'The Change Myth' (Anonymous 2008). In other words not all changes are feared or resisted; merely those which we fear may affect us negatively.

Before people make changes, they have to have a desire to change, a desire which may be based on feedback from others, from something they have learned or an insight they have gained from a positive or negative experience. The choice of whether to change is the client's, not the coach mentor's. Furthermore, just because something can be changed, does not necessarily mean that it should be changed (Megginson and Clutterbuck 2005). It is also important to accept that people cannot change other people, although they can help create the awareness and motivation which may inspire others to want to change (Berg and Szabo 2005).

Coach mentors use their listening and questioning skills to help re-frame opportunities, visualise the future, and reflect on learning, thus helping people cope with change and to create the future.

In this chapter, we look at changes at the individual level. As organisations consist of people, applications of coaching and mentoring at the individual level can also be applied at the organisational level which we discuss in Chapter 9.

Reasons for change

Individuals may desire change for many reasons. A common reason for managers is that they have become aware through feedback that something in their current pattern of behaviour is negatively affecting either their current performance or relationships or their future ambitions or dreams. A common reaction is for managers to reject negative feedback which conflicts with their self-image, as illustrated in Vignette 4.1.

Vignette 4.1   Not ready to change

Robert sat at his desk and looked at his 360° feedback, then at the HR manager sitting across the desk, then back at the results. Surely there was some mistake? He and his team got on well, they had a monthly meeting where he gave them an update on the company's performance and each of his staff had an annual appraisal. Yet, according to the survey results, his team didn't feel well informed and they didn't think he paid enough attention to their career development. What more did they want? His team were lucky – his manager rarely gave him any feedback. Must be a Gen Y thing, he thought, people said they were always looking for feedback. Now the HR manager was speaking. At first the words didn't make any sense. She was talking about bringing in a coach, not for his team who were clearly the problem, but for him! He had never lost his temper at work before but he could feel anger welling up inside. He took the only option he could think of, and walked out before he said something he would regret. He returned to find a note on his desk, informing him that an appointment had been made for him with an executive coach who would 'help him to address the issues in the survey'. Well, he would see this executive coach, explain things to him, and then get back to work as usual.

Coaching or mentoring at this stage would not be a useful intervention, unless the coach mentor can quickly establish credibility and rapport and if the client is willing to see things from a different perspective. Only then can the coach mentor help the manager develop insights into why they are perceived in a way that differs from their self-perception. This in turn may result in managers developing a desire to change in some way. Here again, the coach mentor can help identify the client options, choose, and plan actions.

Women returning to work after maternity leave may have changed their worldview and benefit from coaching or mentoring to re-assess their values and career direction, to identify options for work–life balance, as well as identifying whether and how their values and goals now align with the organisation's values and goals. The organisation's goals may have changed during the maternity period or there may have been re-structuring or changes in personnel. Other returners may also benefit, e.g. people returning after a major illness, or those returning from overseas assignments. In each case, the person returning has had experience of personal change. Such 'trigger events' (Cooper, Scandura et al. 2005) facilitate leadership development. Investing in coaching and mentoring helps experienced employees to make sense of their experience, providing space in which people can process what has happened and decide how best to cope with or take advantage of them. It also makes it more likely that these people will be retained by the organisation.

Other reasons for being coached or mentored, such as transitions to new roles, are discussed in Chapter 5.

Learning and change

As noted in Chapter 2, there is a strong link between coaching and mentoring and learning. Bachkirova, Cox et al. state that:

The concept of change, which is at the heart of coaching, is also inherent in the concept of learning. Any discernible change in behaviour or cognitive development suggests that learning has taken place. (Bachkirova, Cox et al. 2010: 6)

Cameron and Green agree that:

Learning is not just an acquisition of knowledge but the application of it through doing something different in the world. (Cameron and Green 2009: 14)

Cameron and Green (2009) categorise learning theories as theories of individual change. If people are to change, they need to learn to do something new, listen to their employees' ideas or learn to do something in a new way, such as give feedback in a constructive way to their employees.

Both of these texts confirm Kolb's (1984) concept of experiential learning, where the learner learns about something in the abstract, does something, reflects and generalises from that experience, and as a result, plans to do something different. Coach mentors are thinking partners who challenge clients to think more deeply, to reflect on their experience and to choose options for the future. The choice of what to do and how to do it rests with the client.

Learning requires commitment both on the part of employees and on the part of their managers (Hunt and Weintraub 2010). Learning increases clients' self-efficacy as well as their competence, thus increasing the likelihood of goal attainment (Kurt-Südhoff 2012). Learning also requires humility, an acknowledgement that a person does not already know everything and that there may be better ways of doing things. The notion of humility in leadership is gaining currency, as it encourages self-awareness and reflection (Morris, Brotheridge et al. 2005). Willingness to learn from experience is a hallmark of authentic leaders, according to Cooper, Scandura et al. (2005). Coach mentors can work with clients to set learning goals rather than performance goals, e.g. to learn how to articulate and communicate their vision effectively. Focusing on learning rather than on performance has been shown to be linked with higher levels of motivation, which in turn lead to higher levels of performance (Ordóñez, Schweitzer et al. 2009; Grant 2012).

Theories of change

An understanding of how people change is useful in choosing the most appropriate coaching and mentoring approaches. In Cameron and Green's (2009) view, behavioural change means either encouraging a positive behaviour or discouraging a negative one. Rewards may take various forms, not only financial but also non-financial rewards such as feedback and social reinforcement. In coaching and mentoring, behavioural change relies less on direct reward and punishment and more on increasing self-awareness in clients so that they relate their personal motivation to the change.

Stages of change

A coach mentor is an agent of change but does not make the changes (Skiffington and Zeus 2003). Skiffington and Zeus describe the role of the coach as helping people to self-change, facilitating changes, and supporting people in maintaining changes. Their approach is based on research by Prochaska et al. (Prochaska, Norcross et al. 1994; Prochaska, Redding et al. 2008), where the stages of change are identified as:

- Precontemplation, when people may think about change but do not intend to do anything;

- Contemplation, when they think seriously about making a change;

- Preparation, in which they actively prepare to implement a change;

- Action, when they start to implement the change;

- Maintenance, when they sustain the change; and

- Exit.

Skiffington and Zeus combine the precontemplation and contemplation stage, renaming it as the reflection stage, but otherwise remain true to the original model. They propose a number of techniques which are appropriate in this approach including reviewing the impact of behaviour on the people in the coachee's environment, changing or avoiding triggers for the old behaviour, developing alternative behaviours, developing support networks, and rewarding changes.

Table 4.1   Coaching skills for stages of change, based on Prochaska and DiClemente (1982)

Stage	Coaching/Mentoring Skill	Purpose
Precontemplation	Listening	Understand current situation
	Asking questions	Raise awareness
Contemplation	Listening	Raise awareness
	Asking questions	Challenge assumptions
		Reframe
Preparation	Listening	Explore options and consequences
	Asking questions	Establish level of commitment
	Goal setting	Help increase self-efficacy
	Rehearsal	
Action	Listening	Encourage client to carry out specific actions and to continue implementation
	Asking questions	
	Monitoring performance	
	Feedback	
Maintenance	Listening	Understand to what extent client has changed
	Asking questions	Encourage positive changes
	Feedback	Challenge lack of action or lack of positive change
Exit	Change is embedded and no longer seen as change	

Table 4.2 Questions for stages of change (adapted from Scoular 2010)

Stage	Example Questions
Precontemplation	How might things be better?
	What are the implications of not changing?
Contemplation	So, you think it might be helpful but on the other hand, you're concerned that it might not work?
Preparation	So how could you explore this further?
	Any thoughts about how you might go about it?
Action	What specifically could you do?
	What specifically will you do?
	How did that work out?
Maintenance	How important is it for you to continue doing this?
Exit	

The stage that their clients are in determines the purpose of the conversation and hence influences the coaching and mentoring approach. Table 4.1 illustrates the use of coaching and mentoring skills at various stages of change. Scoular (2010) suggests questions for coaches to explore at each stage, as exemplified in Table 4.2.

Unless clients are ready for change, i.e. at the preparation stage, it is pointless to set goals. Clients are likely either to procrastinate and avoid making progress, or alternatively to go through the motions, attaining a goal which they do not find motivating and which does not enhance their well-being. Signs that a client is not ready to change include phrases such as 'that sounds interesting' (no indication that it has any meaning for the client nor that the client has any intention to do anything about it) or when the client explains several reasons for not doing something. At this point, the client might benefit from listing the pros and cons of the change. Where the benefits outweigh the disadvantages, the client may be ready to commit. If the benefits outweigh the disadvantages but the client is not ready to commit, there may be other disadvantages which the client has not yet articulated or the change may in some way conflict with the client's personal motivation, which needs to be explored before the client can move forward.

The process of change is not linear. Relapse may happen at any stage. The coach mentor and client then recommence at the appropriate stage. If a client slips from the action stage back to contemplation again and again, it may be that the chosen action is not one which the client really wants or feels able to take. Unless this is addressed, the client will feel stuck, knowing and feeling they should do what they have said, but reluctant to take the first steps. Clients may be at different stages of the model for different goals (Williams 2008). As a result, coach mentors may work in different ways with clients on the different goals the client has selected.

Grant (2010) warns that it takes time to embed change. Using Prochaska's 'stages of change' model, Grant explored changes by managers learning to adopt a coaching style at work. Grant found that it took about six months for the benefits of becoming a coaching manager to become apparent. This indicates a need for additional support during this period, until the new behaviours are the norm and not something the manager has to remember to do. While some clients may achieve their goals, reaching the exit point in Table 4.1 within the lifetime of a coaching mentoring contract, the mainte-nance stage may last long after the coaching engagement has finished (Skiffington and Zeus 2003). It is therefore important for the client to have other supportive networks around them to help keep them on track, to be aware of what may trigger relapses, and to have strategies ready if these triggers eventuate. Such support is valuable at all stages, because, as Zeus and Skiffington point out, *'change does not occur in a vacuum'* (Zeus and Skiffington 2000: 200). An on-going mentoring relationship is one way in which to provide this support.

Cascade of change

A similar set of stages is identified by Megginson and Clutterbuck (2005) in their cas-cade of change:

- Awareness
- Understanding
- Acceptance
- Commitment
- Plan of action
- Implementation
- Positive feedback.

Coach mentors can support people at any of these stages, particularly, according to Megginson and Clutterbuck, if the person has at least reached the stage of awareness. Listening and asking questions are important at every stage, helping raise awareness in the early stages and helping define action plans and establish levels of commitment at the later stages. If the client has not yet reached the commitment stage, there is no point developing detailed action plans. As noted in Chapter 3, people sometimes jump into setting SMART goals too soon. On the other hand, if the person has already begun to implement, then listening to their progress and giving positive feedback on their achievements reinforces commitment to sustaining the change.

Self-determination theory

A further way to conceptualise change in individuals is through self-determination theory. Ryan and Deci (2000) found that people have three basic needs which foster motivation and growth: competence, relatedness and autonomy. In order to change, people need to develop competence in the new area, feel a sense of relatedness to oth-ers, and be free to make a choice to deploy the new behaviour. Gagne and Deci (2005) say that support for manager's autonomy leads to more job satisfaction and greater acceptance of organisational change. Coach mentors help clients understand their own motivation, whether intrinsic or extrinsic, and how to make the most of their strongest motivators, in order to achieve their new goal. To be sustainable, goals have to be self-concordant, i.e. fit with the client's underlying motivators. Goals that are self-concordant are associated with greater well-being as well as a greater likelihood of implementation (Sheldon and Elliot 1999).

Intentional change theory

Intentional change theory offers another way to think about change and the phases involved (Smith, Van Oosten et al. 2009):

- ideal self
- real self
- learning plan
- testing new behaviours
- relationships.

In the 'ideal self' phase, the coach mentor helps the person visualise the person they would like to become and to be remembered as. This helps the person heighten their self-efficacy, i.e. their belief in their ability to reach that state, and arouses an emotional commitment, which helps motivation. As Bandura (1977) found, if people do not believe their efforts will be successful, then they do not try very hard. Their efforts are affected not only by their beliefs about their own capabilities but also by their beliefs about the complexity or difficulty of the task (Bandura 2012). Coach mentors challenge clients' beliefs, which may lead to an increase in self-efficacy and likelihood of success. Moen and Allgood (2009) found that while executives tend to have high levels of self-efficacy, executives who were coached increased their levels of self-efficacy significantly beyond that of the control group of executives. Self-efficacy can be built, for example, through helping people articulate their thoughts around the changes to be made and how they are to be made, considering worst possible scenarios and rehearsing alternative scenarios. Smith et al. (2009) discuss the positive emotions of hope and excitement which follow the visualisation of the ideal self. The coach mentor's role at this stage is to help the person tap into their deep desires.

When the ideal self is clear, the coach mentor then helps the client to have a clearer view of their current real self, including how they are seen by others, so that the client does not discount others' opinions or ignore those with whom they disagree. A variety of assessment tools may be used at this stage, for example Values-In-Action (VIA) and Realise 2, both of which are validated tools which can be used to identify strengths, prior to deciding which strengths to develop (see links at the end of this chapter). The coach mentor should become proficient, and where appropriate, licensed in the interpretation and use of the tools they use.

Having helped clients to identify their strengths, coach mentors then help clients choose how to build on them (Biswas-Diener and Dean 2007). Strengths use is associated with progress towards goals, which in turn leads to an increase in well-being and further progress towards goals (Linley, Nielsen et al. 2010). Garvey, Stokes et al. (2009), however, warn that a strengths approach may run into opposition from Human

Resource managers, who have traditionally worked more from a deficit perspective, addressing employees' weaknesses.

In Smith et al.'s model, the gap between ideal and current self may initially distress or depress the client. However, they then decide what they need to learn and to do, in order to move closer toward their ideal self. In the fourth phase, clients try out new behaviours which are congruent with their ideal self. The coach mentor creates a safe environment for this rehearsal which builds clients' confidence and self-efficacy. In the final phase, clients identify supportive relationships which help them sustain their behavioural change.

Coaching and mentoring for change

Mentoring is about '*transition, change and transformation*' (Megginson, Clutterbuck et al. 2006: 28). Within a mentoring relationship, change may occur slowly or may result from a flash of insight. Coaching is typically a more time-constrained process than mentoring, but it too relates to some form of change, with the person being coached or mentored identifying a gap between where they are now and where they want to be. Hawkins and Smith regard the essence of coaching as '*facilitating personal change*'(Hawkins and Smith 2006: 20) while Passmore suggests that '*most people are, at least initially, drawn to coaching to be different*' (Passmore 2010: 165). This of course applies where the client wants to be coached. As Coutu and Kauffman point out, executives who get the most out of coaching are those who are highly motivated '*with a fierce desire to learn and grow*' (Coutu and Kauffman 2009: 94). Clients who are not willing to change are not coachable (Niemes 2002; Carey, Philippon et al. 2011).

The beliefs of the humanist psychology school, according to Cameron and Green (2009), are that people are inherently capable of change. Open communication and appreciation of people's contribution to the goals of the organisation help create an environment where individuals can grow. These same beliefs underpin coaching and mentoring. Dubrin suggests that one of the main benefits of coaching is that it '*generates new possibilities for action and facilitates breakthroughs in performance*' (Dubrin 2010: 301). Rostron defines coaching as 'a process that creates sustained shifts in thinking, feeling and behaviour – and ultimately in performance' (Rostron 2009: 53). Rostron stresses that changes in the client's self-awareness and relationship awareness should result in visible changes in workplace behaviour, so that it is possible to measure what has changed as a result of coaching. Hawkins and Smith (2006) agree that the main focus is on behaviour, but they also look for changes in the way people think. Cox (2010) argues that one of the differences between counselling and coaching is that while the focus of coaching is on change, it is usually external change, although this may result in some psychological change. Wales (2003) identifies changes both in internal qualities such as self-awareness and external competencies in managing others.

In the cognitive approach to change, Cameron and Green (2009) argue that by changing their thought processes, individuals can change the way they respond to situations. Cameron and Green focus on Albert Ellis's rational emotive therapy and Aaron Beck's cognitive therapy, the latter also underpinning cognitive behavioural coaching. A technique used in coaching and mentoring which derives from this approach is the ABCDE approach discussed in Chapter 8, where coach mentors help clients recognise the beliefs which affect their response to events, and help clients to dispute these thoughts and to choose a new response (McMahon 2009). Some authors add an additional step to make the acronym ABCDEF, where the final step is a future focus, including goal setting (Williams, Edgerton et al. 2010).

Despite the strength of the cognitive approach and its applicability to coaching and mentoring, Cameron and Green (2009) warn that some difficulties cannot simply be reframed or talked through, but rather have to be worked through. They also note that this approach ignores emotions which can impact on change. The psychodynamic approach to change explores the many emotions which may affect our response to change, including denial, anger, grief, relief, experimentation and discovery (Cameron and Green 2009). In a psychodynamic approach to coaching, the coach mentor creates a safe environment in which not only thoughts but also feelings and hopes can be shared (Lee 2010). The trained psychodynamic coach recognises when clients use certain defence mechanisms, such as displacement, where clients keep busy with unimportant things, or projection where they blame other people. Lee (2010) notes that in practice, coaches whose approach is underpinned by psychodynamic theory may also use techniques from cognitive, solution-focused or other coaching approaches. As with all coaching and mentoring approaches, this approach should only be adopted by those with adequate training and supervision. Furthermore, Lee warns that not all clients want the depth of a psychodynamic approach. Coach mentors need to select approaches in which they are competent and which suit their clients.

Choosing how to change

Having decided to make a change, the client or team member may benefit from someone helping them to identify options and choose between them. Using the skills identified in Chapter 3, the coach mentor prompts the client to go beyond their first thoughts and identify a range of options, using simple prompts such as 'Let's think of more ways you could tackle this' and then using a 'What else?' question several times until no more ideas emerge. It can be useful to think about how someone else might tackle the change, e.g. 'Let's say your team member John were working on this, how might he address it?' This helps people recognise that other people may have different perspectives. It also helps to frame the discussion as one where nothing is off limits, e.g. 'Let's say there were no budget restrictions and you could do anything you wanted, what would you do then?' or 'Imagine that you had an extra day in the week just to work on this, how would you go about it?' It also helps people to visualise the change having been achieved, for example, 'Looking back in five years time, what would you like people to say about your leadership?'

Goal setting

When several options have been identified, coach mentors can use the tools and techniques for selecting options which are discussed further in Chapter 8. The selected option is a goal to which clients commit. It is meaningful to them, because they have selected it, it fits with their internal motivation, and it achieves a change which they desire.

Coach mentors can influence the effort clients put into achieving their goals through exploring the client's implementation intentions. Chatzisarantis, Hagger et al. (2010) found that simple prompts such as asking clients to write down when and where they plan to use the new behaviour increased the likelihood that the client would in fact implement their plan, even when the goal was not concordant with their internal motivators.

Coach mentors use goal setting and scaling questions with their clients both to determine the level of commitment to change and to generate commitment to it. Passmore (2010) suggests that on a scale of 1 to 10, where 10 is that the client has already made the change and 1 is the client has no interest in making the change, clients with a score less than 8 are unlikely to make the change.

Clients need to believe that the goal is attainable and that achieving it will result in some reward, whether that is a positive feeling, satisfaction with the improvement, or a more tangible reward. Follow up on progress towards goals is important until the change is habitual, i.e. the person's usual way of being and doing.

Reframing

A technique advocated by Cameron and Green (2009) and commonly used by coach mentors is reframing, where the coach mentor helps the client think about the situation in a different way, perhaps identifying the opportunity in a difficult situation or re-defining one's belief in the attainability of a goal from impossible to possible. Cameron and Green describe rational analysis as '*a cognitive technique par excellence*' (Cameron and Green 2009: 35). They suggest that the person writes down their specific belief and then all the reasons why it is not true, so that the person can see for themselves that it is an irrational belief and hence will stop believing it. The 'thinking errors' in Table 8.1 (see p. 136) provide further examples of how people can use rational analysis to address the underlying beliefs leading to a behaviour they wish to change. Palevsky (2010) states that one of the reasons for not implementing changes is related to a belief that change is not possible – thus by not implementing the change, one can prove that one had been right all along. Understanding what is blocking us helps to remove the block.

Rehearsal

While the coach mentor is not usually present when the client is actually implementing their change (unless they are a coaching manager), clients may choose to rehearse a new behaviour in the safety of a coaching session (Zeus and Skiffington 2000; Passmore 2007), either talking it through or rehearsing a possible scenario. Rehearsal allows coach mentors to observe and to give feedback in a constructive way. There are many reasons why clients do not follow through with a change in behaviour they discussed in a previous coaching session. Their workplace has not changed and it may be difficult for the client to start doing something different. It can be difficult for the client to visualise the change in practice. Peltier (2010) suggests using covert or mental rehearsal to help them gain confidence in their new behaviour. The coach mentor can help the client think through what it will be like to implement a change in behaviour, discussing the feelings this may evoke, e.g. 'it feels awkward or artificial'. Such fears may then be discussed, strategies developed to minimise the likelihood that they will arise, and to address them, if they do materialise. The coach mentor can give feedback on how the client is approaching the topic and explore alternatives. It also helps if coach mentors model the desired behaviour, e.g. ways of giving constructive feedback or challenging an employee who has not kept a commitment. Rehearsal increases the likelihood that the client or employee will implement the agreed change, similar to the 'plan-making effect' (Lawton 2013).

Sustaining change

If clients do not have strategies for dealing with difficulties as they arise, they may give up when it proves more difficult to implement in reality than in the safety of a coaching or mentoring session. Thornton observes how truths that appeared *self-evident in the clear light of a coaching session can evaporate on return to normal work routine*' (Thornton 2010: 241). Coach mentors offer varied strategies to help clients deal with 'roadblocks' (Megginson and Clutterbuck 2005). Examples of such strategies may include visualisation of when the goal is achieved, reviewing the reasons the client wants to change, identifying any possible benefits to not implementing the change, rehearsal, and third party viewpoints, where the client imagines what someone else would see and say if they looked at his/her progress. Kets de Vries and Korotov (2007) state that anticipating problems, rehearsal, reframing and on-going encouragement increase self-efficacy and motivation to implement agreed changes.

If the client has tried to change a number of times already, they may find it helpful to identify the unsuccessful pattern and to 'change the script' (Megginson and Clutterbuck 2009). The client describes the pattern and is asked to notice when it is played out again at work. The coach mentor then invites the client to select a point in the script where they would like to make a change. The client chooses a way where a slight change could be made and tries this next time the script starts to play out. Over time, clients can change the whole conversation so that it no longer prevents them implementing the desired change.

Unfortunately many people find that when they attempt to change behaviour, their colleagues are cynical and 'wait for it to wear off'. When nothing else has changed in the workplace, it can be hard not to lapse into old ways of doing and relating. Coach mentors and other supportive people provide on-going encouragement, reinforcement and feedback on the new behaviour, until it is so embedded that it has become the new norm. With respect to change, Peltier (2010) suggests that changes which only affect the individual and not the system, are likely to be temporary. Changes in the system make it easier for individuals to maintain change. Thornton (2010) suggests that some tolerance of relapses is important, enabling people to renew their efforts to implement the new behaviour.

Resilience

Coaching and mentoring for resilience helps individuals cope with change, whether personal or organisational. Baeijaert and Stellamans define resilience as 'the capacity to deal with challenges, bounce back from difficulties, adapt to changes and to learn from these experiences' (Baeijaert and Stellamans 2010: 87). They argue that a solution-focused coaching approach nurtures resilience, making the client more aware of their own resources and ability to move forward. Barrett (2004) suggests that one can target specific elements of resilience, such as flexibility. In coaching clients to develop flexibility, she encourages them to consider diverse scenarios and to draw on the resources in their networks, and not only on their own resources. Another element is proactiveness, where Barrett sees the coach as playing a particularly useful role, helping people decide to try something new, considering what the worst outcome might be, having the client rehearse to meet that eventuality, and help them take risks and learn from their experience. These approaches build self-efficacy and reduce stress by increasing people's confidence in their ability to cope.

Conclusion

This chapter highlights how coach mentors help clients recognise the need to change and take steps to achieve change. Theories of change offer useful platforms on which coach mentors can base their approaches. Changes which are in line with the client's internal motivation, and which focus on learning, are more likely to be implemented successfully. Coach mentors also help clients to recognise that change takes time and that there may be relapses. Rehearsals help build self-efficacy and increase the chances of successfully implementing change. On-going support during the implementation helps clients reflect on their actions and the reactions of their colleagues, to modify their approach if needed, and to find ways to succeed.

Useful links

The links in this chapter highlight resources to support learning about individual change.

American Psychological Association – http://www.apa.org/helpcenter/road-resilience.aspx

Tips for developing resilience and coping with change.

Businessballs – http://www.businessballs.com/personalchangeprocess.htm

Fisher's model of personal transition and other theories.

Center for Creative Leadership – http://www.ccl.org/leadership/podcast/index.aspx

Podcasts on topics such as leading in times of transition and reflection for resilience.

International Journal of Learning and Change – http://www.inderscience.com/jhome.php?jcode=ijlc

Topics include learning processes and sustainable change.

Mind Tools – http://www.mindtools.com/pages/article/coping-with-change.htm

Approaches to coping with change such as the change curve.

Realise 2 – http://www.cappeu.com/Realise2.aspx

Strengths assessment and development tool.

University of Oregon – https://sites.google.com/site/reflection4learning/why-reflect

Summarises major theories relating to reflection for learning.

Values in Action – http://www.viacharacter.org/www/

Inventory of strengths.

References

Anonymous (2008) The Change Myth. *Pfeiffer 2008 Annual Consulting*, E. Biech. San Francisco, Wiley.

Bachkirova, T., E. Cox, et al. (2010) 'Introduction', in E. Cox and T. C. Bachkirova, *Complete handbook of coaching*. London, Sage, pp. 1–20.

Baeijaert, L. and A. Stellamans (2010) 'Coaching for resilience', in T. S. Nelson (ed.) *Doing something different: solution-focused brief therapy practices*. New York, Taylor & Francis, pp. 87–92.

Bandura, A. (1977) 'Self-efficacy: towards a unifying theory of behavioral change', *Psychological Review*, 84(2): 191–215.

Bandura, A. (2012) 'On the functional properties of perceived self-efficacy revisited', *Journal of Management,* 38(1): 9–44.

Barrett, F. (2004) 'Coaching for resilience', *Organization Development Journal*, 22(1): 93–6.

Berg, I. K. and P. Szabo (2005) *Brief coaching for lasting solutions*. New York, Norton.

Biswas-Diener, R. and B. Dean (2007) *Positive psychology coaching*. Hoboken, Wiley.

Cameron, E. and M. Green (2009) *Making sense of change management: a complete guide to the models, tools and techniques of organizational change*. London, Kogan Page.

Carey, W., D. J. Philippon, et al. (2011) 'Coaching models for leadership development: an integrative review', *Journal of Leadership Studies*, 5(1): 51–69.

Chatzisarantis, N. L., M. S. Hagger and C. K. Wang (2010) 'Evaluating the effects of implementation intention and self-concordance on behaviour', *British Journal of Psychology*, 101(4): 705–18.

Cooper, C. D., T. A. Scandura and C. A. Schriesheim (2005) 'Looking forward but learning from our past: potential challenges to developing authentic leadership theory and authentic leaders', *The Leadership Quarterly*, 16(3): 475–93.

Coutu, D. and C. Kauffman (2009) 'What can coaches do for you?', *Harvard Business Review*, 87(1): 91–7.

Cox, E. (2010) 'Last things first: ending well in the coaching relationship', in S. Palmer and A. McDowall (eds) *The coaching relationship*. Hove, Routledge, pp. 159–81.

Dubrin, A. J. (2010) *Leadership: research findings, practice and skills*. Mason, OH: Cengage.

Gagne, M. and E. L. Deci (2005) 'Self-determination theory and work motivation', *Journal of Organizational Behavior*, 26: 331–62.

Garvey, R., P. Stokes, et al. (2009) *Coaching and mentoring theory and practice*. London, Sage.

Grant, A. M. (2010) 'It takes time: a stages of change perspective on the adoption of workplace coaching skills', *Journal of Change Management*, 10(1): 61–77.

Grant, A. M. (2012) 'An integrated model of goal-focused coaching: an evidence-based framework for teaching and practice', *International Coaching Psychology Review*, 7(2): 147.

Hawkins, P. and N. Smith (2006) *Coaching, mentoring and organizational consultancy: supervision and development*. Maidenhead, Open University Press.

Hunt, J. M. and J. R. Weintraub (2010) *The coaching manager*. Los Angeles, Sage.

Kets de Vries, M. F. and K. Korotov (2007) 'Transformational executive programs: an owner's manual', in M. F. Kets de Vries, K. Korotov and E. Florent-Treacy (eds) *Coach and couch: the psychology of making better leaders*. Basingstoke, Palgrave Macmillan, pp. 142–62.

Kolb, D. (1984) *Experiential learning*. New York, Prentice Hall.

Kurt-Südhoff, A. (2012) 'Using positive psychology tools in coaching to increase wellbeing', *Praxis der Wirtschaftspsychologie II*, 2: 149.

Lawton, G. (2013) 'Nudge in the right direction', *New Scientist,* (2922): 32–6.

Lee, G. (2010) 'The psychodynamic approach to coaching', in E. Cox, T. Bachkirova and D. Clutterbuck (eds) *The complete handbook of coaching*. London, Sage, pp. 23–36.

Linley, P. A., K. M. Nielsen, R. Gillett and R. Biswas-Diener (2010) 'Using signature strengths in pursuit of goals: effects on goal progress, need satisfaction, and well-being, and implications for coaching psychologists', *International Coaching Psychology Review*, 5(1): 6–15.

McMahon, G. (2009) 'Cognitive behavioural coaching', in D. Megginson and D. Clutterbuck (eds) *Further techniques for coaching and mentoring*. Oxford, Butterworth-Heinemann, pp. 15–28.

Megginson, D. and D. Clutterbuck (2005) *Techniques for coaching and mentoring*. Oxford, Butterworth-Heinemann.

Megginson, D. and D. Clutterbuck (eds) (2009) *Further techniques for coaching and mentoring*. Oxford, Butterworth.

Megginson, D., D. Clutterbuck, B. Garvey, P. Stokes and R. Garrett-Harris (2006) *Mentoring in action*. London, Kogan Page.

Moen, F. and E. Allgood (2009) 'Coaching and the effect on self-efficacy', *Organization Development Journal*, 27(4): 69.

Morris, J. A., C. M. Brotheridge and J. C. Urbanski (2005) 'Bringing humility to leadership: antecedents and consequences of leader humility', *Human Relations*, 58(10): 1323–50.

Niemes, J. (2002) 'Discovering the value of executive coaching as a business transformation tool', *Journal of Organizational Excellence*, 21(4): 61–9.

Ordóñez, L. D., M. E. Schweitzer, A. D. Galinsky and M. H. Bazerman (2009) 'On good scholarship, goal setting, and scholars gone wild', *Academy of Management Perspectives for Managers*, 23(1): 82–7.

Palevsky, M. (2010) '360-degree group coaching from the inside out', in M. F. Kets de Vries, L. Guillen, K. Korotov and E. Florent-Treacy (eds) *The coaching kaleidoscopye: insights from the inside*. Basingstoke, Palgrave Macmillan, pp. 102–17.

Passmore, J. (2007) 'An integrative model for executive coaching', *Consulting Psychology Journal: Practice and Research*, 59(1): 68–78.

Passmore, J. (2010) 'Integrative coaching', in *Excellence in coaching: the industry guide*. London, Kogan Page, pp. 157–71.

Peltier, B. (2010) *The psychology of executive coaching: theory and application*. New York, Routledge.

Prochaska, J. O. and C. C. DiClemente (1982) 'Transtheoretical therapy: toward a more integrative model of change', *Psychotherapy: Theory, Research & Practice*, 19(3): 276–88.

Prochaska, J. O., J. C. Norcross and C. DiClemente (1994) *Changing for good*. New York, Avon.

Prochaska, J. O., C. A. Redding and K. E. Evers (2008) 'The transtheoretical model and stages of change', in K. Glanz, B. K. Rimer and K. Viswanath (eds) *Health behavior and health education: theory, research and practice*. San Francisco, Jossey-Bass, pp. 97–121.

Rostron, S. S. (2009) *Business coaching international*. London, Karnac.

Ryan, R. M. and E. L. Deci (2000) 'Self-determination theory and the facilitation of intrinsic motivation, social development and well-being', *American Psychologist*, 55(1): 68–78.

Scoular, A. (2010) *Business coaching*. London, Financial Times.

Sheldon, K. M. and A. J. Elliot (1999) 'Goal striving, need satisfaction, and longitudinal well-being: The self-concordance model', *Journal of Personality and Social Psychology*, 76: 482–97.

Skiffington, S. and P. Zeus (2003) *Behavioral coaching: how to build sustainable personal and organizational strength*. North Ryde, NSW, McGraw-Hill.

Smith, M. L., E. B. Van Oosten and R. E. Boyatzis (2009) 'Coaching for sustained desired change', *Research in Organizational Change and Development*, 17: 145–73.

Thornton, C. (2010) *Group and team coaching*. Hove, Routledge.

Wales, S. (2003) 'Why coaching?', *Journal of Change Management*, 3(3): 275–82.

Williams, H., N. Edgerton and S. Palmer (2010) 'Cognitive behavioural coaching', in E. Cox, T. Bachkirova and D. Clutterbuck (eds) *The complete handbook of coaching*. London, Sage, pp. 37–53.

Williams, P. (2008) 'The life coach operating system: its foundations in psychology', in D. B. Drake, D. Brennan and K. Gortz (eds) *The philospy and practice of coaching: insights and issues for a new era*. Chichester, Jossey-Bass, pp. 3–25.

Zeus, P. and S. Skiffington (2000) *Complete guide to coaching at work*. Sydney, McGraw-Hill.

5

COACHING AND MENTORING FOR LEADERS

Introduction

Expectations of leaders have changed. Traditional ideas of the leader as a great man (usually a man) who would lead the troops into battle have given way to ideas of situational leadership, where the form of leadership exercised varies with the situation and the people being led, and to discussions of the differences between transformational and transactional leadership and between leadership and management. More recent theories of leadership include stewardship, servant leadership, distributed leadership, spiritual leadership and followership. To learn more about the different theories of leadership, see e.g. Lussier and Achua (2010). The focus here is not the form of leadership practised but rather on how coach mentors support leaders in their increasingly demanding roles.

The cost of leadership failure is high, both to the individual and the organisation, which is one of the reasons for the rapid growth of executive coaching, transitions coaching and various forms of 'on-boarding', helping people to adjust to new roles quickly (Smith, Van Oosten et al. 2009; Dai, De Meuse et al. 2011). This chapter explores applications of coaching and mentoring for leaders. Coaching and mentoring is useful at various points in people's careers when they are experiencing change or situations which require them to change. This chapter thus builds on the discussion of coaching for individual change in Chapter 4.

Coaching and mentoring for leadership development

As discussed in Chapter 4, coaching and mentoring help people make choices about what and how to change. Leadership is an on-going learning exercise entailing continuous leadership development. Mentoring potential high-flyers has long formed part of leadership development activities in large organisations. Senior executives often have external mentors who act as sounding boards. As coaching has increased in popularity in the business world, the initial target market for external coaches has been executives, while internal coaches have focused primarily on middle managers and other employees. As forms of leadership development, both coaching and mentoring offer the opportunity for leaders at all levels of the organisation to reflect on their leadership practice, make sense of feedback, set goals and take action – a continuing cycle of reflective leadership practice. While leaders can do this on their own, it is helpful to have a 'thinking partner' who listens attentively, because this improves the quality of our thinking (Kline 1999).

Neither coaching nor mentoring by itself is sufficient, if executives lack skills and need training. Kiel, Rimmer et al. (1996) reported that the majority of leadership weaknesses were due to skills the leaders had never acquired, such as developing teams, communicating a vision or managing conflict. Executives, according to O'Shaughnessy (2001), must understand their own need for self-development, in order to perform at their best and to stay ahead of those who wish to take their places. The coach mentor needs to be able to diagnose when a coaching mentoring intervention is appropriate and sufficient, when it needs to be supplemented with training, and to help the client choose appropriately. As discussed previously, combining training with coaching and mentoring helps leaders implement what they learn in training and sustain their changed behaviour until it is their natural way of doing things.

Part of the initial assessment is to choose the appropriate leadership development activity or combination of leadership development activities for a particular context, rather than automatically design a coaching or mentoring intervention on request.

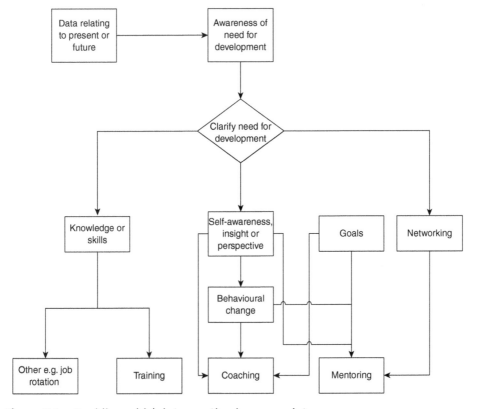

Figure 5.1 Deciding which intervention is appropriate

Some questions to consider are: Does the person need knowledge or skills? Does the person need networks? Is it a question of gaining clarity on perspectives, challenges, goals and accountability? Is anything blocking the person from reaching their potential or performing their best? The flowchart in Figure 5.1 suggests possible decision points to determine the best fit, e.g. if the purpose is to gain knowledge or skills, then training or job rotation might meet the need, while if the purpose is to gain insight or to achieve behavioural change, then either coaching or mentoring could prove useful.

A combination may also be useful, e.g. coaching to enhance the transfer of skills to the workplace following a training intervention.

Even where coaching or mentoring is aimed at personal development rather than strategy, it is useful for the coach mentor to understand the environment in which the client is operating, in other words to adopt a systems approach (Stern 2004). It may be, for example, that the client genuinely cannot implement desired changes because of external constraints. It is also important for the coach mentor to engage with the client's stakeholders to understand perceptions and expectations. The coach mentor needs to be sufficiently aware of the context to know when and how to challenge the client effectively.

Contexts for leadership coaching and mentoring

Whether new leaders join an organisation or move up within its ranks, there is a period where they are less than 100% effective, as they learn about their new role and possibly about the organisation as well. Coach mentors shorten the learning curve, by helping clients to understand what is required in their new role, how to capitalise on their existing strengths and the support available, to set goals for their new roles, and to navigate their new environments. They thus reduce the time it takes for a leader to become effective and reduce the likelihood of failure. The more senior the leadership position, the more expensive the cost of failure. Yet failures are still common, with as many as 50% of leaders failing within the first 18 months of their appointment (Reynolds 2011). Sometimes the failure is because the person is ineffective in a different industry or context, while at other times, new leaders take a long time to adjust their behaviour to the requirements of their new position. The goal for coaching and mentoring is to help leaders to succeed and avoid failure or burn-out. After all, leaders are hired or promoted because of the organisation's need for their abilities. An investment in coaching and mentoring can protect the investment in these leaders, who have the potential to inspire other people to achieve their potential or may instead prove ineffective or worse, damaging their own performance and careers or those of others.

On-boarding

On-boarding coaching or mentoring begins even before new appointees take up their role, according to Berman and Bradt (2006), observing that everything executives do or do not say or do is interpreted by the team that will work for them. The earlier the support starts, the higher the chances of success. Newly appointed leaders are often anxious about their new role and appreciate the support of coach mentors in helping them develop their personal, social and strategic capabilities (Reynolds 2011). Building self-efficacy is crucial to successful transition. Coaching has been shown to develop self-efficacy in a study of 144

CEOs and middle managers in Norway (Moen and Allgood 2009), although the partici-pants had quite high levels of self-efficacy before coaching began. Furthermore, coaching increased the self-awareness of participants, helping them to analyse what they needed to do and to recognise where they needed to learn more. Coach mentors help leaders to develop more accurate self-perceptions, to be neither under nor over confident.

Transitions

Organisational changes such as mergers or re-structuring may mean that managers need to change behaviours which had been valued previously. Managers promoted from technical operational roles may need to become more strategic or better at motivating people. Motivation to change is highly important as managers who are not convinced of the need to change may either not try or simply go through the motions, and through their lack of authenticity, lose the trust of their people. Senior leaders need to develop their external networking skills. This may not be easy initially, particularly for those who do not naturally enjoy networking or presentations. They may need to learn how to develop people more broadly, and not only consider where team members need to acquire technical skills. An honest conversation about the challenges for an individual manager transitioning to leadership from a more hands-on role helps develop realistic expectations and target resources effectively.

Mentoring is essentially about transition and change, according to Megginson et al. (2006). Mentors help new leaders or leaders in new positions become aware of the require-ments of their new role, sharing their own experience of what helped ease the transition and shorten the learning curve. Many leadership coaches specialise in transitions, helping leaders become aware of behaviours which have previously served them well, but which now may block their path to further success. For example, a strong focus on technical detail may lead to technical managers being promoted. However, unless they can develop their emotional intelligence, their ability to motivate people and their ability to develop and communicate a strategic vision, they may not be able to succeed at a higher level, as demonstrated in Vignette 5.1.

Vignette 5.1   From technician to leader

Joanne arrived at work for her new role as Research and Development Manager. This was the job she had wanted since she had started as a laboratory technician. Yet, for some reason she didn't understand, she was feeling very nervous. She switched on her computer and opened her email. One of the emails was from Mark, requesting leave for family reasons. She wasn't sure about company policy on this. As she looked through her Inbox, she thought 'well, at least I know why I'm feeling nervous … a lot of this is new to me'. She decided to start by finding company policies on the Intranet and started reading. Other employees arrived for work, most glanced her way as they came in, but seeing her engrossed in reading, did not disturb her. About 10.30 Andrew, the R&D Director called in.

'Good morning Joanne, how is your first day going?', he asked.

(Continued)

(Continued)

'Oh hi, Andrew, okay I think, but there's a lot I need to learn about company policies etc. so I thought I'd start there.'

'How about we take a wander around the lab so everyone can see you in your new role without your lab coat?'

'Uh ... okay.' She wasn't sure why he thought that was a good idea, she knew everyone already, but he was the boss. When she saw Tim, one of the trainee technicians, struggling with setting up a piece of equipment, she instinctively moved towards him.

'Hang on, Joanne', said Andrew. 'What are you going to do now?'

'Set up that machine, I know how to do that', she replied.

'I know you do,' he said, 'but are there any other ways you could handle it?'

'Well, I could ask Mary or Chris to help.'

'Any other options?'

'If we just let him do it by himself, it will take too long', she replied. 'It will be quicker if I do it.'

'Then Tim will need to keep coming back for help. How capable do you think Tim is?'

'Oh very', she said.

'And would he ask if he needed help?'

'Mm, well, he might be afraid people would think less of him.'

'How about you ask Mary or Chris to keep an eye on him and help if it becomes necessary?' said Andrew.

'Okay', she said, realising this was the first time she would be asking someone to do something, not as a co-worker, but as a manager.

'And then maybe you and I can go for a coffee. We all know you're brilliant technically. We appointed you to this role because we think you can make a difference as a leader in the lab. Let's see how we can support you to excel in your new role.'

'That would be really helpful', she replied.

With each transition, leaders need to review their capabilities, evaluate how their capabilities match what is needed in the new context and decide where they need learning or support. Coach mentors help leaders do this in an honest way, neither overly harsh nor lenient. For example, encouraging a leader lacking in confidence about the strengths or previous successful experiences that they bring to their new role helps clients recognise that they are not starting from zero but do actually have a basis for success. On the other hand, leaders who are over-confident may be challenged to provide evidence about their claim to be good at managing meetings – particularly if the coach mentor has had the opportunity to sit in on meetings led by the client and has seen evidence to the contrary.

Moving on

An executive may also choose to work with a coach mentor on their transition out of the organisation, sometimes opting to work with not-for-profit organisations or other organisations where they believe they will find more meaningful outlets for their talents. Such transitions may arouse mixed emotions, from pragmatic concerns about lower salaries to fear of failure in a new environment, and excitement about the challenge of 'giving something back' to society. The coach mentor can help the executive gain clarity about their motivation and their values, and decide on steps to fulfil their new ambition.

Rather than leaving an organisation by choice, coach mentors also work in outplacement situations, helping those whose jobs are disappearing to identify their strengths and find new opportunities. This broader approach contrasts with the job and organisation focus provided by many organisations in down-sizing situations (Gandolfi 2007). The focus on people's strengths helps both practically in terms of increasing the likelihood of finding new employment but also psychologically, offsetting the blow to one's self-esteem which can arise when a previously successful person's job is made redundant. Providing coaching and mentoring as part of the outsourcing service can help reduce 'survivor guilt' among those left in the organisation.

Assessment tools

Assessments vary from performance data, e.g. a sales executive's sales figures or staff retention for a general manager, to perception data, such as appraisals or 360° assessments, aptitude tests and validated personality measures such as DisC (Slowikowski 2005), Myers Brigg Type Indicators (MBTI) and Neo/Wave (Big Five)(Furnham 1996). Stothart (2011) provides a useful example of how MBTI was used together with 360° feedback and coaching in a manufacturing organisation. While some managers had initial difficulties in accepting their 360° feedback, MBTI helped them better understand how others might perceive their behaviour. In a different organisation, DisC was used to help an executive understand how others might perceive him and what he needed to do as a result (Furlong 2011). Such tools are used more often in coaching than in mentoring (Joo 2005), whether this is because coaching is a commercial venture with a need both to demonstrate effectiveness and a budget to purchase appropriate tools or licences, or because mentoring is more informal and reliant on the relationship between the two people, is unclear. However, tools such as MBTI can be very useful in a mentoring relationship.

Validated tests for emotional intelligence also exist, such as Bar-on (Bar-On 2000; 2004) and Schutte, Malouff et al. (1998). Grant notes that '*Leadership, emotional intelligence and good coaching skills are inextricably interwoven*'(Grant 2007: 258). There are also assessments for specific aspects such as team roles, e.g. Belbin (1993), and learning styles, e.g. Kolb and Kolb (2005), and tools which prompt reflection, such as the Life Balance Audit (Smewing and McDowall 2010). Strengths tests such as the Realise 2 instrument are becoming increasingly popular as both coach mentors and organisations begin to realise the benefits of focusing on people's strengths and values, rather than on their deficits. Assessment tools are discussed in more detail in Passmore (2008).

With all these assessments, it is important to note that the descriptors are not permanent labels. As people go through different experiences, their behaviours and preferences can and do change. An out of date psychometric profile may no longer reflect the person and their current preferences. Although these instruments can suggest areas for exploration, the coach mentor should not treat the output generated by a psychometric profiling instrument as a definitive judgement any more than they would treat a cultural stereotype as fact.

Many psychometric tests require licensing and training to administer but users report that they are helpful in helping people to acknowledge that there are areas for improvement, providing a form of data which some executives are more willing to accept than anecdotal evidence from their colleagues. Smewing and McDowall (2010) suggest that if used at the beginning of the relationship, assessment tools help provide context for an external coach and may suggest relevant questions. Assessment tools can also be used during the coaching process, if conversations keep re-visiting old ground. If used at the conclusion of a relationship, a repeated assessment provides the opportunity to measure changes since the beginning of the contract. However, a mentor familiar with the organisational context and the individual in question and with less drive to demonstrate a return on investment, may find such tools less useful.

360° reviews

Of the various tools mentioned, the most common in organisations today is the 360° review. Intended to give a more rounded view of a person than a purely top down assessment of a subordinate by a manager, 360° assessments use multiple sources for ratings, including some from subordinates and peers as well as from the manager to whom the person reports. 360° assessments have been criticised for many reasons, such as potential bias, wording of the questions, the risk of more weighting being attached to ratings by senior managers or that a temporary issue may skew results. While the scores may not always be fair, they do represent people's perceptions at a point in time (Sherman and Freas 2004). More inputs can produce a more accurate picture, however, it may be that only one of the feedback givers has consciously noted a particular behaviour, and yet this may be the behaviour that is holding the client back. In other words, it is not enough to look at average scores but to consider the comments carefully, rather than defensively, and try to understand what has led to each comment.

Applications of coaching and mentoring skills

Coaching and mentoring are powerful forms of leadership development. As discussed below, a leader who works with a coach mentor can identify their own blind spots, accept and reflect on feedback, and set goals to address.

Challenging self-perceptions

Some leaders may be over-confident, unaware of their own weaknesses or how they are perceived. '*Often executives self-delude themselves because too few have been honest with them or because their self-confidence overwhelms their self-awareness*' (Ulrich 2008: 105). Furthermore, Gregory, Beck et al. (2011) note that executives are likely to have previously been successful but then receive little feedback in their leadership roles, so that their self-image and self-efficacy are not necessarily applicable to their new role, where different skills may be required. Depending on their previous experience, leaders may believe that they need to behave in a certain way in order to be effective. Exploring such beliefs is important because they may prevent leaders from making changes. One of the ways in which we develop our self-awareness is through feedback from colleagues, team members, managers and others with whom we interact. However, feedback, particularly honest feedback, becomes rarer as people rise through the ranks of an organisation (Kaplan 2011). People are understandably reluctant to give negative feedback to someone who can affect the feedback giver's chances of development, promotion, remuneration and job retention.

The coach mentor is not dependent on clients in the same way as internal employees, and can fill this feedback void, helping leaders to calibrate their self-perception with the perceptions of others and address discrepancies where they exist. Particularly where the leader's self-awareness is low, it is useful to have data as stimulus material for a conversation. The leader may be completely unaware of how their behaviour impacts on others, whether they are aggressive or merely display some mildly annoying behaviours or perhaps regard the perceptions of others as unfortunate (Crawshaw 2010). Furthermore, the less skilled the leader is in some of the competencies they are now required to master, the more likely they are to over-estimate their ability (Kruger and Dunning 1999).

Making use of feedback

It has been found that combining assessments such as 360° reviews with coaching makes it more likely that the feedback will be acted upon, just as combining coaching with training increases the rate of implementation of what was learned in training. London and Smither (2002) suggest that the widespread availability of coaching and mentoring, whether by peers, subordinates, supervisors or external partners, is one of the hallmarks of a strong feedback culture. They also note that coaching improves people's willingness to accept and act on feedback. Feedback is a powerful stimulus for individual learning and growth.

Hooijberg and Lane (2010) report that executives now expect coaches to help them to interpret the reports, and help them decide which issues to focus on. Leaders may initially reject feedback which contradicts their self-image. Coach mentors help leaders process feedback and acknowledge that there are issues to be addressed, whether they are performance or perception-related. Then the coach mentor helps the leader explore options to address the issues identified, choose options and track progress, as the leader carries out the planned actions. In other words, the interaction does not stop when the feedback is analysed, rather the feedback is one of the inputs into a cycle of leader self-development, for which the leader takes responsibility and the coach mentor provides guidance and encouragement. For example, feedback from 360° assessments may lead to a focus on improving communication skills so that the manager changes how they communicate what they do rather than change the substance of what they do (Gregory and Levy 2010). Roche and Hefferon (2013) report that a non-judgemental, strengths-based conversation to debrief a strengths-based assessment was a powerful way to help participants capitalise on their strengths.

Some individuals are more likely than others to make use of feedback. The factors influencing an individual's 'feedback orientation' are the extent to which they: are willing to seek feedback; are sensitive to the views of others; value feedback; process feedback mindfully; and feel accountable to use feedback (London and Smither 2002).

Feedback orientation can be measured using the Feedback Orientation Scale developed and validated by Linderbaum and Levy (2010). Regular coaching and mentoring increase people's positive response to feedback.

Reflection

It is often difficult for senior leaders to think out loud, as they may not be able to discuss strategic options freely with their colleagues or direct reports, all of whom have a vested interest in the outcome. Hunt and Weintraub observe that coaching can:

> *help mitigate the isolation associated with leadership roles and the potential damage that such isolation can cause to the leader's psyche and ability to function on a sustainable basis.* (Hunt and Weintraub 2010: 7)

Kilburg (1996) notes that one of the most helpful aspects of coaching is that it forces executives to take time out from their busy schedules to reflect on their own performance and the performance of their organisation.

Blackman (2006) found that the coach's ability to help clients identify their blind spots and to take appropriate action was among the most important aspects of executive coaching as rated by clients. An outside person such as a coach mentor can bring an unbiased fresh perspective, challenge stereotypes and blinkered thinking, and help leaders think openly and critically about the possibilities in each situation. Coach mentors also help people think through what Trompenaars and Hampden-Turner (2012) call dilemmas and Glunk and Follini (2011) call polarities. Both describe situations when someone is faced with seemingly opposite choices. Faced with these extremes, executives can get so attached to one or other end of the spectrum, that they underestimate the value of the other option or swing like a pendulum from one extreme to the other. Coach mentors help clients reconcile such dilemmas and find ways to tolerate the resulting ambiguity. This can take the form of asking questions about both extremes, developing an understanding of what both offer, and exploring options which capitalise on both, rather than falling back on a compromise between the two.

Goals

Chapter 3 stated the importance of personal goals and organisational goals being aligned. Coaching and mentoring conversations help leaders to develop a broader perspective on their development, their role with their teams, their organisation and society more broadly. Leaders may be very focused on organisational goals but may not have stopped to reflect on what they personally want to achieve in life and on their personal drivers. Managers faced with conflicting goals may not enact any change or may enact change which is not valued by their organisation. Morriss, Ely et al. (2011) suggest that the narrow pursuit of personal goals can lead to self-protection and self-promotion. Leaders can become blocked when they only focus on their own careers. Instead Morriss et al. argue that focusing on helping other people succeed helps leaders succeed in their own goals.

It has long been known that motivation relates to both intrinsic and extrinsic factors, intrinsic being internal factors such as a personal desire to do a job well, and extrinsic being external factors such as rewards. The outcome of motivation is action of some kind, the duration and extent of the action being related to the degree of motivation. Unless people find their goals motivating, they are unlikely to strive to attain them.

Grant, Curtayne et al. (2009) report that executive coaching increased personal goal attainment in a sample of 41 executives, as well as increasing resilience, reducing stress and increasing well-being. Although a small sample, this suggests that if goals are chosen well, then coaching helps increase the likelihood of the goals being achieved. A simple technique is to ask clients to reflect on previous actions they have implemented which align with the proposed goal (Fitzgerald, Moss et al. 2010). Clients who recognise that the new goal is consistent with their previous actions show increased commitment to the new goal. Spence (2007) suggests a practical approach for coach mentors, first of all agreeing with the client a scale representing progress toward attaining a goal, then using that scale to monitor progress. Coach mentors and clients agree on the so-called 'Goal Attainment Scale', defining what would constitute the expected outcome, what would be better than expected and what would be the best possible outcome (using whatever labels the client finds useful). Spence suggests that one of the outcomes of these discussions is that the client becomes more committed to the goal as they visualise the outcome.

Coach mentors help leaders to understand how their personal goals align or do not align with organisational goals, visualise and gain commitment to the set goal, generate options for achieving the goal, and give feedback on progress towards achieving it. As noted in Chapter 3, challenging goals generate higher performance than easy goals, with participants showing greater effort, focus, and persistence. Achieving goals heightens people's sense of satisfaction. Where people have previously experienced this satisfaction, they are likely to work to achieve new goals in order to experience this again.

Conclusion

Leadership is regarded as a critical competency for organisations and leaders today. In down-sized and flatter organisations, people have less chance to develop their leadership skills in low risk contexts. Coaches and mentors apply their skills to help leaders raise their self-awareness, reduce their blind spots, and make successful transitions to new roles in the same or different organisations. These applications of coaching and mentoring increase the return on investment in other forms of leadership assessment and development, whether 360° reviews, training, induction or outplacement.

Useful links

The links in this chapter highlight resources to support learning about leadership.

American Management Association – http://www.aman

Podcasts and articles on topics such as emotional intelligence and leadership values.

Center for Creative Leadership – http://www.ccl.org/leadership/podcast/index.aspx

Podcasts on topics such as strategic and global leadership and evaluation of leadership development.

Chartered Institute of Personnel and Development – http://www.cipd.co.uk/hr-topics/leadership.aspx

Podcasts and written resources on topics such as distributed leadership and conflict management.

Insead – http://knowledge.insead.edu/leadership-management

Interviews from around the world on diverse leadership topics.

Values Based Management – http://www.valuebasedmanagement.net/

Short summaries of a wide range of leadership topics.

References

Bar-On, R. (2000) 'Emotional and social intelligence: insights from the Emotional Quotient Inventory', in R. Bar-On and J. D. A. Parker (eds) *The handbook of emotional intelligence: theory, development, assessment, and application at home, school, and in the workplace.* San Francisco, CA, Jossey-Bass, pp. 363–88.

Bar-On, R. (2004) 'The Bar-On Emotional Quotient Inventory (EQ-i): Rationale, description and summary of psychometric properties', in G. Geher (ed.), *Measuring emotional intelligence: Common ground and controversy.* Hauppauge, NY: Nova Science.

Belbin, R. M. (1993) *Team roles at work.* Oxford: Butterworth-Heinemann.

Berman, W. and G. Bradt (2006) 'Executive Coaching and Consulting: "Different Strokes for Different Folks"', *Professional Psychology – Research & Practice*, 37(3): 244–53.

Blackman, A. (2006) 'Factors that contribute to the effectiveness of business coaching: the coachees perspective', *The Business Review, Cambridge*, 5(1): 98.

Crawshaw, L. (2010) 'Coaching abrasive leaders: using action research to reduce suffering and increase productivity in organizations', *International Journal of Coaching in Organizations*, 29(8): 1.

Dai, G., K. P. De Meuse and D. Gaeddert (2011) 'Onboarding externally hired executives: avoiding derailment, accelerating contribution', *Journal of Management & Organization*, 17(2): 165–78.

Fitzgerald, P., S. Moss and J. Sarros (2010) *Sustainable coaching: a primer for executives and coaches.* Prahan, VIC, Tilde University Press.

Furlong, C. (2011) 'Leading in difficult times: the role of executive coaching in developing constructive behaviours', *The Performance Solution*: 23.

Furnham, A. (1996) 'The big five versus the big four: the relationship between the Myers-Briggs Type Indicator (MBTI) and NEO-PI five factor model of personality', *Personality and Individual Differences*, 21(2): 303–307.

Gandolfi, F. (2007) 'Downsizing, corporate survivors, and employability-related issues: a European case study', *Journal of American Academy of Business*, 12(1): 50–6.

Glunk, U. and B. Follini (2011) 'Polarities in executive coaching', *Journal of Management Development*, 30(2): 222–30.

Grant, A. M. (2007) 'Enhancing coaching skills and emotional intelligence through training', *Industrial and Commercial Training*, 39(5): 257–66.

Grant, A. M., L. Curtayne and G. Burton (2009) 'Executive coaching enhances goal attainment, resilience and workplace well-being: a randomised controlled study', *The Journal of Positive Psychology: Dedicated to furthering research and promoting good practice*, 4(5): 396–407.

Gregory, J. B., J. W. Beck and A. E. Carr (2011) 'Goals, feedback, and self-regulation: control theory as a natural framework for executive coaching', *Consulting Psychology Journal: Practice & Research*, 63(1): 26–38.

Gregory, J. B. and P. E. Levy (2010) 'Employee coaching relationships: enhancing construct clarity and measurement', *Coaching: An International Journal of Theory, Research and Practice*, 3(2): 109–23.

Hooijberg, R. and N. Lane (2010) 'Using 360° feedback coaching effectively in executive education', *Perspectives for Managers*, 181: 1.

Hunt, J. M. and J. R. Weintraub (2010) *The coaching manager*. Los Angeles, Sage.

Joo, B.-K. (2005) 'Executive coaching: a conceptual framework from an integrative review of practice and research', *Human Resource Development Review*, 4(4): 462–88.

Kaplan, R. S. (2011) 'Top executives need feedback – here's how they can get it', *McKinsey Quarterly*, Spring: 1–11.

Kiel, F., E. Rimmer, K. Williams and M. Doyle (1996) 'Coaching at the top', *Consulting Psychology Journal: Practice & Research*, 48(2): 67–77.

Kilburg, R. R. (1996) 'Foreword: executive coaching as an emerging competency in the practice of consultation', *Consulting Psychology Journal: Practice & Research*, 48(2): 59–60.

Kline, N. (1999) *Time to think, listening to ignite the human mind*. London, Ward, Lock, Cassell.

Kolb, A. Y. and D. A. Kolb (2005) 'Learning styles and learning spaces: enhancing experiential learning in higher education', *Academy of Management Learning & Education*, 4(2): 193–212.

Kruger, J. and D. Dunning (1999) 'Unskilled and unaware of it: how difficulties in recognizing one's own incompetence lead to inflated self-assessments', *Journal of Personality and Social Psychology; Journal of Personality and Social Psychology*, 77(6): 1121.

Linderbaum, B. A. and P. E. Levy (2010) 'The development and validation of the Feedback Orientation Scale (FOS)', *Journal of Management*, 36(6): 1372–405.

London, M. and J. W. Smither (2002) 'Feedback orientation, feedback culture, and the longitudinal performance management process', *Human Resource Management Review*, 12(1): 81–100.

Lussier, R. N. and C. F. Achua (2010) *Leadership: theory, application and skills development*. Mason, OH, Cengage.

Megginson, D., D. Clutterbuck, R. Garvey, P. Stokes, and R. Garrett-Harris, (2006) *Mentoring in action*. London, Kogan Page.

Moen, F. and E. Allgood (2009) 'Coaching and the effect on self-efficacy', *Organization Development Journal*, 27(4): 69.

Morriss, A., R. J. Ely and F. X. Frei (2011) 'Stop holding yourself back', *Harvard Business Review*, 89(1–2 Jan–Feb.): 160–3.

O'Shaughnessy, S. (2001) 'Executive coaching: the route to business stardom', *Industrial and Commercial Training*, 33(6/7): 194–7.

Passmore, J. (ed.) (2008) *Psychometrics in coaching*. London: Association for Coaching/Kogan Page.

Reynolds, G. (2011) 'Exploring the meaning of coaching for newly appointed senior leaders in their first twelve to eighteen months in role', *International Journal of Evidence-Based Coaching and Mentoring*, Special Issue No. 5: 39–53.

Roche, B. and K. Hefferon (2013) '"The assessment needs to go hand-in-hand with the debriefing": the importance of a structured coaching debriefing in understanding and applying a positive psychology strengths assessment', *International Coaching Psychology Review*, 8(1): 20–34.

Schutte, N. S., J. M. Malouff, L. E. Hall, D. J. Haggerty, J. T. Cooper, C. J. Golden and L. Dornheim (1998) 'Development and validation of a measure of emotional intelligence', *Personality & Individual Differences*, 25(2): 167–77.

Sherman, S. and A. Freas (2004) 'The Wild West of executive coaching', *Harvard Business Review*, 82(11): 82–9.

Slowikowski, M. K. (2005) 'Using the DISC behavioral instrument to guide leadership and communication', *AORN*, 82(5): 835–43.

Smewing, C. and A. McDowall (2010) 'Assessment in coaching', in S. Palmer and A. McDowall (eds) *The coaching relationship: putting people first*. Hove, Routledge, pp. 79–100.

Smith, M. L., E. B. Van Oosten, et al. (2009) 'Coaching for sustained desired change', *Research in Organizational Change and Development*, 17: 145–73.

Spence, G. (2007) 'GAS powered coaching: Goal Attainment Scaling and its use in coaching research and practice', *International Coaching Psychology Review*, 2(2): 155–67.

Stern, L. R. (2004) 'Executive coaching: a working definition', *Consulting Psychology Journal: Practice & Research*, 56(4): 154–62.

Stothart, C. (2011) 'Coaching with 360 and MBTI: a case study', *Assessment and Development Matters*, 3(3): 5.

Trompenaars, F. and C. Hampden-Turner (2012) *Riding the waves of culture*. New York, McGraw-Hill.

Ulrich, D. (2008) 'Coaching for results', *Business Strategy Series*, 9(3): 104–14.

6

COACHING AND MENTORING BY LEADERS

Introduction

This chapter will explore applications of coaching and mentoring by leaders, both with individuals and teams. It first explores the role of leader as coach, and then examines current understanding of group and team coaching, concluding with developing a coaching and mentoring culture.

Leader as coach

Expectations of contemporary leaders have moved beyond an expectation that a single leader at the top of an organisation will have all the traits of a 'great man'. Instead there is an expectation that leadership will be demonstrated at all levels of an organisation, and that leaders within the same organisation will share a set of values which guide their behaviours (Yukl 2010). Leaders are role models, and any discrepancies between actions and words are noted by employees and other stakeholders. Where there are discrepancies, employees respond to the leaders' actions rather than their words. A hallmark of contemporary leadership is an emphasis on authenticity and ethics, with the leader being true to himself or herself and honest with employees and other stakeholders. Discrepancies between what leaders say and do are seen as a lack of authenticity. George (2007) found that authentic leaders became and remain authentic through honest reflection, learning, and enhancing their self-awareness.

These contemporary leadership characteristics are also found in the leader as coach or mentor. However, while managers may occasionally mentor their employees about their career development, it is more common for mentors not to have a direct line relationship with their mentees. In contrast, managers are increasingly being expected to deploy coaching skills. While a cynic might suggest that this is due to a desire in companies to reap the benefits of coaching without paying for external coaches, a more positive interpretation is that coaching matches the expectations of modern leadership, providing practical guidance to managers, for example on how to improve communication with their employees or how to go beyond a simple tick-box exercise when setting goals with team members. As Connor and Pokora note:

> *Senior leaders are relying less on external coaches to help transform teams and departments. There is now increasingly the expectation that all managers and leaders should use coaching skills to encourage learning and development throughout the organization as well as to increase productivity.* (Connor and Pokora 2012: 13)

The skills of a contemporary leader strongly overlap with the skills of a coach mentor outlined in Chapter 3. In fact, Dubrin argues that '*effective leaders are good coaches*' (Dubrin 2010: 300), while Clegg, Kornberger et al. claim that '*the ability to coach is now becoming a core challenge for good leaders*' (Clegg, Kornberger et al. 2011: 149)'. Lussier and Achua (2010) suggest that regardless of whether or not people are managers, they can be leaders who coach others. They argue that developing coaching skills is an important part of leadership development. Prominent among the relevant skills are: two way communication; incorporating active listening; asking powerful questions; goal setting; and feedback. Garvey et al. (2009) identify additional factors that contribute to high performance, such as being innovative, flexible and able to learn quickly, to tolerate complexity and to work collaboratively. They suggest that coaching and mentoring can contribute to all these factors. The time managers spend coaching their teams members not only helps improve individual performance and a deeper quality of thinking, but also fosters relationships and trust, which has previously been shown to lead to effective team performance, commitment, strategy implementation and productivity (McCarthy 2007). A simplified version of the managerial coaching process is shown in Figure 6.1.

Aligning goals and values with the organisation leads to people taking ownership, being empowered, feeling motivated and engaged. This in turn results in higher quality (and often quantity) of work from employees, ultimately resulting in better individual performance. The coaching manager's opportunity to continue to observe, listen and ask questions, helps team members develop self-confidence and self-efficacy and to identify

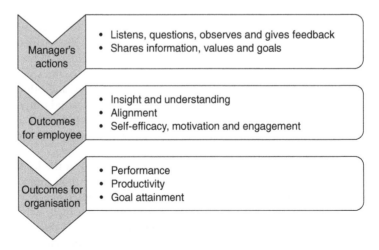

Figure 6.1   Managerial coaching

further opportunities for improvement. The flow-on effects may be seen in improvements in a range of organisational key performance indicators such as productivity, ideas generated, ability to attract quality applicants for new jobs, talent retention and development, and an ability to achieve organisational goals.

Emotional intelligence

Managers have to deal with human beings whose emotions vary every day (Cox and Patrick 2012). Managers need to recognise the importance of emotional issues in the workplace and to develop their emotional intelligence so they can support their employees appropriately – perhaps not with sophisticated tools or techniques, but by providing a safe space for employees to discuss issues and being authentic in their way of being with employees. Emotional intelligence leads to documented gains in employee engagement, productivity and well-being (Langley and Francis 2012). Grant regards coaching skills and coaching behaviours as '*in part, a manifestation of an individual's emotional intelligence*' (Grant 2007: 259). Mentoring develops emotional intelligence by helping managers think through judgement issues, which are often involved in managing people (Berman and West 2008). A combination of one-to-one and group coaching has been shown to help people to develop their emotional intelligence and to provide '*a more positive, emotionally literate approach to emotion in the workplace*' (Cox and Patrick 2012: 47). Emotional intelligence helps develop rapport, a key ingredient in a successful coaching and mentoring relationship.

Alignment

Today's managers are expected to set clear expectations of what is expected of each employee and to ensure that employees understand the alignment between their roles and that of the organisation (Yukl 2010). Coaching managers ask employees to articulate their understanding of what is expected of them and share their own view, so that managers and employees develop a shared understanding. Only once expectations are clear, can discussions about alignment and goals take place. A person will only achieve his or her goals if those goals are aligned with the person's intrinsic drivers and values (Rostron 2009).

Riddle and Ting (2006) describe how coaching managers help their team members gain insights into their own motivation and the degree to which they are committed to change. In focusing conversations around goals and alignment, the coaching manager and the employee develop a keener understanding of each team member's motivation. This may lead to a conversation about the fit between the person and the organisation and indeed may sometimes lead to a person choosing to leave an organisation or changing their current role within it. A similar outcome may arise with external coaches. Scoular (2010) recommends that in their discussions with potential client organisations, coaches should highlight the possibility of people deciding to leave. This is not to be feared, if the end result is that those who stay in the organisation are those whose goals and values are aligned with those of the organisation and who are committed to the organisation's success.

The importance of goals

Some approaches to coaching are particularly useful for managers because they are goal-oriented and thus support the manager in working towards organisational success (Ellinger, Beattie et al. 2010). An example is the solution-focused approach and other goal-focused approaches, discussed in Chapter 2. These approaches are more tightly focused on solutions, and more structured than some other coaching approaches, although they are still very much about exploring where the coachee wants to go and how they want to get there.

Even if a goal is well chosen, people may lose sight of it because of day-to-day pressures (Longenecker 2010). Coaching managers and mentors have the opportunity for on-going conversations which help people differentiate between what is urgent and what is important, in the light of the organisation's direction and the person's own motivation. As highlighted in Chapter 3, for these conversations to be effective, managers need to be able to give feedback constructively, to ask questions which open up conversations with employees, and to listen attentively both to what is said and what is left unsaid.

Strengths and challenges of leader as coach

The coaching manager has some clear advantages over the external coach, one of which is their familiarity with their team members as well as with the company, the industry and the context. Warren Bennis (cited in Korn 2011) names Falstaff in *Henry IV Part I* as the first executive coach, noting Falstaff's advice to the king as '*you want to lead people, you better understand their world*' – advice which is still relevant today.

A further advantage for coaching managers is that they have a variety of opportunities to interact with their team members, whether face-to-face or electronically. They see how their team members behave with others. They may get more honest inputs from colleagues about a problematic team member than an outsider would do. The drawback is that they lack the independent perspective of an outside coach mentor and may be so immersed in a situation that they fail to recognise salient points or to recognise their own blind spots or biases. However, their ability to give frequent feedback to motivate, challenge and develop employees is a great asset (Frisch 2001).

Relationship

As noted previously, the relationship between coach and coachee has been described as the most critical success factor in coaching (Bluckert 2005). Because of the importance of the relationship, organisations carefully match external coaches with their clients. Mentors are usually chosen freely. Managers, however, are appointed for many reasons, often for their technical competence and previous successes. The existence of a positive relationship between manager and team members should not be taken for granted. If a positive relationship does not exist, that should be addressed prior to coaching taking place (Ellinger, Beattie et al. 2010; Ladyshewsky 2010). In other words, organisations should not issue an edict declaring that all managers will henceforth coach all their employees, as this would most likely result in some unwilling coaches and coachees.

Relationships with immediate managers are known to have a strong impact on well-being, performance and on employees' intention to stay or leave a company. A coaching style has been shown to enhance this relationship. In listening to their team members, coaching managers grow to understand the thought processes and motivation of their team members more deeply than traditional managers (Whitmore 2009).

It is important for managers to listen authentically and to respond to what they hear. They may find they learn from the different perspectives and expertise of their employees. Thus there are additional benefits to managers deploying coaching skills, in addition to the direct outcomes of the coaching itself.

Directive versus non-directive

While coaching, at least in the west, is usually described as non-directive (Cox, Bachkirova et al. 2010), being non-directive can be difficult for a manager who is used to providing solutions (Leimon, Moscovici et al. 2005). Employees may be used to asking a quick question and getting a quick answer. However, they then come back again and again to get more answers. This makes the manager feel needed and may reinforce his/her view that employees cannot operate independently. Moreover, if managers provide a solution before the speaker feels that the manager has fully understood the issue, the speaker may simply reject the proposed solution. By contrast, if a manager encourages employees to develop their own solutions and to develop their ability to solve problems, then employees become more autonomous and genuinely empowered, and stronger solutions may emerge through dialogue.

In the early stages of adopting a coaching approach, managers will often focus on performance, feedback and goals (Anderson, Frankovelgia et al. 2009). Over time, as managers develop their skills and their confidence, they ask more powerful questions, spend more time listening than talking, and start to develop genuinely collaborative solutions. An employee's experience of being coached may vary considerably depending on their manager's experience of coaching and their coaching skills.

Vignette 6.1 illustrates a conversation between an employee and a manager who is relatively new to coaching, and an alternative by a more experienced coaching manager.

Vignette 6.1   A collaborative approach?

a)

Okay, thought Jack, this is my chance. I'm going to do some of that 'corridor coaching' they were talking about in the training session.
'Marty,' he said, 'I couldn't help noticing that you were a bit abrupt on the phone to the suppliers earlier. Can you tell me why?'
'Oh they're always letting us down', said Marty. 'They need to know that they can't treat us like that.'

(Continued)

(Continued)

'Oh I've always found that it's better to work together and have a good relationship', said Jack. 'Maybe they let us down because we don't treat them well.'

'That's rubbish', said Marty heatedly. 'Are you saying it's my fault that we don't get deliveries on time?'

'No, no', said Jack hastily. 'But supplier performance is one of my key performance indicators, and it's not particularly good at the moment. We talked about supplier relationships at our last meeting, remember, and about building partnerships.'

'Well, *you* try building a partnership with that lot,' snapped Marty. 'I've tried everything and nothing works.'

'You have a very negative attitude,' said Jack, 'maybe they're responding to that.'

'So you *are* saying it's my fault,' said Marty, sounding even angrier than before. 'You haven't been here five minutes and you know it all already. Well, when you've got some real suggestions apart from smiling at them over the phone, come back and see me.'

Oh dear, thought Jack, as he walked away, that did not go as planned. This coaching business is harder than it looks. Maybe I'd better stick to using it in their appraisals and times that I can prepare better for.

b)

'Marty,' he said, 'I couldn't help noticing that you were a bit abrupt on the phone to the suppliers earlier. Can you tell me about it?'

'Oh they're always letting us down', said Marty. 'They need to know that they can't treat us like that.'

'Tell me a bit more', said Jack.

'They seem to think that we're not as important as some of their other clients, because we put a lot of small orders through, rather than a couple of big orders.'

'You've been here a long time, Marty. Is there anything we can do or should do, do you think?'

'Well we've tried a few things but I don't know, I was thinking after you said that thing about relationships the other day in the meeting, and you were saying that if you go to the butcher's regularly, and have a chat with them, they give you a better cut of meat than to a stranger, and I was thinking there's probably something in that, so I don't know, maybe we could arrange to visit their factory and get to know them a bit.'

'Sounds like it might be worth trying', said Jack. 'Who do you want to take with you?'

'Oh,' said Marty, 'mm well maybe because it's the first time, maybe you, so they see we treat them seriously, and then maybe Jenna as well, she chases them when I'm on holiday.'

'Okay,' said Jack, 'I'll be happy to come along, I haven't visited any of the suppliers since I started, so I'm glad you've suggested it. Just let me know when.'

'Will do', said Marty.

Challenges

Among the many purposes of questions outlined in Chapter 3 is the ability to use questions to challenge and confront. However, Wheeler (2011) found coaching managers less willing to challenge and confront their team members, perhaps because of their positive relationships. Blakey and Day cited in McGurk (2012) also warn of the danger if coaching is overly supportive, fails to challenge poor performance, and hence does not meet the needs of other stakeholders and the organisation as a whole. If the relationship is genuinely a strong one built on mutual respect and dialogue, then constructive feedback should enhance the relationship rather than threaten it. However, coaching managers need support and help in implementing coaching practices, as it takes time for both them and their teams to get used to new ways of working together to meet both individual and organisational requirements (Grant 2010; McCarthy and Ahrens 2013).

Power

In addition to constraints around the choice of goals and the lack of choice of coach, the issue of power in the coaching manager's relationship with their team members also needs to be considered. While we have mentioned the importance of trust between manager and employee, it remains a fact that the manager has more power, with the power to hire and fire, to recognise and reward, and to provide opportunities for development (Whitmore 2009; Bresser 2010). As a result, team members may be reluctant to speak as freely as they might with an independent coach, whether that is an internal coach who is not a line manager or an external coach.

Of course, there are power issues in every coaching relationship (Welman and Bachkirova 2010). Although the coaching manager cannot create conditions of equality where none exist, if employees have been properly selected and share some goals with the firm, then '*the coaching manager can share responsibility for development with the employee*' (Hunt and Weintraub 2002: 6). A coach does not present as an expert or guru, but rather as someone who will work with the client collaboratively to develop options and solutions. An employee's relationship with a coaching manager is less dependent on the positional power or status of the manager and more on the manager's willingness to listen to and work with the ideas of the employee.

Confidentiality

Confidentiality can pose further dilemmas for the coaching manager. Employees may share more information with a coaching manager who has good listening and questioning skills than they might do with other managers. The trust in the relationship creates a safe place for such sharing to take place. However, this may put the manager in a quandary if the information shared is important for others in the company to know (Riddle and Ting 2006). If a manager breaches confidentiality, then it will be very hard to regain trust both with the individual(s) involved and with others, as the story will spread through the organisation. Coaching by the manager in question will be impossible and indeed any other coach coming into that environment will have to work hard to re-build trust. One way to prevent such issues arising is to agree what levels of confidentiality apply and what can be disclosed. Connor and Pokora (2012) advise against giving a blanket guarantee of confidentiality but to discuss the issue explicitly with employees in advance. Of course, if there is a legal obligation or duty of care, for example if the coachee were at risk of self-harm, then this would over-ride the duty of confidentiality. Chapter 11 discusses ethical and confidentiality issues further.

Role switching

The coaching manager may also use other forms of interaction, such as training or mentoring or consulting – in other words, roles which require more giving of instruction, advice or information (Ellinger, Beattie et al. 2010). In broad terms, we can position each as follows:

- Training is usually to help people develop or improve skills-base.
- In mentoring, someone shares their knowledge or experience to help another person solve their own problems and/or choose their own goals.
- In consulting, the client is given solutions to their problem.

To avoid confusion, Bresser (2010) and Hicks and McCracken (2010) recommend that the coaching manager indicate clearly when he or she is coaching or putting on a different hat. Whitmore (2009) suggests that the choice of role depends on the situation, e.g. in a crisis or other situation where time is of the essence, a directive style may be best, while in other circumstances, where the aim is to enhance quality and/or learning, the optimal approach is coaching. The coaching manager balances the interest of their employees with those of the organisation, considers the context and requirements of the situation, and chooses the approach they regard as effective and ethical. Riddle and Ting (2006) warn that coaching managers may experience role conflict as their relationship with employees will shift, depending on the role they are adopting at a particular time. Managers usually make their choice intuitively and instantaneously. However, if they think about possible situations in advance, possibly in discussion with their own coach or mentor or supervisor, this will help them make decisions in the moment.

Coaching and mentoring teams

The original conception of a mentor was the older adviser to a younger person. This function can also be performed with one mentor meeting a group of clients and exploring options together. Team mentoring is less common where the purpose of mentoring is to help individuals develop their career but is a good alternative to one-to-one mentoring where the purpose is employee development (Zachary 2005), and is particularly effective, when the group members are diverse and willing to learn from each other (Johnson 2013).

Group and team coaching are also becoming popular, the difference between group and team being whether those being coached form a genuine team with a shared purpose or are a group of individuals. The rise in group coaching occurred in parallel with the global financial crisis which might prompt questions as to the motivation of organisations appointing team coaches. However, team coaches often provide a combination of coaching for individual team members as well as the team as a whole and are rarely a cheaper option to traditional individual coaching.

External team coaches are appointed to help the team improve their performance, explore new ways of working together, and help them engage with all their stakeholders (Hawkins 2011). What little research has been done to date on group or team coaching has mostly been carried out in relation to external coaching. Findings are very positive, with group coaching offering a powerful complement to one-on-one coaching, according to Brown and Grant (2010). Team coaching is the best way to develop social intelligence, according to Thornton (2010). Mathieu, Maynard et al. (2008) suggest that coaching teams can have a positive effect on self-management, team empowerment and several other factors which contribute to team effectiveness. Kets de Vries (2005) found that team coaching enhanced commitment and accountability and improved conflict resolution. While an individual coach mentor may not always have an opportunity to observe their client at work, it is very important for an external team coach mentor to observe the team in action before they coach individual team members and the team collectively. This may include observing conversations between the team leader and individual team members, telephone calls and team meetings.

In addition to coaching individual team members, coaching managers also coach their team as a team. In a rare longitudinal study of managers coaching teams, Shipper and Weer (2011) found that coaching enhanced commitment, reduced tensions, and led to increased team effectiveness. There is therefore an incentive for team leaders to adopt a coaching approach to team leadership as well as to managing individual employees. However, little research has yet been done on leaders coaching their own teams.

Developing commitment

In engaging in dialogue with the team, the coaching manager helps team members visualise the future and develop commitment to the organisation's goals. The team works together to generate options for achieving the goal, and review feedback on progress towards achieving the goal. Visser (2009) illustrates how a solution-focused approach can be used to help teams develop a shared view of where they are now and where they would like to be. Each member of the team says where they believe the team is on a scale of 1 to 10. The coach prompts the team to consider situations in which the team has worked well together and to identify what they did that was effective. Then the team coach prompts the team to think about what they could do to move one point up the scale. Before the meeting finishes, each team member commits to actions they will take to improve team effectiveness.

Communication is an area which is often highlighted as an area to address in employee surveys. In eliciting and valuing the tacit knowledge of their team members, managers role model a collaborative approach typically found in high performing organisations. Blanchard notes:

> *Sharing information and facilitating open communication builds trust and encourages people to act like owners of the organization.* (Blanchard 2010: 10)

Blanchard goes on to observe that in high performing organisations, '*participation, collaboration and teamwork are a way of life*' (Blanchard 2010: 12). This highlights the potential benefits of deploying coaching in teams.

If managers do not listen well, according to Hunt and Weintraub (2010), team members become entrenched in their original positions, which makes it harder for them to change their views. A coaching manager focuses on team members, helping them to reflect and make sense of what is happening and what they want to happen, building up their autonomy and confidence in their own judgement.

Meetings

Managers who adopt a coaching style with their employees will often adopt a coaching style in meetings, listening to each person's point of view, asking challenging questions, working with the team on defining or aligning goals, and providing feedback on team achievements and where more needs to be done. Perkins (2009) found that leaders who gave less of their own opinion and asked more questions, chaired meetings which resulted in enhanced engagement, better decision-making and better solutions (see Vignette 6.2).

Vignette 6.2   Team meetings

My first team meeting is next week, thought Joanne. She didn't want it to be like the old ones, with everyone making the same point over and over again. She decided to take up Andrew's offer of a coach and arranged to meet Zac the next day. To her surprise, Zac did not give her a list of things to do with the team. Instead he encouraged her to talk about how she would like to see the team working together and the benefits she could see coming from that. As she spoke, she felt herself become clearer about what she did want. She wanted people to listen to and support each other, she wanted people to come up with new ideas, and she wanted people to support the ideas that they decided on collectively, even if it wasn't their own idea initially.

'What do other people on the team want?' asked Zac.

'I don't know', she said, 'but I'm the team leader so I decide, don't I?'

'You could,' he answered, 'but are your ideas the only ones or the best ones?'

'Oh', she replied, pausing for thought. 'You mean if I am genuine about people coming up with ideas and so on, I should practise what I preach?'

'Yes', said Zac. 'People will judge you by your actions, so role modelling is important. What other difference might it make if you ask the team how they would like to operate?'

'We might get more ideas or build on these ones. I think people will feel more ownership because they helped develop them. And our meetings will change because we agree on how they should be, not because I'm the team leader laying down the law. I'm much more comfortable with that and I think the outcome will be stronger for the team as well.'

'Great. Is there anything you would like to do to prepare for the meeting?'

'Yes, I'd like to practise how I would introduce the topic and think about how I might handle responses from different people.'

'Fine, well let's start now'.

> Walking into her meeting a few days later, Joanne was confident she could handle whatever would come up. She felt she had already moved a long way from her previous technical role. She didn't have all the answers but she trusted the people she was working with. Together she was sure they would come up with some really good ideas.

Unlike external coach mentors, coaching team leaders have the opportunity for regular on-going observation of team performance and can address issues as they arise, with individuals or with the team as a whole. Stern (2004) notes that executives may need repeated feedback and opportunities to practise new behaviours before they abandon destructive habits they display with their teams. Videos are useful in letting people see their own behaviour and recognise patterns of which they were previously unaware.

Specific team or meeting analysis tools also provide useful data as a starting point for discussion. These include:

- self-reviews completed by the team leader and members
- commenting on how well the team adopts recognised good practices such as having the right people at the meeting, who are well-prepared and fully present (i.e. not taking phone calls, replying to emails or otherwise being inattentive)
- spending appropriate amounts of time in the meeting on appropriate issues
- ensuring everyone is listened to respectfully and that actions are recorded.

Other tools rely on an observer (e.g. a coach mentor) to categorise the various types of interactions in the meeting, such as whether people listen to each other or interrupt each other, and whether people support each other's ideas or reject them. It also allows a quick review of whether one or two people dominate a meeting or whether everyone gets a chance to participate. If it becomes apparent that some people are rarely heard, the team leader can actively solicit their views, or ensure everyone takes turns in sharing their views. Alternatively, if some people always knock other people's ideas, everyone can be asked to say something positive about ideas they have heard before any criticism is voiced. The role of finding problems with an idea can be rotated, so that the same people are not always seen as naysayers.

Virtual teams

Increasingly teams are geographically dispersed, adding the challenge of technology as well as additional challenges such as time zones, culture and language, as will be discussed in Chapter 10. The coaching leader has to make additional efforts to develop and maintain a relationship with each team member as well as with the team as a whole, interspersing individual conversations with team conversations and activities, and using an array of different technologies to keep in touch. Similar efforts are needed when some or all team members telecommute, working from home or from teleworking hubs. Such environments are easier to manage if there is a coaching and mentoring culture, where each person takes responsibility for their performance, shares an understanding of the organisation's purpose, and is in regular dialogue with their team and team leader.

Developing a coaching and mentoring culture

Leaders have an important role to play in role modelling the organisation's values. Indeed, acting as role models is one of the key recommendations for developing a coaching culture in Anderson, Frankovelgia et al. (2009). If managers use coaching and mentoring skills themselves, this focuses attention on coaching and mentoring throughout an organisation, leading to more widespread adoption of these behaviours. Managers must first be trained in coaching skills and then they must be motivated and supported to use their coaching skills. Being coached or mentored themselves is helpful, as it demonstrates that they personally see the value in being coached or mentored and they can also learn some of the tools or techniques their coach mentor uses with them.

Leaders can experiment with ways to develop a culture where people feel comfortable voicing challenges or feedback constructively and where the leader listens to other opinions, in other words fostering a coaching or mentoring culture. Some organisations are naturally more aligned with a coaching and mentoring culture than others. Zachary (2005) warns that without cultural congruence, it is very difficult to develop a mentoring culture. For example, Zachary highlights that if the organisation does not value learning, than mentoring is unlikely to flourish. On the other hand, where mentoring fits with the organisation, there are additional benefits. For example, the improved skills in feedback and goal setting gained through mentoring can also be deployed for performance improvement throughout the organisation.

Friday and Friday (2002) advocate developing a corporate mentoring strategy that aligns with the overall corporate strategy, clearly defines its purpose and justifies the allocation of resources. Zachary (2005) suggests that conversations not only about the content of mentoring, but about the mentoring process and the mentoring relationship, improve the quality of mentoring in organisations.

Coaching helps employees to be clear on what is expected of them, to receive regular feedback on their progress, and helps managers to be clear on how they can help. According to Lindbom (2007), a mix of regular, frequent, formal and informal coaching conversations becomes self-reinforcing. Informal coaching is referred to by a variety of terms such as 'corridor coaching' and 'coaching on the fly'. It is coaching which takes place ad hoc, as opportunities present. It is often focused on what has been observed or reported. The coaching manager and coachee make sense of the data and perception together, and together develop a solution. Informal coaching is less frequently about longer-term goals and employee development, and more a day-to-day approach to enacting leadership.

Where there is a coaching and mentoring culture, coaching and mentoring are seen as the way that the organisation's values are demonstrated and the company's strategy is implemented. In other words, coaching and mentoring are not stand-alone initiatives but integral to the organisation's way of life.

Before attempting to introduce coaching or mentoring in an organisation, it is important to have trust and openness, a willingness to learn from mistakes, and for people to be valued as individuals, according to Hunt and Weintraub (2010). The authors also note that while reward systems which discourage people from spending time coaching make it difficult to introduce coaching, on the other hand, it is not necessarily a good idea to give people monetary rewards for coaching, as this might lead to people coaching for the wrong reasons. It is preferable to hire people with a natural affinity with coaching and mentoring, who are intrinsically motivated to coach and mentor and who can develop their skills over time. Lindbom (2007) suggests that where core competencies have been defined and the organisation is committed to them, then there is a firm foundation for coaching. Organisations may not necessarily describe their culture as a coaching culture although their managers may display many of the behaviours expected of coaching managers (Apthorpe 2011). The more these behaviours occur naturally, the easier it is to develop a coaching culture.

Megginson and Clutterbuck (2006) identify four stages in developing a coaching culture, which they term nascent, tactical, strategic and embedded as shown in Figure 6.2.

The authors offer a useful matrix to help organisations identify how far they are on the journey towards developing a coaching culture. Organisations self-assess against the grid, with each criterion offering an opportunity to explore the views of different stakeholders and how the organisation can best continue its development. Questions relate to whether coaching is linked to business drivers, whether people are encouraged to be coached, whether coaches are trained, whether coaching is recognised and rewarded, how systemic the approach is and who manages the approach.

A different version of a coaching organisation assessment is offered by Hunt and Weintraub (2007), focusing on four areas: culture (e.g. teamwork, learning, developing staff are important), business context (e.g. strategy is well understood), existing HR practices (e.g. expectations are clear and feedback is given) and the experience people in the organisation have already had with coaching. This assessment helps on organisation decide

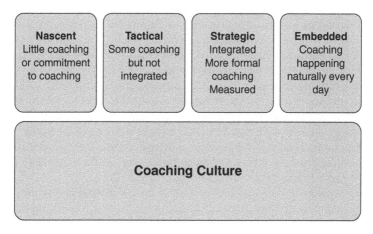

Figure 6.2 Development of a coaching culture, adapted from Megginson and Clutterbuck (2006)

whether it is ready to introduce coaching, and if so, what would be the best approach. Zachary (2005) offers a mentoring culture audit, which focuses on organisational learning, alignment, communication and support. These tools are useful in establishing a baseline so that the organisation knows where they are starting from. For example, if there is already a lot of informal coaching or mentoring in an organisation, the approach to developing a coaching or mentoring culture would be different than in an organisation where there is scepticism and a lack of genuine commitment to change, in other words where hearts and minds must first be won.

Options for introducing a coaching culture include having everyone coached by external coaches, everyone coached by internal coaches, or some combination of the two. Hunt and Weintraub's (2007) recommended approach is to involve senior managers with good experiences of being coached, to use some external coaches and to develop internal coaches. Coaching can then be cascaded through the organisation. Zachary (2005) proposes a mentoring implementation model built around creating readiness for mentoring, creating opportunities for mentoring, and ensuring there are structures and processes to support mentoring. Choosing the right internal people to act as mentors is crucial, as is a clear definition of what the organisation expects of mentoring. Providing the mentors and mentees with training is essential. Zachary suggests having coaches available for mentors. Mentors could also be available for coaches. Organisations need to think about which combination works best for them.

Are there differences between implementing a coaching culture and a mentoring culture? As discussed in Chapter 1, the skills of coaches and mentors overlap. Both coaches and mentors listen to the person with them, ask challenging and possibly provoking questions, give feedback, and help the person set goals. Both coaches and mentors help a person gain insights and take responsibility for their choices and their actions. In both a coaching and a mentoring culture, people, regardless of their formal role, listen, give feedback, are empowered and support each other.

However, in the past few years, more attention has been focused on developing a coaching culture than a mentoring culture. Why might this be? Perhaps the more targeted intervention of coaching, with goals aligned to the organisation's goals, and the conversation more tightly focused on the individual's role within the organisation, is an easier 'sell' to the Human Resources department than the more free-flowing, open-ended conversation of informal mentoring, which focuses more on the individual and their development than organisational objectives. It is quite common for people to have formal mentors at work as well as informal mentors outside the workplace (Barry 2012). Formal mentoring programs provide similar levels of visibility as coaching programs, with the availability of mentors controlled by a central unit, usually HR or Learning and Development and some form of reporting also managed by that unit. Informal mentoring however may just happen between two people who find it productive. In fact, there is a suggestion in the literature that informal mentoring is more powerful than formal structured programs. This may be because informal approaches are primarily for the benefit of the individual. However, informal mentoring can have negative outcomes if the mentoring relationship is abused (Hurst and Eby 2012).

Mentoring is often an optional activity, one in which managers may engage because they want to help new starters or because they want to give something back or some other altruistic motive, but it does not necessarily help the manager to achieve his or her own objectives. It may be seen as a 'good thing to do' but not necessarily one which leads to any short-term gains. However, a mentoring culture leads to engaged employees who are committed to the organisation and use their discretionary effort to help achieve the organisation's goals and hence is a worthwhile approach to enhancing engagement and productivity. There is no research to suggest whether either a coaching or a mentoring culture is more effective in achieving individual and organisational benefits. Furthermore, many organisations use the terms coaching and mentoring interchangeably. Coaching and mentoring help achieve objectives – the employee's, the manager's and the organisation's, provided there is alignment between the three sets of objectives. The purpose of coaching or mentoring will determine the choice of which to introduce or what combination is likely to work best.

Conclusion

Leadership is regarded as a critical competency for organisations today. Leaders deploy coaching and mentoring skills as a practical way to demonstrate the attributes expected of leaders today. Coaching and mentoring conversations in which people feel genuinely listened to and know their voices are heard are highly motivational. Goal-setting conversations in which the person's values and personal goals are taken into account can lead to a close alignment with organisational goals. Coaching and mentoring skills thus help leaders to embody leadership and role model positive organisational values.

Traditionally one-to-one activities, group and team coaching are becoming more popular and one-to-many mentoring is also appearing. With coaching and mentoring appearing at many levels, a coaching and mentoring culture may evolve unforced. Alternatively, organisations may decide to promote a coaching and mentoring culture, recognising and rewarding those who deploy coaching and mentoring skills. However, caution is needed that people do not adopt coaching or mentoring for purely instrumental gain but that they use the power of coaching and mentoring to help clients and employees to be their best selves.

Useful links

The links in this chapter highlight resources to support learning about coaching and mentoring by leaders for individuals and teams.

American Management Association – http://www.amanet.org/Individual-Solutions.aspx

Podcasts and articles on topics such as coaching for emotional intelligence and challenging conversations.

Belbin – http://www.belbin.com/rte.asp?id=397

Free resources for team roles and team building.

Center for Creative Leadership – http://www.ccl.org/leadership/podcast/index.aspx

Series of podcasts on topics including coaching teams and team dynamics.

David Clutterbuck – http://www.davidclutterbuckpartnership.com/articles-blogs/

Articles and blogs on topics such as toxic mentors/mentees and questions for coaches to ask themselves.

International Mentoring Association – http://mentoring-association.org/standards/

Outlines standards for mentoring programs.

Christine Thornton – http://www.thorntonconsulting.org/free-resources

Articles and checklists including topics such as organisational dynamics and managing people who dominate in groups.

References

Anderson, M. C., C. Frankovelgia and G. Hernez-Broome (2009) 'In focus/coaching: business leaders reflect on coaching cultures', *Leadership in Action*, 28(6): 20–2.

Apthorpe, L. (2011) *Can coaching behaviours exist naturally within an organisation.* Master of Business Coaching Unpublished Research Report. Sydney, Sydney Business School, University of Wollongong.

Barry, N. H. (2012) 'The gentle art of mentoring in higher education', *To Improve the Academy: Resources for Faculty, Instructional, and Organizational Development*, 31: 103.

Berman, E. and J. West (2008) 'Managing emotional intelligence in U.S. cities: a study of social skills among public managers', *Public Administration Review*, 68(4): 742.

Blanchard, K. (2010) *Leading at a higher level: Blanchard on leadership and creating high performing organizations.* Upper Saddle River, NJ, FT Press.

Bluckert, P. (2005) 'Critical factors in executive coaching – the coaching relationship', *Industrial and Commercial Training*, 37(6/7): 336–40.

Bresser, F. (2010) *The global business guide for the successful use of coaching in organizations.* Cologne, Frank Bresser Publishing.

Brown, S. W. and A. M. Grant (2010) 'From GROW to GROUP: theoretical issues and a practical model for group coaching in organisations', *Coaching: An International Journal of Theory, Research and Practice*, 3(1): 30–45.

Clegg, S. R., M. Kornberger and T. Pitsis (2011) *Managing & organizations.* London, Sage.

Connor, J. and J. Pokora (2012) *Coaching and mentoring at work.* Maidenhead, Open University Press.

Cox, E., T. Bachkirova and D. Clutterbuck (eds) (2010) *The complete handbook of coaching.* London, Sage.

Cox, E. and C. Patrick (2012) 'Managing emotions at work: how coaching affects retail support workers' performance and motivation', *International Journal of Evidence-Based Coaching and Mentoring*, 10(2): 34–51.

Dubrin, A. J. (2010) *Leadership: research findings, practice and skills.* Mason, OH, Cengage.

Ellinger, A. D., R. S. Beattie and R. G. Hamlin (2010) 'The "manager as coach"', in E. Cox, T. Bachkirova and D. Clutterbuck (eds) *The complete handbook of coaching.* London, Sage, pp. 257–70.

Friday, E. and S. S. Friday (2002) 'Formal mentoring: is there a strategic fit?', *Management Decision*, 40(1/2): 152–7.

Frisch, M. H. (2001) 'The emerging role of the internal coach', *Consulting Psychology Journal: Practice and Research*, 53(4): 240–50.

Garvey, B., P. Stokes and D. Megginson (2009) *Coaching and mentoring theory and practice*. London, Sage Publications Ltd.

George, B. (2007) *Finding your true north: a personal guide*. San Francisco, Jossey-Bass.

Grant, A. M. (2007) 'Enhancing coaching skills and emotional intelligence through training', *Industrial and Commercial Training*, 39(5): 257–66.

Grant, A. M. (2010) 'It takes time: a stages of change perspective on the adoption of workplace coaching skills', *Journal of Change Management*, 10(1): 61–77.

Hawkins, P. (2011) *Leadership team coaching*. London, Routledge.

Hicks, R. P. and J. P. McCracken (2010) 'Three Hats of a Leader: Coaching, Mentoring and Teaching', *Physician Executive*, 36(6): 68–70.

Hunt, J. M. and J. R. Weintraub (2002) *The coaching manager*. Los Angeles, Sage.

Hunt, J. M. and J. R. Weintraub (2007) *The coaching organization*. Thousand Oaks, Sage.

Hunt, J. M. and J. R. Weintraub (2010) *The coaching manager* (2nd edn). Los Angeles, Sage.

Hurst, C. S. and L. T. Eby (2012) 'Mentoring in organizations: mentor or tormentor?', in N. P. Reilly et al. (eds) *Work and Quality of Life*. Springer, pp. 81–94.

Johnson, S. J. (2013) 'Toward a useful model for group mentoring in public accounting firms', *International Journal of Business and Social Research*, 3(6): 1–7.

Kets de Vries, M. F. (2005) 'Leadership group coaching in action: the zen of creating high performance teams', *Academy of Management Executive*, 19(1): 61–76.

Korn, M. (2011) 'Where business thinkers learn their lessons', *Wall Street Journal* (28 Dec.).

Ladyshewsky, R. K. (2010) 'The manager as coach as a driver of organizational development', *Leadership & Organization Development Journal*, 31(4): 292–306.

Langley, S. and S. Francis (2012) *Emotional intelligence at work. White Paper*. Mossman, NSW, Emotional Intelligence Worldwide.

Leimon, A., F. Moscovici and G. McMahon (2005) *Essential business coaching*. Hove, Routledge.

Lindbom, D. (2007) 'A culture of coaching: the challenge of managing performance for long-term results', *Organization Development Journal*, 25(2): 101–06.

Longenecker, C. O. (2010) 'Coaching for better results: key practices of high performance leaders', *Industrial and Commercial Training*, 42(1): 32–40.

Lussier, R. N. and C. F. Achua (2010) *Leadership: theory, application and skills development*. Mason, OH, Cengage.

Mathieu, J., M. T. Maynard, T. Rapp and L. Gilson (2008) 'Team effectiveness 1997–2007: a review of recent advancements and a glimpse into the future', *Journal of Management*, 34(3): 410–76.

McCarthy, G. (2007) 'Toolkit for managing virtual teams', *The Human Factor*, 2(1): 26–9.

McCarthy, G. and J. Ahrens (2013) 'Managerial coaching: challenges, opportunities & training', *Journal of Management Development*, 32(7): 768–79.

McGurk, J. (2012) *Coaching: the evidence base*. London, CIPD.

Megginson, D. and D. Clutterbuck (2006) 'Creating a coaching culture', *Industrial and Commercial Training*, 38(5): 232–7.

Perkins, R. D. (2009) 'How executive coaching can change leader behavior and improve meeting effectiveness: an exploratory study', *Consulting Psychology Journal: Practice & Research December*, 61(4): 298–318.

Riddle, D. and S. Ting (2006) 'Leader coaches: principles and issues for in-house development', *Leadership in Action*, 26(2): 13–18.

Rostron, S. S. (2009) *Business coaching international*. London, Karnac.

Scoular, A. (2010) *Business coaching*. London, Financial Times.

Shipper, F. and C. Weer (2011) *A Longitudinal Investigation of the Impact of Positive and Negative Coaching on Team Effectiveness. 2011 Academy of Management Annual Meeting*. San Antonio, Texas, Academy of Management.

Stern, L. R. (2004) 'Executive coaching: a working definition', *Consulting Psychology Journal: Practice & Research*, 56(4): 154–62.

Thornton, C. (2010) *Group and team coaching*. Hove, Routledge.

Visser, C. (2009) 'Solution focused scaling questions', from http://articlescoertvisser.blogspot.com.au/2009/02/solution-focused-scaling-questions.html (accessed 04/05/2013).

Welman, P. and T. Bachkirova (2010) 'Power in the coaching relationship', in S. Palmer and A. McDowall (eds) *The coaching relationship: putting people first*. Hove, Routledge, pp. 139–58.

Wheeler, L. (2011) 'How does the adoption of coaching behaviours by line managers contribute to the achievement of organisational goals?', *International Journal of Evidence Based Coaching and Mentoring*, 9(1): 1–15.

Whitmore, J. (2009) *Coaching for performance*. London, Nicholas Brealey.

Yukl, G. (2010) *Leadership in organizations*. Upper Saddle River, NJ, Prentice-Hall.

Zachary, L. J. (2005) *Creating a mentoring culture*. San Francisco, CA, Jossey-Bass.

7

COACHING AND MENTORING FOR STRATEGY

Introduction to strategy

Following on from the earlier chapters where we explored coaching and mentoring skills and models as well as coaching of and by individuals, we now turn our attention to the application of coaching and mentoring at the organisational level. In this chapter, we explore how coaching and mentoring can be used to help in the development and implementation of strategy. Woods (2010) defines the difference between 'strategic coaching' and 'strategy coaching'. According to Woods, all effective coaching should be strategic in that it benefits both the organisation and the individual. Here, we focus on what Woods describes as strategy coaching: *'coaching to support the strategy creation, development and implementation process in organizations'* (Woods 2010: 245).

A coach helps managers to think creatively about how to realise their advantage (Leimon, Moscovici et al. 2005). Similarly, mentoring helps direct and support strategy, thereby contributing to competitive advantage, according to Mathews (2006). Morgan, Harkins et al. (2005) see the role of the strategy coach as coaching the leader or leadership team in an in-depth analysis of its competitive environment and in the choices through which it will thrive in that environment in the future. They argue that this may include coaching for change as well as coaching individual or team behaviour. Bartlett describes the coach's role as

> to hold up a mirror to help the organization see and evaluate its current position and future options, and to decide what path it should align around moving forward. (Bartlett 2005: 200).

As coaching and mentoring do not offer pre-defined solutions, this approach allows managers to work with their employees to develop relevant solutions and goals appropriate for changing external contexts. In other words, coaching and mentoring help managers to translate high level strategic priorities into practical actions through meaningful conversations.

What is strategy?

First of all, what is strategy and why does it matter? Johnson, Scholes et al. define strategy as:

> *the direction and scope of an organisation over the long term, which achieves advantage in a changing environment through its configuration of resources and competences with the aim of fulfilling stakeholder expectations.* (Johnson, Scholes et al. 2008: 3)

Developing and implementing strategy is important for success, according to Hanson, Dowling et al. (2008) in an environment categorised by rapid change, with threats and opportunities arising from globalisation, information communication technology, and a blurring of boundaries between industries, e.g. entertainment, technology, and information, as well as a blurring of boundaries between competitors, customers and suppliers. Govindajaran (2005) comments that not only has the world become more complex but also what he terms 'the half-life of knowledge' has become much shorter, in other words, ideas become dated more quickly. Bartlett (2005) notes that the most important constraint for organisations today is not capital but information, knowledge and expertise which reside throughout the organisation and are not the sole preserve of the top team. Leleur (2012) advocates the deployment of a coach, moderator or facilitator to help organisations cope with the level of complexity facing today's decision-makers.

In such a rapidly changing business environment, risk management is increasingly important. Managers have to identify and manage risks, not only at an early stage of strategy development, but also monitoring changes to known risks and emergence of new risks on an on-going basis, so that strategy may be adjusted as necessary. Strategy is no longer a lengthy sequential process undertaken every few years but an iterative process where the organisation is constantly adapting to new information.

An important criticism of the traditional linear model of strategy development is that it is slow and prevents people from responding effectively to a rapidly changing environment. The alternative to this deliberate, rational or intended strategy is 'emergent strategy', defined by Hill and Jones as 'unplanned responses to unforeseen circumstances' (Hill and Jones 2008: 24). Although the phases of strategy development are often described sequentially, strategy nowadays is often conceived as a hybrid, combining rational and visionary, incremental and other processes (Smith 2009).

A further critique of traditional strategy levied by Johnston and Bate (2003) is that strategic planning is often numbers-based and lacking creativity, and as a result, it merely extends existing strategy, which may not be appropriate in a changed or changing environment. The response proposed by Johnston and Bate is strategy innovation, 'shifting a corporation's business strategy in order to create new value for both the customer and the corporation' (Johnston and Bate 2003: 4). Woods (2010) observes that one role for the strategy coach is to help executives spend time on value-adding strategic activities rather than on fire-fighting day-to-day issues. Strategic leaders need time to think. In addition to using coaching tools and techniques, strategy coaches and mentors facilitate the use of strategy tools and techniques, making managers aware of useful ways to understand their environment and to decide on their strategic direction and implementation.

While both coaches and mentors help managers think through how to develop and implement strategy, there are differences in the roles they play. Wycherley and Cox suggest that *'Executives requiring practical advice may need to consider internal mentors or consultants'* (Wycherley and Cox 2008: 47). Mentors offer the benefit of their experience, thus potentially shortening the learning curve for new managers with little previous experience of strategy development. The mentor's role here is to help clients test their ideas and to have confidence in the strategy development process. They also make clients aware of where they may need further education and training. The downside, if mentors offer advice, is that previous experience may or may not be relevant to the current scenario and that a strategy which worked well in the past may not work well now.

Lyons describes coaching as the preferred vehicle for emergent strategy, *'responsive enough to reduce the risk in successfully travelling toward that ever-changing destination'* (2006: 93). Coach mentors add value by bringing in ideas from elsewhere, either from their experience with other organisations (without revealing any confidential information) or from research. Govindarajan (2005) suggests that one of the strengths of a strategy coach is knowledge of world class practices from other industries. In the complex and sometimes chaotic environment in which managers operate, the coach, according to Lane and Down (2010), must adopt a systems approach in order to support the person and their key relationships both inside and outside the organisation.

It is important to note that a coach mentor deploys strategy tools within a coaching or mentoring approach, asking questions, listening and reflecting back to managers, rather than as a consultant delivering an answer to the client. As Bartlett says, the *'strategy coach should not be seen as the guru with all the answers'* (Bartlett 2005: 200). Managers should not treat the coach mentor as an authority whose opinion is absolute but as a source of possible ideas as well as a sounding board. A relationship of mutual respect between manager and coach mentor facilitates learning for both parties.

Applications of coaching and mentoring to strategy development

A key role for coaching and mentoring in strategy is helping managers think. According to Ulrich (2008), coaching helps an executive *'gain clarity about the results he hopes to accomplish and how to make them happen'* (Ulrich 2008: 109). Similarly a mentor helps focus on things that matter.

A safe sounding board

Govindajaran (2005) states that it is very difficult for a CEO to have an open and honest conversation about strategy. Indeed, Kets de Vries (2007) refers to the loneliness of the CEO, driven by perfection and afraid to let others see their flaws, while Prahalad (2005) argues that a CEO cannot discuss many of his/her ideas internally because of the vested interests of those involved, as illustrated in Vignette 7.1.

Vignette 7.1   Sounding board in a merger

Mike, the newly appointed CEO of a European manufacturing company, created as the result of a merger between an Italian company and a British company, was struggling to decide who should be on his top team. If all the top team were from Britain, the Italians would resent it and feel undervalued. On the other hand, Mike did not yet know whom he could trust on the Italian side. He did not think that the Italian director with the best English was necessarily the best person to choose, as a couple of the older Italian directors seemed to be regarded both with more affection and with more respect, than the fluent English speaker. His coach, Anna, helped Mike re-frame the selection in strategic terms. First she helped Mike to articulate how he would like the company to look in five years time. By then, Mike felt it would not matter where people were from, the company would be genuinely one company, trust would be established, and the best person would be appointed for each role. Next Anna helped Mike identify options to get to the long-term goal. Mike chose to appoint people from what were previously the two separate companies so that neither would feel alienated. He also created some 'special project' roles, to which he allocated people he was unsure about. This would give them the chance to prove themselves, as well as providing additional resource to address some major post-merger issues.

Leaders may deliberately isolate themselves, according to Frisch, '*in order to avoid being petitioned by those affected*' (2005: 23). Prahalad (2005) warns against relying on former colleagues or new reports that may be interested in expanding their sphere of influence but may not present a full or honest picture. In contrast, a coach mentor can be an independent ally, allowing CEOs to test their ideas in a safe and confidential environment, to develop their ideas in a robust fashion, and decide on how best to take those ideas forward. Lyons (2006) supports this role of the coach, describing the coaching session as '*a safe and supportive theatre*' in which to refine their ideas, as well as '*a platform for practical action directed toward intelligent and strategic intent*' (Goldsmith and Lyons 2006: 97).

Managers can be so convinced that their position is correct that they listen only in order to convince others of their own position. A coach mentor models a different way of listening, which is about genuinely understanding the viewpoint of others.

Blind spots

A major risk for companies is that executives have blind spots and are not aware of them. Blackman (2006) found that the coach's ability to identify clients' blind spots was the most important factor as rated by clients. Lack of awareness is compounded by the fact that senior managers are rarely given honest feedback by their team members.

> *Often executives self-delude themselves because too few have been honest with them or because their self-confidence overwhelms their self-awareness.* (Ulrich 2008: 105)

The coach mentor challenges in a constructive way, either in relation to the executive's behaviour or in relation to the strategic options they are considering, thus helping the manager to heighten their self-awareness and acknowledge blind spots. According to King and Eaton:

> *coaching creates the ideal forum for exploring new solutions and developing action plans, while providing continuous support and feedback.* (King and Eaton 1999: 147)

Biases and framing

In complex environments, where there is so much information that it is difficult to make sense of it, people often turn to internal or external experts. The risk, according to Waldersee and Tywoniak (2007) is that as expertise increases, so do biases, because experts automatically filter out information that is incompatible with their existing knowledge. A coach mentor operates differently to an expert consultant, helping elicit tacit knowledge from people in different functions of the organisation, without imposing an expert view or succumbing to the bias of long-term membership of that organisation. Coach mentors of course have their own biases but their heightened self-awareness helps them guard against their biases impacting unduly on the client.

Vogt, Brown et al. (2003) illustrates how a coach mentor can shift an organisation's thinking by reframing an issue, for example, instead of asking:

> *How can we compete with the Chinese?*

the coach mentor could ask:

> *How can we collaborate with the Chinese?*

Such questions force managers to think the unthinkable and to become aware of assumptions they have been making about what is or is not possible. While some assumptions may be perfectly valid, the coach mentor surfaces these assumptions, so that they are not accepted automatically but are evaluated for their relevance to the company's current situation. One way to do this is simply to reflect back what the coach mentor is hearing. People may agree on a position but for different reasons. They may disagree because they are not all in possession of the same facts. This reflective role ensures that everyone compares their view of reality and frees people to think about options they may have discarded unthinkingly.

Scenario planning

While coach mentors add significant value by listening to people, asking questions and giving feedback, their role is greatly enhanced when they combine their mentoring and coaching skills with frameworks developed for strategic management. Once managers are aware of their blind spots, coach mentors facilitate scenario planning (Sterling 2003), where managers define alternative versions of the future, based on forecasts of key variables. Coach mentors help managers visualise these different futures, recognising risks and consequences and identifying options for managing the risks identified. Coach mentors apply the same skills they use in helping individuals to visualise the future, using, for example, variations on the miracle question deployed within a solution-focused coaching approach.

Inputs to strategy

Developing a powerful strategy depends in part on the quality of the inputs to the strategy. Involving others in developing strategy not only improves the quality of inputs to the strategy but also helps develop buy-in to the strategy. According to Sterling (2003), the best way to ensure people understand a strategy is to involve them in developing the strategy. A common reason for failure to implement strategy is a lack of understanding of or buy-in to the strategy. However, many employees have strategies imposed upon them (Hamel cited in Prahalad 2005). Stacey argues that the role of leaders is '*to participate actively in local interactions to widen and deepen communication*' (2007: 301). Lane and Down see the role of management less as driving or inspiring people to achieve a pre-defined vision but about developing '*a process for sharing the wisdom of many different and contrary perspectives*' (2010: 525), noting that different perspectives encourage creativity, if that diversity can be harnessed effectively.

Listening to different voices

The much under-estimated skill of listening is a fundamental pre-requisite to the ability to respond to complex situations, which, according to Lane and Down, need '*listening openly and reflectively to different perspectives in order to be open to new possibilities and the emergence of an agreed purpose*' (Lane and Down 2010: 519). Listening helps shift people from entrenched positions and enables new solutions to emerge. Colleagues or employees may secretly have reservations but be reluctant to voice them. DeLisi (2010) warns that if employees feel their input will not be valued, they will either not provide input or will not be committed to the approved strategy.

Gast and Zanini (2012) give an example of a company which invited employees to comment on a new strategic initiative. However, as employees knew that senior management was very attached to the new initiative, none of them voiced their doubts and concerns. The new initiative failed in a short time, despite many people being aware that failure was the most likely outcome and despite managers inviting inputs. It is clear therefore that managers need to find ways to demonstrate to their employees that it is safe to voice doubts or alternative opinions.

With reference to the Global Financial Crisis, Lane and Down (2010) comment that some people claimed they had foreseen the risks but could not get their voices heard. The dominant thinking was only concerned with performance and growth. One of the characteristics of a coaching and mentoring organisation is that people feel listened to. This encourages them not only to respond to the suggestions of management but to put forward suggestions of their own. Yet in their book, *The Power of Appreciative Inquiry*, Whitney and Trosten-Bloom observe that: '*Surprisingly little has been written about the experience of being heard in organizations*' (2010: xiv). Alvesson and Sveningsson (2003) also comment on how rare it is for management literature to discuss listening.

Appreciative Inquiry

Appreciative Inquiry is one approach to encourage more voices to be heard. Lewis, Passmore et al. (2008) describe how Appreciative Inquiry was used with a regional sales team, resulting in better understanding of the strengths and resources they possessed, a shared vision of the future, and ultimately in more targets being achieved. Salespeople are often on the road and may lack a shared understanding of each other's strengths or those of their organisation, unless there is a determined effort to encourage conversations.

Prevailing beliefs and stories

Pounsford (2007) warns that an organisation's traditional recipes for success may become a dangerous orthodoxy. Prevailing beliefs which have been the source of competitive advantage in the past may become obsolete and prevent the organisation recognising sources of future competitive advantage (Woods 2010). Woods sees the role of the coach as helping executives to differentiate between past and future sources of competitive advantage.

Lane and Down (2010) warn of further dangers when certain stories come to dominate leading managers to exclude possible alternatives. They suggest that managers need both to understand the impact of the stories they tell and to tell stories better suited to more unpredictable times. The importance of storytelling in organisations is increasingly recognised by researchers such as Collison and Mackenzie (1999) and Conroy (2011) but managers do not always understand its power.

Storytelling enables people to share assumptions, frame experiences, and make sense of organisational life (Reissner and Du Toit 2011). Pounsford (2007) reported that engaging employees in conversations about change in BAE Systems resulted in an increase in understanding of the business strategy from 54% to 82%, and optimism about the future at BAE increased from 43% to 68%. Pounsford notes the difference between debates which are useful in evaluating proposals and coaching conversations which lead to improvements in engagement. Both may be useful at different points in the strategy development process.

Lapp and Carr introduce the term 'storyselling' which they describe as a story which sells the organisation's message in order *'to stimulate employee engagement'* (Lapp and Carr 2008: 248). Storytelling establishes an emotional connection which can reduce the likelihood that the listener reflects or challenges a story. While this emotional connection provides a foundation for a positive response to change, storytelling can also be used to exert or abuse power, according to Reissner and Du Toit (2011). The coach mentor needs to ensure that people are not so swept up in the story that they fail to consider what the story reveals about the organisation, its values and its intentions.

Geiger and Antonacopoulou (2009) warn that when managers uncritically retell dominant success stories, people accept these stories as truth and lose the ability to question the assumptions on which they are based. In this context, it is useful for an outsider, external to the company and possibly the industry, to ask naïve questions, prompting people to think about whether their assumptions are in fact justified. Given the complexity of the modern business environment, Bartlett suggests that an outsider can recognise *'deeper questions or more embedded problems that may otherwise remain unrecognized or even taboo'* (Bartlett 2005: 199). Conway recommends that a mentor use candour '*to force re-examination and reprioritization without becoming a crutch*' (Conway 1995: 27).

Stakeholder analysis and systems approach

Stakeholder analysis is not only useful for managers but also heightens the coach mentor's awareness of the environment and of how managers view the environment. Furthermore, according to Hawkins and Smith, stakeholder analysis enables the coach mentor to '*recognize where there may be critical gaps in the story*' (Hawkins and Smith 2006: 172). With regard to internal stakeholder analysis for business unit level strategy, Champion suggests going beyond a mere listing of internal stakeholders to ask the following questions:

> *Whose support do you need the most to succeed in your objectives?*
>
> *How can these identified stakeholders support you in your future priorities and challenges?*
>
> *What tactics will you use to engage each stakeholder?* (Champion 2010: 245)

Coaching and mentoring help managers move out of functional silos, in order to '*conceive of the whole rather than just the parts of the situation facing an organisation*' (Johnson, Scholes et al. 2008: 15). Woods (2010) highlights the value the strategy coach adds by facilitating conversations across the organisation, cutting across functional divides. A mentor also helps managers to network both internally and externally, enabling managers to appreciate different viewpoints and to test their own understanding. Johnson et al. argue that strategic management is a major challenge for managers trained to undertake operational tasks, relevant to their function, and in detailed planning and analysis. Coach mentors help managers conceptualise and take a helicopter view of complex issues. Managers often start to ask themselves the same questions they have been asked by coach mentors, and develop their skill in strategic thinking.

Coach mentors also help managers make the transition to a strategic role by asking questions relating to different levels of analysis, discovering patterns and relationships, and exploring different perspectives, e.g. competitors or the public (Watkins 2012). Sull (2007) recommends people be clear on the purpose of each conversation, e.g. is the intention to make sense of the environment, make choices, to make things happen or to revise assumptions?

Strategy development

Crompton and Smyrnios (2011) found that entrepreneurs valued attentive listening and thought-provoking questions which enabled them to gain awareness and identify new opportunities. Instead of seeing conversations as a way to explore strategy, Beaudan sees strategy as '*an opportunity to generate powerful conversations inside the organization*' (Beaudan 2001: 68). Such conversations enable organisations to develop a strategy that will be implemented because people will own it and will have contributed to making it robust.

Increasing the number of participants in the strategy development process is one way to increase the amount of the information available and hence increase the likelihood of making good decisions (although of course by no means a guarantee of a good decision). Brockmann and Anthony (2002) argue that better decisions are made when tacit knowledge is made explicit and used in strategic decision-making. Coaching and mentoring are more appropriate for the transmission of tacit knowledge than training, according to Joia and Lemos (2010).

The 'different and contrary perspectives' advocated by Lane and Down (2010) can be explored in a variety of ways, both face-to-face and electronic. Weisbord and Janoff (2005) describe how Ikea brought 'the whole system into one room', with each participant having relevant knowledge and authority to make decisions, in what they term 'Future Search'. Whitney and Trosten-Bloom (2010) emphasise the importance of bringing together everyone who has an interest or influence and of giving an equal voice to everyone in the process. Using Appreciative Inquiry within a strategy process can create a shift from an analytical and purely intellectual exercise to a more holistic, energising process. According to Steil and Gibbons-Carr (2005), the use of large group interventions differs from standard scenario planning in that many stakeholders have a voice in determining the future that is chosen and the process is efficient as it occurs in a single event. The accuracy of the prediction is less important in their view than unfreezing the organisation from the way it has been thinking about the future. Sull (2007) recommends a spirit of open enquiry in this initial sense-making stage, i.e. not attempting to convince other people of one's own point of view but seeking to understand everyone's point of view. This is in keeping with a coaching and mentoring approach. In fact, Bond and Seneque (2013) argue in favour of incorporating coaching within a systems-wide approach to change and to organisational development as a way of promoting sustainable learning.

Bringing together stakeholders with different perspectives may however result in polarised debate and even chaos, according to Hurley and Brown (2009). The alternative they recommend to generate positive outcomes is the World Café process. They list a series of design principles for 'conversations which matter' (Hurley and Brown 2009: 6):

- Clarify the context
- Create hospitable space
- Explore questions that matter
- Encourage everyone's contribution
- Cross-pollinate and connect diverse perspectives
- Listen together for patterns, insights and deeper questions
- Harvest and share collective discoveries

A simple example of how this works is hosting a strategy development meeting in a casual environment which allows people to work together on one aspect of the strategy at one table and then move onto another table, meeting different people and learning about different perspectives. Meanwhile, one person stays at each table, drawing together the insights on that topic. A whole group discussion then allows patterns and consensus to develop. What is noticeable in the World Café approach is that although the leader must be well prepared in order to create the infrastructure for the meeting to succeed, and to be effective in coaching and mentoring techniques such as listening and questioning in order to enable ideas to emerge, the leader does not come with a pre-defined solution or decision.

Leith (2004) offers a useful guide to facilitating large group interventions, advising against 'selling ideas' to participants, lest they may later experience 'buyer's remorse'. Instead he suggests fostering ownership by allowing people to participate in developing the plan. Lewis, Passmore et al. (2008) suggest that Appreciative Inquiry works very well in combination with Future Search, World Café and other conversational approaches to large group interventions.

Identifying strengths

An important part of strategy development highlighted by Sterling (2003) is the ability to recognise the organisation's true strengths, in particular, where these strengths span multiple functions. Once strengths have been identified, the organisation can examine the marketplace to identify opportunities and focus on applying its strengths to those opportunities. A strengths-based coaching approach (Biswas-Diener and Dean 2007) can be adapted from a focus on the strengths of the individual to identify the strengths of the organisation. Twenty-two signature strengths have been identified by Peterson and Seligman (2004), including, for example, leadership, open-mindedness, creativity and curiosity. An organisation with strengths in these areas but low on prudence might be innovative and entrepreneurial. The coach mentor would work with the organisation on maximising opportunities while managing risks. Another organisation might have strengths in perspective and persistence, leading to a reputation for addressing stakeholder needs. Signature strengths are not a diagnosis but an opportunity to collectively explore strengths which may not previously have been recognised.

A systems approach also helps identify organisational strengths. The coach mentor and managers explore in depth the nature of the organisation's resources, its capabilities and competencies. They then consider whether the organisation has any distinctive capabilities, i.e. capabilities which are difficult for the competition to imitate, which can be leveraged in a variety of ways, and which add value for the customer (Coulter 2010). Either the coach mentor or a manager can take the role of 'devil's advocate', challenging any claims for distinctive capabilities which cannot be supported by evidence. This needs to be repeated periodically as the organisation may hold on to perceptions of distinctive capabilities which no longer have value for customers or internal stakeholders. Managers may be inclined to discount any evidence which does not support their existing view of the organisation's strengths. The coach mentor's ability to challenge and confront is particularly important here, even if they thereby put the potential for further contracts with the organisation at risk. Not to do so would not be in the best interest of the client.

Many managers are familiar with a traditional SWOT analysis. However, in completing it without an external party, managers are sometimes satisfied with a superficial level of analysis. Indeed as Kearns warned, a SWOT analysis can be *either a powerful management tool or a superficial and even misleading exercise* (1992: 3). The coach mentor's skill at questioning, probing and challenging, generates insight and awareness so that this simple tool becomes a vehicle for an in-depth exploration of both the internal and external environment. Similarly, a PESTLE (Political, Economic, Social, Technological, Legal and Environmental) analysis combined with coaching or mentoring helps managers examine how external drivers impact their business environment. Coaching and mentoring offer a way to address the recommendation by Etzold and Buswick (2008) to free strategy from a toolbox approach.

Applications of coaching and mentoring to strategic choice

Processes such as the World Café generate a range of options. Options may also be generated using the creativity tools in Chapter 8. Coach mentors help organisations think through options, make strategic choices, and articulate the reasons for their choices. Many entrepreneurs are adept at spotting opportunities. However, they may want to tackle all of them simultaneously although they lack the resources to do so successfully. Coach mentors help entrepreneurs face reality and prioritise according to potential risks and rewards. Conte (2002) argues that the coach also plays a useful role in helping entrepreneurs define their goals and establishing a way to monitor progress towards them. Furthermore, Conte argues, a coaching approach is more appropriate for entrepreneurs than consultancy as coaching leaves ownership with the entrepreneur, in tune with the entrepreneur's independence and desire for control.

Awareness of biases

We now know that many of our decisions are not rational but are in fact based on instinct and subject to a variety of biases of which we may not be consciously aware. Murray, Poole et al. (2006) observe that while we like to think of ourselves as rational decision-makers, evaluating all options against a set of logical criteria, in the real world this is often not the case. We may not have all the information which would allow us to make rational decisions and we may need to make a decision before having such information. Our emotions also affect the choices we make. Murray et al. (2006) highlight a number of biases which affect our decision-making. For example, something which is easier to remember is regarded as more likely to happen (availability bias). The confirmation bias (Douglas and Jones 2007) occurs where people only make use of evidence which confirms their point of view. If numbers are mentioned prior to the decision, those numbers affect the decision made, e.g. Douglas and Jones refer to an experiment where people who played with a rigged 'wheel of fortune' which stopped at the number 10, gave a lower estimate of the percentage of Africans in the United Nations than those who played with a wheel rigged to stop at the number 65. Many other forms of bias have been demonstrated experimentally, such as:

- The law of small numbers, where we may make faulty judgements based on stereotyping or small samples;

- Loss aversion, where we believe a loss will hurt more than a corresponding gain will please; and

- Sunk cost fallacy, where we stick with a decision in which we have already invested, when it would be more sensible to cut our losses (Douglas and Jones 2007).

The latter may also lead to escalation of commitment, where people throw good money after bad. Fitzgerald, Moss et al. (2010) suggest that the role of coaches in situations of escalation of commitment is to help managers recognise that sunk costs should be ignored as they cannot be recovered. Escalation of commitment is heightened among groups who understand each other's perspectives according to Gunia, Sivanathan et al. (2009) and hence is a risk which coach mentors must guard against, both in themselves and their clients. Team members who get on well together may be reluctant to comment negatively on each other's ideas or indeed may accept each other's ideas unthinkingly, thus increasing the risk of group think, with the associated confirmation bias, i.e. not seeking information which would challenge a proposal, not identifying all the relevant risks, and not evaluating consequences thoroughly. An external person such as a coach mentor is invaluable at this stage.

Another risk is that senior managers tend to be optimistic about the future and this leads them to believe that they will definitely gain the benefits identified, e.g. in a merger proposal, despite the fact that 75% of mergers fail to achieve the synergies predicted (Schuler and Jackson 2002). Lovallo and Kahneman argue that

> *Managers make decisions based on delusions and optimism, rather than a rational weighting of gains, losses, and probabilities. They underestimate benefits and overestimate costs.*
> (Lovallo and Kahneman 2003: 58)

McKenzie, van Winkelen et al. (2011) report that some organisations identify potential biases and manage potential distortions in important decision-making through targeted coaching or mentoring or alternative governance process.

Imperfect information

As noted earlier, we often lack information which would allow us to make perfect decisions. Indeed McKenzie, van Winkelen et al. claim that '*Strategic decision makers are mired in uncertainty and ambiguity*' (McKenzie, van Winkelen et al. 2011: 404). Given this imperfect information, coach mentors help clients consider scenarios which may arise and the impact of each decision on finance, marketing, employees, operations, customers and other stakeholders in the community.

While there is a risk in making decisions with less than perfect information, the more common risk for most organisations, according to Sterling (2003), is 'analysis paralysis', when companies do nothing while waiting for all the information relevant to their decision. An alternative is to review a series of scenarios and establish the likelihood of each. The outputs of these scenarios are then compared against a series of criteria. If, for example, the organisation is happy to accept lower returns in return for market growth, then that may lead to one choice, whereas if instead the organisation wants to maintain high prices and remain a niche player, this is likely to lead to a different choice. Sull describes this approach as '*Place your bets and take your chances*' (Sull 2007: 30), in other words, choosing the best option available in an uncertain world. Unlike a consultant, a coach mentor does not recommend a solution but instead helps managers think through options, make the best choice they can with the information and resources available, and follow through to implementation.

Decision-making

Kurtz and Snowden (2003) propose the Cynefin framework as a way to deal with the complexity of decision-making. In this framework, environments are categorised as known, knowable, complex or chaotic. In a known environment, we can use what has been identified as good practice. In a knowable environment, the use of scenario planning, systems thinking, expert advice and adaptive learning, helps people move from a knowable to a known environment, taking care to articulate and challenge assumptions. In the complex environment, it is important not to be bound by what has hitherto been regarded as best practice but to consider multiple perspectives and seek to recognise emergent patterns. Narrative techniques can be effective in the complex space. In the chaotic space, decisions need to be taken quickly but the organisation needs to be alert to responses within the system and take corrective action as needed. A similar categorisation is proposed by Courtney, Kirkland et al. (1997) who describe an environment with a clear enough future, an environment with a small number of alternative futures, an environment with a range of futures, and an environment characterised by true ambiguity. Conversations in which managers discuss how they view the future in these terms are helpful in establishing exactly what is known and knowable about the future and achieving a shared understanding within the organisation.

A complementary approach is the application of pattern thinking to strategy (Slywotzky and Morrison 2000). Patterns are repeated events and offer short cuts to understanding a complex environment, thus enabling people to make decisions quickly. For example, deregulation leads to some predictable outcomes, such as a rapid increase in the number of suppliers, while vertical integration generates opportunities in selling additional products to existing customers at each level. Coach mentors help managers recognise these patterns and predict their likely impact while simultaneously helping managers avoid assuming that such patterns will always generate the predicted impact.

Organisations need to be able to justify their choices in terms of their strategy and values, and to communicate their reasons clearly. Otherwise, the grapevine may attribute reasons for the choice, e.g. that the CEO plays polo with another CEO may be perceived as the reason for a strategic alliance (Hubbard and Beamish 2011).

Commitment

It was noted in Chapter 3 that open questions are the most common form of question in coaching and mentoring. However, at this late stage of the strategy development process, when the coach mentor wants to encourage the client to make a decision, closed questions have a role to play. Does the client wish to choose x or y? Is the client clear on what is important versus what is urgent? How committed is the client to their choice? Scaling questions may also be used here, e.g. on a scale of 1 to 10, where 1 is not committed at all, and 10 is completely committed and starting to implement today, where does the client see him/herself? As with individual goals, if it is clear that the client is not very committed, the coach mentor explores what is holding the client back. Not to face up to this lack of commitment is likely to result in a failure of implementation, as identified by Chermack et al. (2005). Potential road-blocks may relate to many different reasons, for example:

- Self-efficacy: the client does not really think the strategy will work and so does not want to waste effort on it. This needs to be explored to identify whether the perceived problems are real, and if so how they can be addressed.

- Fear of negative stakeholder reactions: perhaps more data is needed on the stakeholders' views or a more detailed plan to engage with them.

- Perceived lack of alignment between the top level strategy and operational plans: address alignment if real, or articulate alignment if perceived.

- Emotional issues, e.g. an attachment to the previous strategy: celebrate the achievements of the previous strategy and generate commitment to the new, through involvement and visioning.

The source of road-blocks needs to be understood as each will be tackled in a different way. Simply urging people to be committed is ineffective.

Applications of coaching and mentoring to strategy implementation

Chermack et al. (2005) note that most strategy literature focuses on articulation and development of strategy, but pays little attention to implementation. Similarly in organisations, most of the effort appears to be in strategy formulation, with many organisations simply failing to implement their chosen strategy. Indeed, Sterling (2003) cites research reporting that nearly 70% of strategies were not successfully implemented. Causes of implementation failure include lack of buy-in by staff, lack of alignment throughout the organisation, and a lack of follow-through. In such cases, strategy is not part of the everyday life of the organisation.

Strategy communication

A key aspect of implementation is inspiring communication of the strategy, so that everyone in the organisation understands where the organisation is heading and how they personally can contribute. Coach mentors may need to challenge the organisation's traditional way of communicating strategy, for example if this has previously relied on a series of slide shows or one-way communication. Groysberg and Slind (2012) argue that one-way broadcasting is now a relic. Kouzes and Posner note that although it may seem counter-intuitive, *'the best way to lead people into the future is to connect with them deeply in the present'* (Kouzes and Posner 2009: 21). Vignette 7.2 gives an example of one way to involve people in the process.

Vignette 7.2   Post merger

Mike explored with Anna some of the various ways to get people involved in developing, sharing and implementing the vision. While the company was well-equipped with video conferencing technology, Mike felt that it was important for

---

people to have face-to-face time together also. He instituted meetings with his new top team and their direct reports, which rotated between different factory sites. Mike introduced a process for people to write questions on notes, and have those grouped on a wall for the top team to respond to. This had a number of advantages, the number of notes indicated how hot a topic was, and the anonymity of the notes gave people courage to ask some difficult questions. As Mike and his team responded honestly to these questions, trust began to develop. Mike noticed himself asking the sort of questions Anna asked him. Over time, people started coming up with suggestions and solutions, rather than expecting him to solve their problems or complaining because his solution wasn't what they had in mind. His direct reports started following his lead, resulting in a perceptible shift in the climate: people felt listened to and knew they could contribute and make a difference.

A coaching or mentoring approach based on trust and on positively valuing one's team members offers a way for leaders to connect with people. Employees can quickly tell if a leader is not authentic but is attempting to deploy such an approach purely to attain organisational objectives. Fitzgerald, Moss et al. (2010) warn that the timing of communicating a vision is important, as attempts to communicate a vision before trust is established risk making individuals feel threatened or patronised. Fitzgerald et al. also note that a shared vision helps lower anxiety in times of crisis, and engenders greater loyalty and engagement than a tight focus on goals and targets.

Goal setting

Goal setting makes explicit exactly what it is that the organisation plans to achieve in order to implement its strategy. One of the common causes of failure, according to Chermack et al., is a lack of focus or '*unclear goals that don't translate to other levels*', while another contributory factor is '*misalignment among business processes, units and their goals*' (2005: 1260). This is perhaps partly due to the fact that strategy research has not drawn on insights from motivation and commitment research to identify how people might be inspired to implement strategy (Smith 2009). Coaching and mentoring can play an important role here. Coaches help executives '*gain clarity about the results he hopes to accomplish and how to make them happen*' (Ulrich 2008: 109). Coaching managers cascade strategy to their team, helping each individual to see where they fit in and to see the benefits both for the organisation as a whole and for them as employees.

Goals fit well within the rational strategy paradigm, where the future can be extrapolated from the past (Lane and Down 2010). It is, however, considerably more difficult where rapid change prevails as is the case for many if not most organisations nowadays. However, in all environments, leaders need to provide some direction or key goals, according to Lane and Down. When people throughout the organisation are clear on the overall direction, they make appropriate decisions, without referring constantly to their managers. This then frees the manager to have more time for strategic thinking.

King and Eaton (1999) suggest that coaching helps to close the gap between current and desired performance, by helping people set specific goals, identify issues in the current environment, generate options for achieving the goal, and develop commitment to a plan to achieve the goal. Ulrich (2008) identifies strategy realisation as one of the two main coaching outcomes, behavioural change being the other. McDermott, Levenson et al. (2007) found that coaching was positively correlated with strategy execution.

Once goals have been set and measures agreed to track progress, it is the role of managers to hold people accountable for delivering what has been agreed. Coach mentors may be involved in the review progress, challenging lack of implementation and questioning for example the continued relevance of the strategy or whether the organisation is putting enough resources into implementation. Coaching managers hold their own people to account, giving frequent feedback to encourage positive behaviour and quickly addressing omissions or negative incidents. Failure to hold people accountable is another common factor leading to failure in strategy implementation identified by Chermack et al. (2005). Efforts to include people in strategy development and to minimise potential road-blocks result in a higher level of commitment. However, issues may arise at any time during implementation and some reduce people's motivation. The coaching manager's willingness to listen and to ask non-judgemental questions enables him/her to monitor progress, understand the issues and explore options to address. Goal attainment scaling, outlined in Chapter 3 in relation to individuals, can also be used to track progress toward organisational goals.

Coaching and mentoring SMEs and family businesses

Many start-up businesses fail. Despite passion and enthusiasm for their idea, entrepreneurs often lack the business acumen and people skills to take their idea from the drawing board to continuing business success. Research around the world has found that coaching and mentoring increase the success rates of start-up businesses. Al-Mubaraki and Busler (2010) identify the availability of business coaching and mentoring as one of the factors to consider when reviewing the viability and likely long-term effectiveness of a business incubator program. Their research found that lack of expertise and management know-how were among the prime obstacles to start-up companies in the Gulf States. Porter (2000) describes a coaching program for 'small and medium enterprises' (SMEs) in the UK, based on a diagnostic package of where businesses saw themselves, where they wanted to get to, and the changes required to get where they want to be – the three basic questions asked when coaching individuals. Interestingly, UK clients reported that meeting with a coach helped motivate them to complete the exercises as well as providing useful ideas. Kutzhanova, Lyons et al. (2009) highlight the success of a coaching program for entrepreneurs in the USA, where coaches are used both as sounding boards and as ways for entrepreneurs to become aware of their weaknesses and obstacles and how to overcome them.

Many of the issues involved in transitioning from a technical role to a general management role discussed in Chapter 4 are relevant in the context of developing new businesses. Entrepreneurs are often self-taught with little formal business training. They may not know how to demonstrate leadership (Kempster and Cope 2010). They may not trust others to have the same knowledge or passion for their idea and may feel a need to control all aspects of production and sales which will stifle innovation and initiative. Coach mentors help make entrepreneurs aware of the impact of their behaviour, rehearse new ones, and support them until the changed behaviour becomes the default. A mentor may be more valued than a coach in this context, offering trusted advice and sharing experience (Biggs 2010).

According to Kutzhanova, Lyons et al. (2009), individual coaching helps entrepreneurs learn and prepare for change, through reflection, feedback, challenging pre-conceived ideas and providing support. They also found that peer coaching helped learning through the support of the group, gaining multiple perspectives and identifying innovative solutions. St-Jean (2012) reported that mentoring helped entrepreneurs to learn as well as to identify opportunities and develop a coherent vision. Helping entrepreneurs articulate and evaluate risks is also an outcome of coaching and mentoring. This differs from employing a consultant to come and do a risk evaluation in that the clients learn how to recognise risk on an on-going basis.

Conte (2002) summarises the characteristics of entrepreneurs as need for achievement (including goals), need for independence and control, and propensity for risk. She argues that coaching serves these needs well. Entrepreneurs' need for independence and control suits a coaching approach as coaching is a partnership where the client, in this case the entrepreneur, retains control and takes decisions. Through coaching, entrepreneurs learn to articulate their vision and communicate it effectively to their teams. According to Conte, entrepreneurs are not more risk averse than others but simply fail to see some risks. Because entrepreneurs are so passionate about their ideas, others may find it difficult to challenge them or raise doubts about their ideas. External coach mentors highlight blind spots and challenge over-optimistic assessments, not in a negative way, but in a way that helps the client and his/her team to develop stronger solutions. Particularly in small companies, managers may not be familiar with different ways of visualising their company's products portfolio or of useful tools and techniques. While coach mentors are not trainers, they do make their clients aware of relevant approaches and how to make use of them.

Coach mentors offer non-judgemental support and can be justified as a business investment as there is a clear focus on business outcomes. However, there is often an added benefit which takes the form of being a 'critical friend'. Entrepreneurs can be lonely as their drive to make their business succeed may leave little time for friends or family (Kets de Vries, Floreant-Treacy et al. 2007). Sharing their point of view with someone with a fresh perspective is valuable. Despite their usually optimistic nature, the length of time it takes to get businesses started can take its toll. Coach mentors affirm the entrepreneurs' strengths and help them reframe problems as opportunities (Crompton and Smyrnios 2011).

A study of female entrepreneurs found a consensus that coaching by women for women addressed a need for more emotional support and affirmation than that provided by business support agencies (Fielden, Davidson et al. 2009). Research relating to positive psychology suggests that these findings may be applicable across the gender divide, addressing a human need for relatedness and social support. St-Jean and Audet (2012) also found that mentoring helped entrepreneurs develop self-efficacy and resilience. Public and private sector organisations which advise entrepreneurs would do well not only to focus on the technical detail but to support the whole person.

Family businesses face more challenges than other SMEs, as emotions can cloud judgement. Coaches working with family businesses benefit from drawing on resources for family coaching in addition to business coaching (Shams and Lane 2012). Sometimes people avoid addressing issues for fear of inciting conflict or hurting each other's feelings. Founders of a company usually have strong personalities. Their children, even when grown up, may find it difficult to challenge their parents. In all these situations, coach mentors help people recognise their blind spots, voice their opinions and consider issues carefully from different perspectives, in order to reach the best decision for all stakeholders. A particularly tricky situation is when it is time for the founder to let someone else take over the business but the founder may not admit that the time has come for a change.

Some business owners are happy to keep their business small and enjoy running it themselves. They may, however, need prompting to recognise the talents and capabilities of younger employees and/or family. Others are keen to expand. Yet others are keen to sell, some as early as possible and others at a point where it becomes clear to them that the business has reached a stage where others would better lead it. Depending on the founder's age, it may be time to retire and allow a younger person to run the business their way, as in Vignette 7.3. The coach mentor can help the client see the necessity to allow the new person to take their own decisions and possibly choose different directions, and to cope with feelings of loss of control or grief at giving away the organisation they have founded.

Vignette 7.3   Time to pass on the baton

Jack sighed as he got into his car. It had been another exhausting day at the office. He felt the day had been one long argument. His elder son Joe was still trying to get Jack to agree to letting customers order online rather than through the sales team. His younger son Will wanted to expand into China. Both propositions struck Jack as risky. He didn't feel he understood enough about online ordering to make a decision and he certainly didn't know much about China. He was glad he was meeting his old boss Glen, for one of their regular catch-ups at the golf club. When he arrived, Glen was already there, smiling and looking relaxed.

'How's it going?', Glen asked.

'Not so great', replied Jack, not wanting to disparage his sons even to Glen, but not sure what else to say.

'Business?', asked Glen.

'Yes, well the business itself is fine, going really well actually, it's just, well it's Joe and Will, they want to do new things, and I just don't know if they're right. We had a pretty big row, they feel I'm not letting them make any decisions.'

'And are you?'

'Not big decisions, I mean it's my company, I've built it up, but now the industry is changing – sometimes I think maybe they're right, maybe the company does need younger people. It's not fun any more. But you look great, Glen since you retired. How have you coped?'

'Well I focus on the things I enjoy, I do some mentoring with the university start-ups – they have some really bright kids there but they don't know much about business, so we learn from each other. I play golf a couple of times a week and I'm on the board of a couple of not-for-profit organisations, so I feel I'm still useful. I was a bit like you before I retired, not really enjoying it anymore. Now my daughters are running it, maybe not how I would have, but I leave it to them, and the company seems to be thriving. And our relationship is a million times stronger than when we were all in the company. Seriously, I think retiring was the best decision I made, for myself, for the business and for my daughters.'

'Well, maybe I need to think about whether it's my time to do something different', said Jack, looking thoughtful. 'I might need some help to adjust though.'
'You know where to find me', said Glen.

Supporting tools

Coach mentors share tools and how to use them, still working in a collaborative way with clients, rather than coach mentors using the tool and providing clients with the output. Table 7.1 is a short list of tools that are useful in strategy coaching and mentoring.

There are many more tools which can be used in coaching and mentoring, not as an end in themselves but as an opportunity for dialogue and questions.

Table 7.1   Tools for strategy

Tool	Application	More information	Use in coaching and mentoring
Strategy map	Summarises different perspectives	Kaplan and Norton 2001	Elicits tacit knowledge and facilitates shared understanding
VRIN – valuable, rare and/or difficult to imitate or substitute	Strategic capabilities	Barney 1991	Honest assessment and shared understanding
Stakeholder analysis	Strategic analysis	Champion 2010	Consider different perspectives
Boston matrix	Product portfolio analysis	Morrison and Wensley 1991	Is existing portfolio adequate?
Adoption curve	Product adoption analysis	Nicholls 1986	Can current products be moved along curve?
Scenario planning	Strategic options	Sterling 2003; Steil and Gibbons-Carr 2005	Visualise possible futures
Cynefin	Strategic choice	Kurtz and Snowden 2003	Decision-making
World Café	Strategy communication	Hurley and Brown 2009	Engaging employees
Goal setting	Strategy implementation	King and Eaton 1999	Translating into action
Goal attainment scaling	Strategy monitoring	Spence 2007	Holding to account

Conclusion

The use of coaching or mentoring skills or the fact of having a coach or mentor is not a goal in itself. It is important for both internal and external coach mentors to understand their role and their purpose. The external coach mentor provides an independent sounding board, using a coaching and/or mentoring approach in combination with tools and techniques which are helpful in both strategy development and implementation. Internal coaches use the same approaches and have the advantage of familiarity with the organisation and its industry, but lack the independence of an external coach.

Coaching managers use listening, questioning, and visualisation skills in the development of strategy, followed by a focus on decision-making and goal setting, and finally putting emphasis on holding people to account for implementation, giving frequent constructive feedback. In doing so, the managers' style of leadership becomes more inclusive and generates more commitment which in turn leads to systematic implementation of the chosen strategy and to enhanced competitive advantage through motivated and productive staff.

Strategic choices often require some form of innovation, whether in product, service, process or innovation related to choice of markets, for example. Coaching for strategy is therefore closely linked with coaching for innovation which we explore in Chapter 8. Furthermore, strategy implementation often leads to organisational change, which is discussed in Chapter 9.

Useful links

The links in this chapter highlight resources to support learning about strategy.

12 Manage – http://www.12manage.com/i_s.html

Resources for strategy development and deployment.

Jack Martin Leith – http://www.jackmartinleith.com/

Includes topics such as co-creation and value creation.

Large Scale Interventions – http://www.largescaleinterventions.com/

Principles and methods for large-scale interventions.

Mind tools – http://www.mindtools.com/pages/main/newMN_STR.htm

Tools and techniques for strategy.

University of Washington – https://depts.washington.edu/oei/tools-and-templates#section1

Templates for strategy tools such as SWOT analysis and balanced scorecard.

Value Based Management – http://www.valuebasedmanagement.net/

Summary of strategic frameworks such as Michael Porter's Value Chain.

World Café – http://www.theworldcafe.com/

Resources for using the World Café process.

References

Al-Mubaraki, H. M. and M. Busler (2010) 'Business incubators', *Global Business Review*, 11(1): 1–20.

Alvesson, M. and S. Sveningsson (2003) 'Managers doing leadership: the extra-ordinarization of the mundane', *Human Relations*, 56(12): 1435–59.

Barney, J. (1991) 'Firm resources and sustained competitive advantage', *Journal of Management*, 17(1): 99–120.

Bartlett, C.A. (2005) 'Coaching the top team', in H. Morgan, P. Harkins and M. Goldsmith (eds) *The art and practice of leadership coaching*. Hoboken, NJ, John Wiley, pp. 199–202.

Beaudan, E. (2001) 'The failure of strategy – it's all in the execution', *Ivey Business Journal* (Jan–Feb): 64–8.

Biggs, D. (2010) *Management consulting*. Andover, Cengage.

Biswas-Diener, R. and B. Dean (2007) *Positive psychology coaching*. Hoboken, NJ, John Wiley.

Blackman, A. (2006) 'Factors that contribute to the effectiveness of business coaching: the coachees perspective', *The Business Review*, Cambridge, 5(1): 98.

Bond, C. and M. Seneque (2013) 'Conceptualizing coaching as an approach to management and organizational development', *Journal of Management Development*, 32(1): 57–72.

Brockmann, E. N. and W. P. Anthony (2002) 'Tacit knowledge and strategic decision making', *Group & Organization Management*, 27(4): 436–55.

Champion, C. K. (2010) 'Stakeholder mapping for success and influence', in G. McMahon and A. Archer (eds) *101 Coaching strategies and techniques*. Hove, Routledge, pp. 244–5.

Chermack, T. J., J. Provo and M. Danielson (2005) 'Executing organizational strategy – a literature review and research agenda', *Academy of Human Resource Development International Conference (AHRD)*. Estes Park, CO, 54: 1255–62.

Collison, C. and A. Mackenzie (1999) 'The power of stories in organisations', *Journal of Management Development*, 11(1): 38–40.

Conroy, M. (2011) 'Unravelling sutured stories: coaching NHS managers out from under the quilt', *Journal of Management Development*, 30(3): 270–83.

Conte, S. D. (2002) 'Business coaching and the entrepreneur: a well-suited association', *Journal of Business and Entrepreneurship*, 14(2): 123–32.

Conway, C. (1995) 'Mentoring in the mainstream', *Management Development Review*, 8(4): 27–9.

Coulter, M. (2010) *Strategic management in action*. Upper Saddle River, NJ, Pearson Prentice Hall.

Courtney, H. G., J. Kirkland and P. Vigurie (1997) 'Strategy under uncertainty', *Harvard Business Review* (Nov–Dec): 81–90.

Crompton, B. and K. X. Smyrnios (2011) 'What difference does business coaching make to entrepreneurs' firm performance and future growth?', *56th International Council of Small Business (ICSB) Conference*, Stockholm, ICSB.

DeLisi, P. S. (2010) *Strategy execution: an oxymoron or a powerful formula for corporate success?* No. 3. Strategy Execution Working Paper, 2010. Available at http://www.strategylinkconsulting.com.

Douglas, K. and D. Jones (2007) 'Top ten ways to make better decisions', *New Scientist*, 2602 (5 May): 35–43.

Etzold, V. and T. Buswick (2008) 'Metaphors in strategy', *Business Strategy Series*, 9(5): 279–84.

Fielden, S. L., M. J. Davidson and V. J. Sutherland (2009) 'Innovations in coaching and mentoring: implications for nurse leadership development', *Health Services Management Research*, 22(2): 92–9.

Fitzgerald, P., S. Moss and J. Sarros (2010) *Sustainable coaching: a primer for executives and coaches*. Prahan, VIC, Tilde University Press.

Frisch, M. H. (2005) 'Coaching Caveats: Part 1: Organizational Context', *HR. Human Resource Planning*, 28(2): 13.

Gast, A. and M. Zanini (2012) 'The social side of strategy', *McKinsey Quarterly* (May): 1–15.

Geiger, D. and E. Antonacopoulou (2009) 'Narratives and organizational dynamics: exploring blind spots and organizational inertia', *Journal of Applied Behavioral Science*, 45(3): 411–36.

Goldsmith, M. and L. Lyons (eds) (2006) *Coaching for leadership*. San Francisco, CA, Pfeiffer.

Govindarajan, V. (2005) 'Coaching for strategic thinking capability, strategy coaching', in H. Morgan, P. Harkins and M. Goldsmith (eds) *The art and practice of leadership coaching*. Hoboken, NJ, John Wiley, pp. 196–9.

Groysberg, B. and M. Slind (2012) 'Leadership is a Conversation', *Harvard Business Review*, 90(6): 76–84.

Gunia, B. C., A. D. Galinsky and N. Sivanathan (2009) 'Vicarious entrapment: your sunk costs, my escalation of commitment', *Journal of Experimental Social Psychology*, 45(6): 1238–44.

Hanson, D., P. J. Dowling, et al. (2008) *Strategic managment: competitiveness and globalisation*. Melbourne, Cengage.

Hawkins, P. and N. Smith (2006) *Coaching, mentoring and organizational consultancy: Supervision and development*. Maidenhead, Open University Press.

Hill, C. W. L. and G. R. Jones (2008) *Strategic management theory: an integrated approach*. Mason, OH, Cengage.

Hubbard, G. and P. Beamish (2011) *Strategic management: thinking, analysis, action*. Frenchs Forest, NSW, Pearson.

Hurley, T. J. and J. Brown (2009) 'Conversational leadership: thinking together for a change', *Systems Thinker*, 20(9): 2–7.

Johnson, G., K. Scholes and R. Whittington (2008) *Exploring corporate strategy*. Harlow, Pearson Education.

Johnston, R. E. and J. D. Bate (2003) *The power of strategy innovation: a new way of linking creativity and strategic planning to discover great business opportunities*. New York, Amacom.

Joia, L. A. and B. Lemos (2010) 'Relevant factors for tacit knowledge transfer within organisations', *Journal of Knowledge Management*, 14(3): 410–27.

Kaplan, R. S. and D. P. Norton (2001) *The strategy focused organization: How balanced scorecard companies thrive in the new business environment*. Harvard Business Press.

Kearns, K. P. (1992) 'From comparative advantage to damage control: clarifying strategic issues using swot analysis', *Nonprofit Management and Leadership*, 3(1): 3–22.

Kempster, S. and J. Cope (2010) 'Learning to lead in the entrepreneurial context', *International Journal of Entrepreneurial Behaviour & Research*, 16(1): 5–34.

Kets De Vries, M. F. (2007) 'Executive "Complexes"', *Organizational Dynamics*, 36(4): 377–91.

Kets de Vries, M. F. Korotov and E. Floreant-Treacy (2007) 'Goodbye, sweet narcissus: using 360° feedback for self-reflection', in M. F. Kets de Vries, K. Korotov and E. Floreant-Treacy (eds) *Coach and couch: The psychology of making better leaders*. New York, Palgrave Macmillan, pp. 76–102.

King, P. and J. Eaton (1999) 'Coaching for results', *Industrial and Commercial Training*, 31(4): 145–51.

Kouzes, J. M. and B. Posner (2009) 'To lead, create a shared vision', *Harvard Business Review*, 79: 20–21.

Kurtz, C. F. and D. J. Snowden (2003) 'The new dynamics of strategy: sense-making in a complex and complicated world', *IBM Systems Journal*, 42(3): 462–83.

Kutzhanova, N., T. S. Lyons and G. A. Lichtenstein (2009) 'Skill-based development of entrepreneurs and the role of personal and peer group coaching in enterprise development', *Economic Development Quarterly*, 23(3): 193–210.

Lane, D. A. and M. Down (2010) 'The art of managing for the future: leadership of turbulence', *Management Decision*, 48(4): 512–27.

Lapp, C. A. and A. N. Carr (2008) 'Coaching can be storyselling: creating change through crises of confidence', *Journal of Organizational Change Management*, 21(5): 532–59.

Leimon, A., F. Moscovici and G. McMahon (2005) *Essential business coaching*. Hove, Routledge.

Leith, M. (2004) *Leith's guide to large group intervention methods*. Martin Leith Limited. Available at http://www.largescaleinterventions.com/documents/leiths_guide_to_lgis.pdf.

Leleur, S. (2012) 'A summing up: the challenge of strategic decision making', in *Complex Strategic Choices*. London, Springer, pp. 95–121.

Lewis, S., J. Passmore and S. Cantore (2008) 'Using appreciative enquiry in sales team development', *Industrial and Commercial Training*, 40(4): 175–80.

Lovallo, D. and D. Kahneman (2003) 'Delusions of success', *Harvard Business Review*, 81(7): 56–63.

Lyons, L. (2006) 'Coaching at the heart of strategy', in M. Goldsmith and L. Lyons (eds) *Coaching for leadership*. San Francisco, CA, Pfeiffer, pp. 10–23.

Mathews, P. (2006) 'The role of mentoring in promoting organisational competitiveness', *Competitiveness Review*, 16(2): 158.

McDermott, M., A. Levenson and S. Newton (2007) 'What coaching can and cannot do for your organization', *HR. Human Resource Planning*, 30(2): 30–37.

McKenzie, J., C. van Winkelen and S. Grewal (2011) 'Developing organisational decision-making capability: a knowledge manager's guide', *Journal of Knowledge Management*, 15(3): 403–21.

Morgan, H., P. Harkins and M. Goldsmith (eds) (2005) *The art and practice of leadership coaching*. Hoboken, NJ, Wiley.

Morrison, A. and R. Wensley (1991) 'Boxing up or boxed in? a short history of the Boston Consulting Group share/growth matrix', *Journal of Marketing Management*, 7(2): 105–29.

Murray, P., D. Poole and G. Jones (2006) *Contemporary issues in management and organisational behaviour*. Melbourne, Cengage.

Nicholls, J. A. F. (1986) 'The S-curve: an aid to strategic marketing', *Journal of Consumer Marketing*, 3(2): 53–64.

Peterson, C. and M. E. P. Seligman (2004) *Character strengths and virtues: a handbook of classification*. Washington, DC, American Psychological Association.

Porter, S. (2000) 'Building business success: a case study of small business coaching', *Industrial and Commercial Training*, 32(7): 241–4.

Pounsford, M. (2007) 'Using storytelling, conversation and coaching to engage', *Strategic Communication Management*, 11(3): 32–5.

Prahalad, C. K. (2005) 'The competitive demands on today's leaders', in H. Morgan, P. Harkins and M. Goldsmith (eds) *The art and practice of leadership coaching*. Hoboken, NJ, John Wiley, pp. 190–5.

Reissner, S. C. and A. Du Toit (2011) 'Power and the tale: coaching as storyselling', *Journal of Management Development*, 30(3): 247–59.

Schuler, R. S. and S. E. Jackson (2002) 'HR activities and responsibilites in mergers and acquisitions', *Management and Corporate Citizenship Programme*. Geneva, ILO. MCC Working Paper No. 3.

Shams, M. and D. Lane (2012) *Coaching in the family-owned business: a path to growth*. London, Karnac.

Slywotzky, A. J. and D. J. Morrison (2000) 'Pattern thinking: a strategic shortcut', *Strategy & Leadership*, 28(1): 12–17.

Smith, B. D. (2009) 'Maybe I will, maybe I won't: what the connected perspectives of motivation theory and organisational commitment may contribute to our understanding of strategy implementation', *Journal of Strategic Marketing*, 17(6): 473–85.

Spence, G. (2007) 'GAS powered coaching: Goal Attainment Scaling and its use in coaching research and practice', *International Coaching Psychology Review*, 2(2): 155–67.

St-Jean, E. (2012) 'Mentoring as professional development for novice entrepreneurs: maximizing the learning', *International Journal of Training and Development*, 16(3): 200–16.

St-Jean, E. and J. Audet (2012) 'The role of mentoring in the learning development of the novice entrepreneur', *International Entrepreneurship and Management Journal*, 8(1): 119–40.

Stacey, R. (2007) 'The challenge of human interdependence: consequences for thinking about the day to day practice of management in organizations', *European Business Review*, 19(4): 292–302.

Steil, G. and M. Gibbons-Carr (2005) 'Large group scenario planning: scenario planning with the whole system in the room', *Journal of Applied Behavioral Science*, 41(1): 15–29.

Sterling, J. (2003) 'Translating strategy into effective implementation – dispelling the myths and highlighting what works', *Strategy and Leadership*, 31(3): 27–34.

Sull, D. N. (2007) 'Closing the gap between strategy and execution', *MIT Sloan Management Review*, 48(4): 30–8.

Ulrich, D. (2008) 'Coaching for results', *Business Strategy Series*, 9(3): 104–14.

Vogt, E. E., J. Brown and D. Isaacs (2003) *The art of powerful questions*. Mill Valley, CA, Whole Systems.

Waldersee, R. and S. Tywoniak (2007) *Strategic analysis: a guide to practice*. North Ryde, NSW, McGraw-Hill.

Watkins, M. D. (2012) 'How managers become leaders', *Harvard Business Review*, 90(6): 64–72.

Weisbord, M. and S. Janoff (2005) 'Faster, shorter, cheaper may be simple; it's never easy', *Journal of Applied Behavioral Science*, 41(1): 70–82.

Whitney, D. and A. Trosten-Bloom (2010) *The power of appreciative inquiry: a practical guide to positive change*. San Francisco, CA, Berrett-Koehler.

Woods, D. (2010) 'Leadership coaching: strategy coaching', in J. Passmore (ed.) *Leadership coaching: working with leaders to develop elite performance*. London, Kogan Page, pp. 245–61.

Wycherley, I. M. and E. Cox (2008) 'Factors in the selection and matching of executive coaches in organisations', *Coaching: An International Journal of Theory, Research and Practice*, 1(1): 39–53.

8

COACHING AND MENTORING FOR INNOVATION

Introduction to innovation

Innovation refers to changes in products, services, processes or structures, ranging from radical or breakthrough innovation to minor or incremental improvements or a hybrid of the two, from strategic innovation redefining a company's business model to a new application of an existing idea or a brand extension. Innovation is not a goal in its own right but should support the organisation's overall goals such as survival, growth or profitability, as well as strategies which support these, such as providing exceptional customer service or becoming an employer of choice. This chapter focuses on how coaching and mentoring enhance innovation capability, enabling people in organisations to identify and prioritise options, and improve implementation rates.

Why should organisations be interested in innovation? Innovation is a powerful driver for competitiveness and growth (Ahmed and Shepherd 2010). The fast pace of change enabled by globalisation and information communications technology pose a threat to established ways of doing business but also offer opportunities. Competitors can be anywhere in the world and so can customers. Developing a habit of creative thinking in organisations helps people remain alert to new opportunities. Coaching and mentoring help with developing different ways of thinking and challenging sloppy thinking. Both also help people become aware of behaviour which impedes innovation, such as autocratic management styles, and behaviour which enables innovation, such as collective learning. They also help with strategic decisions such as which areas of innovation to keep in-house and which to out-source or spin-off.

Entrepreneurs are people who make things happen, whether in a start-up company dedicated to realising a particular innovation, or in a larger company, where an entrepreneur may be dubbed an intrapreneur. The goal of coaching intrapreneurs, according to Pinchot, is to help people '*become more effective in turning ideas and technologies into profitable business success*' (Pinchot 2005: 170). Entrepreneurs are adept at spotting opportunities. However, they may want to tackle all of them at the same time but lack the resources to do so successfully. Conte (2002) argues that the coach mentor plays a useful role in helping entrepreneurs prioritise, and in establishing a way to monitor progress towards their goals. Within a company, new product champions have been described as 'no-nonsense mentors' (Deschamps 2005). Mentors share their experience, knowledge and networks to help others become more innovative and successful. Whirlpool have appointed a number of 'innovation mentors' (Cutler 2003) – creative people with a passion for change, facilitation and project management skills, who understand the business and can build relationships. An innovation mentor in this sense differs from a personal development mentor, in that their purpose is unambiguously to help individuals and teams to be more effective in relation to innovation.

The characteristics of the innovator's DNA identified by Dyer, Gregersen et al. (2009) are also characteristics of a coach mentor, i.e. questioning skills, observing, experimenting, making connections between unrelated ideas, and networking. By modelling these characteristics, the coach mentor helps clients see how new options can emerge, even in difficult economic circumstances, as in Vignette 8.1.

Vignette 8.1   The innovation buzz

Tony ran a small high-tech firm, specialising in electronic test equipment for airplanes. The company was Tony's reason for living. It was his own patent which had generated the funds to set up the company. The company grew slowly at the start. Tony was the driving force of innovation and sales. After three years, a friend suggested he work with a business coach. Initially reluctant, Tony agreed on a trial meeting with James, a business coach who specialised in working with high-tech firms. Tony took James on a tour of the factory, explaining the technology with pride. James responded appreciatively and also asked about the constraints Tony was operating under. Tony explained that time was his main problem, as he was responsible for all the new ideas and for managing all the customers. James asked about the capabilities of the other people working at the company. Tony said that they were very good, they really understood the products and the market. James then asked if any of the other people ever had ideas. That simple question resulted in what Tony later termed an epiphany. Tony realised that he hadn't been giving his people a chance to use their expertise and intelligence for the benefit of the company. He worked with James on ways to involve and encourage his people to put forward ideas. To his astonishment, people in the company already had several ideas to propose, ones that Tony had never thought of, and many of them seemed promising. Tony and his team worked together to prioritise the ideas and plan in a way that their resources allowed for. The first product based on an employee idea was sold three months later. When James walked around the factory with Tony that week, the buzz of excitement was palpable.

In difficult times, Fitzgerald, Moss et al. (2010) observe that clients may feel vulnerable and more inclined to stay with their current mode of operation. However, the authors suggest that when encouraged to question their current modes of operation, the clients themselves are likely to recognise the need for change. Playing safe is not always the safe option and should not be a default position – it is an option, but only one option.

Innovation results in change. Implementation of innovation needs to be managed with the care devoted to any change as discussed in Chapter 9. Coach mentors help their clients to explore options, a process which has a natural affinity with innovation. Enabling people to visualise change makes it easier to shift from the status quo and to imagine a different future. The client can then take steps to achieve this desired future.

Encouraging innovation

A key application of coaching and mentoring for innovation is in helping managers and entrepreneurs become aware of how their behaviour impacts upon the innovation capability of their organisations, how to become more self-aware and how to foster a climate of innovation, as exemplified in Vignette 8.2.

Vignette 8.2   Hard times

After September 2001, airline sales declined and airline companies invested in fewer new planes. There was less demand for innovative new testing products. James recommended a different business coach, Frank. Frank wandered around the factory, and then requested permission to share an observation: employees were concerned about their jobs because sales were down. Tony knew that, of course they were, but he had been putting off having a meeting until he had something to offer his employees. This had fuelled concerns as the employees had become used to regular meetings with Tony. Next Frank asked Tony what he meant by innovation. Tony enthusiastically explained about new products and patents. What about process or service innovation? asked Frank. Tony looked blank. What if you could make things faster or in some way that the end product would be cheaper? Tony thought about it. In the current situation, new product development would be a luxury but reducing costs would ensure that the hopefully temporary decline in sales would have a less severe impact on the company. Frank hadn't finished. The company installed test equipment but airline maintenance crews did on-going maintenance. Might some airlines be interested in outsourcing? Was training airline maintenance crew an option? With renewed energy, Tony called his people together, discussed the order book and financials with them, and invited ideas. With a little prompting, people began to apply the creative thinking they had previously applied to new products and the ideas began to flow. Energy levels and motivation rose as people responded to the crisis. By the time the airline business picked up, Tony's business was in good shape for growth, having not only survived but actually launched some new services which customers valued.

Innovation friendly behaviour

'*Innovation without people is simply not possible*', according to Ahmed and Shepherd (2010: 292). However, some entrepreneurs, particularly those whose creativity lies in technology, are not particularly good at understanding people and their emotions. The excitement of innovation is so obvious to its developers that they are not always aware of the doubts which their followers may experience. Coach mentors help people identify their strengths and how to appreciate the strengths of others. Just as a leadership or transition coach helps people become aware of what is blocking them personally, an innovation coach mentor helps identify the skills needed to develop and implement innovation. Pinchot advocates a strengths-based approach, noting that

> *People can let go of what's blocking them more easily if they are feeling good about moving ahead with strengths that are already working.* (Pinchot 2005: 170)

When coaching for innovation in Spain, Williams, Paulet et al. (2006) found that rather than concentrate exclusively on items directly related to innovation and creativity, it was useful to focus also on what they termed 'companion factors', including leadership behaviours such as a focus on results, communicating the vision, and attracting and developing collaborators.

Fear or punishment of failure is a major inhibitor of ideas in an organisation. Lee, Caza et al. (2003) argue that experimentation facilitates the creation of new knowledge through a trial and error process which generates insights, provided that people learn from the process. In fact, their summary of the research is that failures are an indispensable part of the process of creating knowledge.

Pinchot (2005) observes that ideas go nowhere, unless someone makes them happen. He suggests that coach mentors encourage a participatory leadership style, whilst simultaneously nurturing the ability to make quick decisions when something is not going well. Coach mentors help people to decide when different approaches are appropriate and to have the courage to adopt these behaviours. Fitzgerald, Moss et al. (2010) note the value of questions such as 'Are you prepared to change in order to achieve your goals?' The authors found that clients who were asked this question were more likely to perceive themselves as flexible and in turn became more flexible. Furthermore their receptivity to information increased.

An interesting role for coaches or mentors is to work with the innovation sponsor. Pinchot (2005) warns that an innocent question from a senior person may be interpreted as an order. Coach mentors make sponsors aware of the impact of their interactions or other blind spots which risk reducing the effectiveness and innovativeness of their organisation, while helping them identify actions which they can take to encourage innovation.

Self-awareness and thinking

Self-awareness is vital for business success, and yet, like empathy, is a quality many entrepreneurs lack. Those at the top of an organisation, whether large or small, are often so compelled by their vision that they are blind to their own weaknesses. Indeed Gill (2008: 1) notes a recent US study which found that while over 82% of CEOs believed that they listened to ideas, only half their employees agreed. Yu, Collins et al. (2008) found that solution-focused and cognitive behavioural coaching led to an increase in self-insight, and both of these approaches relate well to innovation, with solution-focused coaching helping visualise and identify a path to a desired future and cognitive behavioural coaching helping improve people's quality of thinking.

Specific weaknesses of entrepreneurs which coach mentors may observe include haphazard planning, acting on impulse, not following through, failure to delegate, failure to develop their employees (Skiffington and Zeus 2003) and a lack of awareness of the amount of risk appropriate for their organisation (Pinchot 2005). It is easier for an external coach mentor to give honest feedback than for a colleague who may be concerned that the recipient may 'shoot the messenger'. Wenson (2010) found that managers who had been coached found the time to think and to strategise, while their team members reported increases in creativity, innovation, participation, and team building. The improvement in their leadership skills was more likely where self-reflection took place.

A systems approach

Coaching and mentoring for innovation focuses not only on the entrepreneur/intrapreneur and their team, but also on the sponsor and other organisational support. A systems perspective allows the coach mentor to help the leadership team understand the interactions of various elements of their organisation, such as structures, processes, strategies, rewards and management styles, and to make choices which enable innovation to thrive. Innovation is not the result of doing one thing well according to Bessant (2003) but rather of adopting and reinforcing a wide range of behaviours, in other words adopting a systems perspective. A manager may be keen to introduce a physical or online suggestion box to encourage ideas from the workforce. The coach mentor helps managers think through the consequences, for example, how ideas will be evaluated, how those putting forward ideas will be rewarded, and how to communicate rejection without discouraging people from putting forward further ideas. Isaksen and Tidd (2006) suggest that leading systematically or ecologically allows people to stay open and look for possibilities.

A coach mentor helps managers cope with the tension that exists between wanting a very high level of competence and tolerating failures that arise in learning through trial and error. The ability to create safe environments in which to experiment is greatly enhanced by coaching, according to Wenson (2010). Adopting a systems approach, coach mentors also help organisations think through the implications of their decisions, reassess their values and how they reward them. This helps avoid unintended conflict between what an organisation says and does, such as, for example, only rewarding individual behaviour, when the organisation says it wants to encourage collaboration.

Isaksen and Tidd (2006) advocate a solutions focus and an ecological approach, exploring the interactions of different elements in a specific context and the options for solutions. The systems-focused coach mentor helps clients think through alternatives from different perspectives, probes how things currently work and how they might work differently, encouraging clients to consider the implications of changes on the system as a whole. As Pinchot observes: '*People struggling with innovation are facing whole system challenges*' (Pinchot 2005: 172).

Innovation culture

For innovation to become part of the regular way people work and are expected to work requires an innovation culture. Bessant (2003) warns that there are many elements in organisations which work against innovation, e.g. people may feel their ideas are not listened to, may not be empowered, may not understand the strategic direction, or may lack skills, while at the group or organisational level, there may be a lack of learning or sharing of ideas, or a lack of recognition and reward for the innovation that does take place. Organisations cannot become innovative simply by implementing a list of success factors suggested by research. Instead organisations need to adapt and adopt the behaviours and routines appropriate for their particular context at a given point in time. A coach mentor helps people think through their choices, rather than implementing a pre-defined solution. Managers can also develop coaching and mentoring skills such as listening, questioning and goal setting to ensure that people's ideas are heard, that people are clear on the organisation's strategy and empowered to take action (McCarthy and Ahrens 2011). This helps organisations become more agile and respond rapidly to emerging opportunities, as people do not have to wait to be told what to do.

Prather (2010) summarises the factors supportive of innovation as:

1. Challenge and involvement

2. Trust and openness

3. Freedom

4. Risk-taking

5. Idea time

6. Idea support

7. Debates on the issues

8. Interpersonal conflict (negatively correlated)

9. Playfulness and humour

10. Value for diversity of problem-solving style.

Prather notes that in his experience, the most crucial are items 1 to 6. Similar characteristics have been identified by other authors, e.g. Barsh, Capozzi et al. (2008) and Klijn and Tomic (2010). In such a culture, people know that their ideas are valued, trust that it is safe to propose ideas, and manage the associated risk. Many of the same factors, e.g. trust and openness, involvement and idea support, have also been identified as a coaching-friendly context (Hunt and Weintraub 2007; Hunt and Weintraub 2010) and a mentoring culture (Mullen and Lick 1999). In other words, where coaching and mentoring are part of the fabric of the organisation, innovation is more likely to happen. Once organisations become conscious of this linkage, they can leverage their investment in coaching and mentoring to become more innovative throughout the organisation and/or leverage their investment in innovation, to foster coaching and mentoring throughout the organisation.

Learning and knowledge management

A key factor in becoming an innovative organisation is becoming a learning organisation, one in which lessons are learned from both successes and failures, and where those lessons are shared. Both coaching and mentoring have deep roots in learning. The characteristics of a learning organisation identified by Dubrin (2010) include employees being empowered to take decisions and being encouraged to experiment – characteristics similar to those of an innovation culture, which in turn are similar to those of a coaching and mentoring culture as mentioned earlier. As Tidd, Bessant et al. point out, *'Organisations do not learn, it is the people within them who do'* (Tidd, Bessant et al. 2005: 503). Coach mentors help people articulate their thinking, share their thought processes and demystify the innovation process. With each cycle of innovation, organisations not only add to their technological knowledge base, but also to their knowledge about the innovation process.

Bessant suggests that it is the ability to learn and adapt which enables firms to develop sustainable competitive advantage (Bessant 2003: 179). In particular, he highlights the fact that the explicit knowledge in an organisation is a tiny fraction of all that is known, with the rest being tacit knowledge, i.e. knowledge which has not been articulated by the organisation and which nonetheless offers the potential for significant competitive advantage (Nonaka, Toyama et al. 2000).

Coach mentors help turn tacit into explicit knowledge, facilitating knowledge sharing, developing the organisation's intellectual capital, and reducing the risk to the organisation of key people leaving and taking all knowledge relating to some products or processes with them (Anonymous 2004).

Mentors, according to Swap, Leonard et al. (2001), challenge their mentees through their questions, prompting them to learn through thinking rather than learn through doing. Mentors may also prompt learning through the stories they tell. Coach mentors may also introduce an innovation audit to help people reflect on their current level of innovation (Gamal, Salah et al. 2011). The purpose of such a tool is not to tick boxes, obtain a score or provide consultancy, but to facilitate awareness and inspire a conversation around innovation. Gaps in certain areas such as collaboration with external partners do not mean that the company should necessarily adopt such measures but that they should consider whether such measures would be beneficial to their strategy.

Sharing knowledge can highlight opportunities for new applications of a firm's competencies (White and Bruton 2007). Coach mentors help organisations to ensure their corporate memory works as a strength and not an inhibitor, used as a reason to reject ideas which had not worked in the past. After all, circumstances, markets or technologies may have changed so that the idea is now one 'whose time has come'.

Networking

Tidd, Bessant et al. (2005) note the value of networking as a source of learning and creativity. Diverse networks can spark fresh insights and new ideas, as well as providing peer support for organisations in the early stages of developing an innovative culture. Tidd et al. say that such networks are particularly helpful for incremental innovation and suggest that a neutral person can help, particularly in the early stages of setting up such networks. Helping develop networks is commonly associated with mentors. Diversity within organisations can also spark creativity as people have different patterns of thinking, different experience and different expertise. Considering all these different ideas takes longer than working with a more homogeneous group but the ideas are often more powerful as a result of the different perspectives considered. Moreover, the constructive discussion of ideas engenders buy-in, leading to more successful implementation.

Applications of coaching and mentoring to generating options

In addition to coaching and mentoring in relation to behaviour and culture, coaches and mentors also help organisations to apply innovation tools and techniques. This is particularly useful in relation to the identification and prioritisation of options. Coach mentors may not have technical knowledge relating to their client's sphere of operation. However, they bring with them their coaching and mentoring skills and a range of processes or techniques which help the client to develop their creative sides. In discussing the solution-focused approach to coaching, Cavanagh and Grant (2010) suggest that effective coaches educate their clients, sharing their mental models and allowing their domain specific knowledge to serve their clients. McMahon (2009) notes that some clients like to understand the theory behind the concepts, while others are experiential learners who are not particularly concerned with the supporting theory. She advises coaches to work with their clients' preferred learning styles in order to be most effective. The key aspects of creativity according to Isaksen and Tidd (2006: 70) are:

1. Information acquisition and dissemination

2. Intelligence, capability to interpret information

3. Sense-making, giving meaning to information

4. Unlearning

5. Implementation.

The coach mentor poses questions at each of these steps, for example at step one, challenging the range of sources which clients choose and the information they share. Then the coach mentor challenges the interpretation and manipulation of the intelligence provided, helps make sense of the data, encourages unlearning of old routines, challenges people to experiment and reflect, to set goals and track implementation. The basis of all of this is the coach mentor's ability to listen, question, observe and give feedback.

As we know from the theory of neuroplasticity (Doidge 2007), human brains develop in response to the way we use them. Wycoff (2003) argues that it takes time to develop innovation competency and that coaching is a critical part of developing this competency. Coaching and mentoring combine well with tools for generating creative solutions, thereby encouraging the development of creative thinking. Richard (2003) suggests that coaches teach creative strategies to the client. While coach mentors primarily adopt a non-directive role, aiming to help clients develop awareness and take responsibility for their actions, nevertheless there are times when a coach mentor may act as a process facilitator, freeing the participants to focus on achieving the desired outcome.

Different pers pectives

Isaksen and Tidd (2006) suggest that challenging the corporate mindset can be achieved through bringing in external perspectives. They cite the example of Lou Gerstner whose success at IBM was partly due to being able to '*ask the awkward questions that insiders were oblivious to*' (Isaksen and Tidd 2006: 62). Similarly Bartlett notes the advantage of the outsider for whom '*it is often easier to challenge the conventional wisdom and question the embedded truths that block creative new thinking*' (Bartlett 2005: 200). The relationship of trust, which is at the heart of coaching and mentoring, allows coach mentors to ask tough questions which others might be reluctant to pose. Adopting this role, the external coach mentor challenges, probes and makes people aware of what they are taking for granted, so that people see things in a new way. Shaw and Linnecar claim that coaching helps key people '*to keep fresh and alert and to push the boundaries of their thinking*' (Shaw and Linnecar 2007: 215), thus fostering creativity and innovation. Useful questions include questions relating to external perspectives, e.g. 'What would your clients like to see?', 'How would your competitors solve this problem?', and 'How could your suppliers help you to find a solution?'

Challenging

Within a business, people may be so attached to products and services that have previously been part of their identity and the basis of their hitherto success, that they fail to recognise new opportunities or are reluctant to take a risk to move in a new direction. Here the coach mentor provokes or encourages through asking unthinkable questions such as 'What if we stopped making computers?' or 'What would be the worst thing that could happen if we started selling eBooks?' Kaplan (2011) cites the example of a company where people were reluctant to suggest killing off old product lines which had originally been developed by the current CEO. People needed encouragement to believe there were no 'sacred cows'.

Cognitive behavioural coaching techniques are useful in challenging 'thinking errors', such as generalisations and over-simplification as listed in Table 8.1. The underlying basis is that people have core beliefs which lead to automatic assumptions which in turn lead to negative automatic thoughts (McMahon 2009) . When people change their underlying assumptions, they can change their automatic response and behaviour. Examples of errors in thinking are shown in Table 8.1 with examples related to innovation and the approach a coach or mentor may take.

Table 8.1 Thinking errors (adapted from Burns (1989) and McMahon (2009))

Thinking error	Example in innovation	Possible approach for coach mentor
All-or-nothing thinking	'The new product is a total disaster!'	Use scaling questions to get more granularity in thinking, e.g. steps between total success and total failure.
Over-generalisation	'(All) Our customers hate it'	Examine the evidence together – are there some customers who like it? How do these customers differ from the others?
Mental filter	'Our customers expect 100% perfection' 'If it's not cheaper than the competition, we'll never sell it'	Help the person to identify the filters through which they see the situation and whether alternative views are possible. If money and time were not a problem and the client had all the expertise needed, what would they do?
Discounting the positive	Positive feedback ignored, negative feedback magnified	Coach the person to adopt a more realistic view, including both positive and negative events.
Jumping to conclusions	'We can't launch a new product in January'	Examine the evidence together, to see if the conclusion can be supported. Try an experiment or pilot project to test whether alternative outcomes are possible.
Magnification	'The competitors' products are much better than ours'	Gather data about whether others experience the same reaction. Identify the elements which lead to this perception. It may be possible to address some elements separately.
Emotional reasoning	'I'm anxious the new product will bomb' (The new product must be poor because I'm feeling anxious)	Use less emotionally loaded statements. Do a risk management assessment or cost benefit analysis, gather data to get a more realistic assessment. Consider the worst that could happen if the event materialises.
Should statements	'I should have consulted more before the launch'	Switch to 'It would be better if …'
Labelling	'I am too inflexible'	Define the terms used and consider the basis for the label. Consider the implications: even if it is true, are there ways this can be useful? How can it become a strength?
Personalisation and blame	'It's all my fault'	Things are rarely the fault of one individual. Consider the different elements of the problem and how they can be addressed and prevented from recurring. Re-frame as opportunity for learning.

Isaksen and Tidd (2006) highlight further problems of limited cognition such as devaluation of alternatives, illusion of control, basing decisions on prior hypotheses and devaluing alternatives. Clients sometimes believe there is no solution to their problems because they have mentally discounted some options, based on assumptions of which they may not be aware. Coach mentors help them get unstuck with questions such as 'If you had a solution, what would it look like?' or 'Do you have solutions for any part of the problem?' For the coach mentor to be effective, they have to challenge in a constructive way, first acknowledging the client's words by reflecting back or paraphrasing, so that the person knows they have been understood the way they intended. Clients become used to being challenged and develop a habit of challenging their own thinking, disputing their negative assumptions, and becoming more evidence-based in their assertions.

Using innovation tools in a coaching mentoring approach

The coach mentor's expertise also helps participants to get more out of processes designed to spark creativity and innovation. This may seem daunting to the coach mentor who is aware of but perhaps not too familiar with the huge number of creativity tools now available. Isaksen and Tidd (2006) identified 1,270 tools and techniques! However, Thornton (2010) provides some reassurance, advising coaches not to use too many tools. She suggests that if a situation is particularly challenging, it is better to use tools with which coaches are familiar. In more straightforward situations, coach mentors may try out different tools and techniques, and reflect on the effectiveness of the approaches they have used in particular contexts. According to D'Alvano and Hidalgo (2012), new tools lead to increased productivity and improved problem-solving, provided they are integrated with formal and informal routines and the culture of the organisation. Ultimately, it is through conversations around the tools that people gain insights, rather than the tools themselves.

Brainstorming

Most people are aware of the technique of brainstorming, first described by Osborn (1953). The basic principles require people to suggest ideas, which are recorded. When people propose ideas, other people often build on those ideas. At the initial stage, there is no comment or judgement on the quality of the ideas, the aim is simply to generate as many ideas as possible. The coach mentor helps ensure this process is more productive by ensuring that the question or challenge addressed is the most useful or challenging one for the organisation at that time. An appreciative inquiry approach (Whitney and Trosten-Bloom 2010) is useful, identifying topics which are positive (stated in the affirmative), desirable, stimulate learning and stimulate conversations. This is different to many brainstorming sessions where the problem is stated in the negative. An appreciative inquiry question for thinking about a new process for booking tickets, for example, might ask 'What is the best a ticket service can be?', rather than a problem-solving question such as 'How can we reduce the number of wrong tickets issued?' Appreciative Inquiry has been found to result in higher levels of group potency (self-belief) and group identification than in groups approaching similar tasks using problem-solving techniques (Peelle 2006). The importance of clearly defining the topic is underscored by Klijn and Tomic (2010).

The coach mentor adds value to the process of generating ideas first of all by encouraging clients to think about the question, rather than coming up with solutions in response to the first thing said. The coach mentor may also need to remind people of the need to incubate at the end of the brainstorming session, i.e. not to go straight from the identification of ideas to the prioritisation. An incubation period allows the brain to continue to work on the given topic so that when the group reconvenes, it is not unusual for people to start by adding some (sometimes very obvious!) ideas which were missed first time round. Teams may be reluctant to allow time for their ideas to incubate. Ahmed and Shepherd (2010) suggest 'cyclical creativity' as a way to address this, alternating periods of focusing on the given topic, switching off from it and then coming together again to bring together new ideas.

There are a number of variations on brainstorming, which the coach mentor may find useful, depending on the group dynamics. For instance, if some people are naturally quieter than others, then taking turns, where everyone suggests an idea, may avoid one or two people dominating. If a senior person is present at the brainstorming session, it may be helpful for each person to write their ideas down, rather than call them out. This avoids people consciously or unconsciously attaching more weight to the senior person's ideas. Written ideas can be posted on a wall. Later, related ideas can be grouped together. In fact, some researchers such as Terwiesch and Ulrich (2007) have found that teams generate more ideas and better quality ideas, when they first work independently and then share their ideas.

The coach mentor may also encourage the use of warm-up exercises which help people activate their creative sides before focusing on the main topic for innovation. Whitaker (2009) offers a range of ways for people to develop their creativity, including both language-based tools as well as music, art and movement. She suggests that using creative methods helps people access deeply held desires and also increases motivation. Warm-up exercises may or may not be related to the main topic. One example of a language-based exercise is ABC where people think of ideas beginning with different letters of the alphabet, e.g. new ice-cream flavours might be avocado, bacon, Christmas cake, dishwater and so on – clearly some ideas may be more promising than others, but the intention is to get everyone contributing and to have some fun while doing so. Playfulness is associated with creativity, hence encouraging play helps us to express our creative sides.

Another approach is the use of analogies (Ahmed and Shepherd 2010) where a word or situation is described in detail, then the focus for innovation (problem or opportunity) is described. People brainstorm associations or analogies, and how the brainstormed list may apply to the focus for innovation. People might, for example, explore ideas for entertainment on a desert island, such as climbing trees, and then see how those ideas might apply to ways of increasing customer satisfaction, e.g. climbing trees gives a different view, a sense of security and a sense of achievement, and people then consider ways in which to generate these positive feelings for customers. Etzold and Buswick (2008) advocate the use of metaphors to free up a conversation and generate new associations. They suggest that when managers see the connection between a metaphor and a business issue, the insights they gain allow them to visualise innovative solutions. In keeping with the non-directive nature of coaching, they state that encouraging people to find the connections themselves is more effective than making the connections for them.

The coach mentor may also encourage clients to imagine the perfect product, using variants of the 'miracle question', such as 'If you woke up in the morning and you had developed the perfect product overnight, what would it look like?' To help the client visualise the product, the coach mentor may prompt with questions about its size ('would it fit in your hand?'), its weight ('how easy is it to lift?'), its colour and various physical attributes as well as exploring its functions, including any in addition to those in the original specification ('what else does it do?'). In teasing out the characteristics of this imagined product, clients often find it easier to define the characteristics of a real product. Brockmann and Anthony (2002) suggest a coach ask team members to visualise a future competitor. People then share their images so that everyone understands how their colleagues see possible threats and opportunities. This shared understanding helps people to develop products and services to meet the needs of the future and withstand emerging competitors.

Other alternatives to free-flowing brainstorming include 'SCAMPER' and 'TRIZ', both of which encourage a systematic approach to developing new ideas. SCAMPER (Whitaker 2009) is an acronym for:

S = Substitute? (What can I substitute for all or part of this product or service?)

C = Combine? (How can I combine this idea with that idea?)

A = Adapt? (What can we change?)

M = Modify? (or magnify, e.g. exaggerate certain features)

P = Put to other uses? (Could other people use this?)

E = Eliminate? (Could we omit part of this product or service?)

R = Reverse? (Could we reverse the order or see from a different angle?)

A more extensive approach is TRIZ, which stands for the Russian translation of 'Theory of Inventive Thinking'. Developed by Altshuller (Ahmed and Shepherd 2010), TRIZ is based on five principles: subtraction (take away something), multiplication (adding a copy of an existing component in a new way), division (break the product into its components), task unification (include one function in another) and attribute dependency (modify characteristics for particular users or environments). Based on these five principles, there are 40 different idea starters within TRIZ. As with other mental habits, people get used to using them and come up with many new ideas.

Another variation is Kasser's Active Brainstorming which aims to maintain a systems perspective rather than break the whole into smaller parts (Kasser 2009). Ideas are generated in relation to the problem, to the solution and to how to implement the solution. This approach looks at issues from different perspectives such as the operators of the equipment or the customer, and also whether similar issues have arisen or might arise elsewhere, and whether the selected solution might also be applied elsewhere.

The point here is not whether one approach is better than another, but whether one approach fits a particular situation and how the coach mentor can add value.

Applications of coaching and mentoring to selecting options

When a large number of ideas are generated, coach mentors assist clients to decide which ideas to choose, shifting from a creative thinking process to a rational one (Ahmed and Shepherd 2010). Coach mentors ensure people consider the consequences of new ideas, adopting a systems approach to incorporate consideration of all stakeholder perspectives.

Ways of selecting options vary from the simple (discuss and decide by consensus or vote and decide by majority) to more complex, where a set of criteria is carefully defined and weighted. The coach mentor helps people articulate the reasons for their preferences. In so doing, people identify the criteria under-pinning their decision. Without explaining their rationale, people may argue and not understand why others cannot see their point of view. When rationales are shared, people find it easier to see each other's point of view and to come to a consensus. In helping people share their thinking, the coach mentor helps build commitment to the decision. This is more powerful than simple voting.

People can use the definition of criteria to manipulate the decision, i.e. defining criteria which will confirm their preferred option, sometimes known as post-rationalisation. Similarly when criteria are weighted, a higher weight could be attached to a criterion at which a desired option has excelled. It may be that this criterion is indeed more important. Through questioning, the coach mentor can ensure that people are aware of the implications of the weighting they attach. Coach mentors are there to serve the interests of the organisation, not that of any individual. They can help people be more imaginative and comprehensive in the criteria they choose and also confront any bias with probing questions. An example of two sets of criteria and their respective weightings are shown in Table 8.2.

In this table, Option 1 emerges the winner because it scored highest on the heaviest criterion. If the weightings had been equal, the results change, as shown in Table 8.3.

Table 8.2   Weighted criterion ranking: Example 1

	Criterion 1 X 2	Criterion 2 X 1	Criterion 3 X 0.5	Total
Option 1	6	4	2	12+4+1 = 17
Option 2	4	2	6	8+2+3 = 13
Option 3	1	6	4	2+6+2 = 10

Table 8.3   Weighted criterion ranking: Example 2

	Criterion 1 X 1	Criterion 2 X 1	Criterion 3 X 1	Total
Option 1	6	4	2	6+4+2 = 12
Option 2	4	2	6	4+2+6 = 12
Option 3	1	6	2	1+6+2 = 9

Using equal weightings, Options 1 and 2 score equally well. The discussion that needs to take place is whether all criteria are equally important and if not, how they relate to each other. A sanity check post voting helps make sure everyone agrees that the outcome is reasonable or if not, that any doubts are aired. The emphasis is on the conversation and developing a shared understanding. The numbers are merely a point for discussion. The coach mentor ensures the discussion is fruitful and that diverse opinions are respected, rather than an argument where each person tries to convince the other that their choice is the correct one.

As noted in Chapter 7, decision-making is rarely completely rational. Coach mentors challenge people about their choices, making them aware of possible biases, and helping them make sure that they are making choices that are right for their organisation. The discussion of decision-making in relation to strategy in Chapter 7 can be applied also to innovation. Simple graphics such as a 2 × 2 grid of implications of choices can be helpful. For example, Figure 8.1 helps people think through the implications for pricing if a new product is given very few features or given many features. This shifts people from wanting to add in every possible feature that has occurred to them and encourages them to decide in which quadrant they wish to position the new product.

The grid can also be used to get people to explore whether it might be possible to make a feature-rich product without proportionally increasing costs, thus allowing more scope for pricing and marketing. Of course, the coach mentor might also challenge whether all the additional features are genuinely valued by customers or if the optimal product might in fact have fewer features, be easier to use or quicker to manufacture.

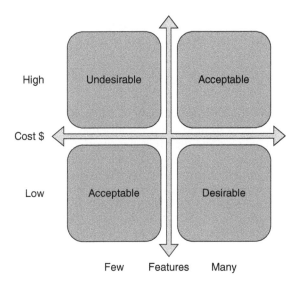

Figure 8.1   2 x 2 grid

Applications of coaching and mentoring to implementing innovation

Megginson and Clutterbuck (2005) comment that it is odd that there are so many books on developing creativity when having ideas is only a tiny part of making change happen. There are several potential pitfalls in implementing innovation, such as, for example, paralysis through analysis and lack of delegation (White and Bruton 2007). A coach mentor helps managers become aware of where their behaviour may be stifling innovation. Klein and Sorra (1996) note that increasingly, implementation failure rather than innovation failure is the cause of organisations failing to achieve the anticipated benefits of an innovation.

Visualisation

For people to commit to implementation, they have to believe that implementation is possible in their specific context. Visualisation is important in building self-efficacy, the belief that one can succeed in doing what one has decided (Bandura 1977). Coach mentors choose a visualisation approach appropriate for the client. For example, Clutterbuck and Megginson (2009) suggest selecting a desired state and imagining what it will feel like. They say the desired state should be something which is important for the client, aligned with their values and achievable, even if stretching. This technique can result in very detailed descriptions of what people will be doing, how others will react, and will include images of what the client regards as success, whether this is in the form of customer feedback, awards, product sales, word of mouth recommendations or other personal sources of satisfaction. The client specifies the date by which their vision will be in place. The coach mentor prompts the person to think about the things that will have made their achievements possible and what else needs to be done to make the vision possible, how they can increase the chances of success, and what their first steps will be.

Commitment

The use of scaling questions, which is common in solution-focused coaching, is a good way to gauge commitment to an innovation. An idea may be brilliant but unless senior management is committed to it and the implementation steps are clear, it is unlikely to succeed. Coaches might also use tools such as force field analysis to help people in an organisation to understand which forces may help them succeed and which may hinder them. An example of a force field analysis is shown in Figure 8.2 for a company about to implement a new website design. Each item is shown as an arrow, the length of each arrow indicating how strong the force is believed to be. The coach mentor then helps people discover options to address the hindering factors and make the most of the helping factors.

An alternative approach is cited in Megginson and Clutterbuck (2005). The coach mentor helps people articulate their commitment and to identify competing commitments which may prevent people from achieving their goal. For example, if the goal is to

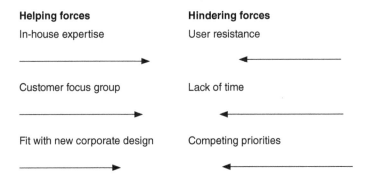

Figure 8.2 Force field analysis

reduce the time it takes to complete a process, a competing priority might be to reduce costs and hence not invest in new technology which would facilitate the first goal. By being clear on conflicting priorities, managers can decide on what makes most sense for the company.

Relationship

The coach mentor's tactics change with a deepening relationship and understanding. In the early stages of a relationship, coach mentors establish trust and credibility and seek to understand how the organisation works. Naïve questions help people to unblock their thinking, so that they themselves question what they previously took for granted. Once the relationship is well established, the coach can challenge more vigorously and with more precision (Bartlett 2005). Because of the strength of the relationship, the coach mentor can be confident that the challenge will be received as intended, i.e. not as a personal attack but relating to the thinking or behaviours observed.

Blocks

Coach mentors use cognitive behavioural coaching techniques to identify and address self-limiting beliefs impeding implementation. Zeus and Skiffington (2000) suggest that once a person notices a self-limiting belief, they should write it down, identify the flaw in their thinking, and counter it with a positive rational alternative. This develops the person's ability to deal with such beliefs rather than be limited by them. McMahon (2009) suggests a number of techniques to address such beliefs, including cost benefit analysis, contingency planning, and use of imagery. In cost benefit analysis, the person is asked to list both the costs and benefits of either continuing with an existing course of action or of implementing a new one. The person can be helped to uncover any 'twisted thinking' such as the examples in Table 8.4, relating to someone who is reluctant to collaborate:

Table 8.4   Benefits and drawbacks of collaboration

Drawback of not collaborating	Benefit of not collaborating
– I won't have all the relevant expertise	– I will have control over the whole project
– I won't have all the right contacts	– My ideas will be implemented
– I do not have time to do everything	– I won't have to rely on others
– I may not succeed	– I will get all the praise/rewards

Scaling questions may be used to assess the importance of each statement, e.g.

I will only succeed if I have total control of the project.

1   2   3   4   5   6   7   8   9   10

If the client rates this at 8, 9 or 10, he/she may have difficulty in collaboration, and will need to convince themselves thoroughly of the benefits of collaboration in order to overcome this belief.

Another basis for a conversation about consequences is a risk identification chart, identifying how likely an event is to happen, and how serious the impacts could be, as shown in Figure 8.3. This suggests that not being first to market is regarded as the most likely event to have serious consequences. This belief can be tested as can other beliefs and the nature of the consequences articulated. Contingency plans are drawn up for high risk events, which are both likely and will have serious impacts if they do. In this case, it is not so much that the technique promotes self-awareness and a change in behaviour, but rather that the technique promotes clear thinking and facilitates decision-making – cognitive coaching rather than cognitive behavioural coaching.

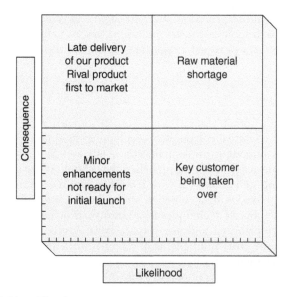

Figure 8.3   Risk identification

Table 8.5 Contingency planning

Situation – What could go wrong?	Action – What will I do if it does go wrong?
Competitor announces an earlier launch date than ours	Check whether our date can be brought forward, e.g. through deploying additional resource.
	Compare our specification to competitor specification – will customers prefer to wait for ours?
Key customer is taken over	Establish relationship with new decision-makers. Understand their requirements, expectations and desires.
	Understand timing of their decisions (may be lengthy due to take over).
	Put added resource into relationships with other customers.

Contingency planning, according to McMahon (2009) can trick the brain into thinking it has already dealt with a situation, so that the thought of the situation becomes less worrying. She says that a similar effect is found when people think through how they would cope with a negative event, as the person realises that none of the dreaded events is fatal. Table 8.5 shows how this applies in innovation.

In addition to beliefs, there may also be an emotional response which inhibits implementation. In this case, Neenan and Palmer (2001) outline an intervention called ABCDE:

- A is the activating event, where the person stops working on the option agreed on.

- B is the beliefs which lead to this, e.g. 'this option will never work and its failure will reflect on me'.

- C is the consequence of these beliefs, such as becoming disengaged or even actively sabotaging the project to ensure it fails, thereby demonstrating the person was right in their evaluation.

- D is disputing these thoughts. If there is a real basis for the belief, this needs to be tackled. If not, the person can be guided using perhaps some of the tactics listed in Table 8.1

- E is an effective reduction in the person's emotional response, enabling a return to more logical thinking and proceeding with implementation.

One of the significant advantages of a thinking partner such as a coach mentor is that the conversation is non-judgemental. Executives are sometimes reluctant to show emotion or to express vulnerability (Kaplan 2011). The coach mentor provides a safe space where clients can say out loud what they think would happen if a project fails or if customers hate an innovation they have personally championed. Having identified the worst, they can then plan to ensure the worst does not eventuate.

Review and learning

As discussed above, coaching and mentoring help people articulate their thoughts, hence making tacit knowledge explicit. One way to access tacit knowledge is through reviewing processes with a 'trusted confidant' (Brockmann and Anthony 2002). Reviewing what has been learned in a project de-brief is an important step, which is too often omitted as people hasten to their next project. A review ensures that lessons have been learned. It is a valuable step in maximising the benefits of innovation and reinforces shared understanding in the organisation. Argyris (1977) categorises learning as single and double loop learning. In single loop or adaptive learning, people focus on what has been learned from the problem solved. In double loop or generative learning, people focus on what can be learned from the way the organisation approached the project and how it can work differently. Ahmed and Shepherd (2010) advocate double loop as the main focus of organisations. Knowledge flows from shared experience according to Forcadell and Guadamillas (2002) and innovation from knowledge. Bessant (2003) suggests that reflection on learning allows an organisation not only to incrementally improve on what they already do, but to challenge the fundamental assumptions by which the organisation operates. Coach mentors not only help an organisation define the technical specifications of a new product or service but also help the organisation articulate its tacit knowledge, challenge its assumptions and identify new ways to operate. When organisations engage in double loop learning, their knowledge becomes a strategic resource for the organisation, a resource which is difficult for others to imitate, as it is embedded in the experience, understanding and culture of the organisation.

To maximise the benefit of this resource, knowledge should be shared across the organisation. Coach mentors often become aware of silos within organisations, although resistance to knowledge sharing may be unspoken. Bringing this behaviour into the light and challenging people to consider the consequences of their actions for their own unit and for the organisation as a whole, can result in a shift in behaviour.

Relevance of team coaching for innovation

According to Pinchot, breakdowns in teamwork are one of the commonest causes of innovation failure (2005: 170). One of the main benefits of working with teams on innovation is the richness of ideas that come from diverse perspectives, particularly where the composition of the team reflects the composition of the customer base. However, this very advantage can also lead to conflict. The practice of developing, selecting and implementing ideas is one where different team members may have strong views. If teams have not already done so, it will be useful, as Thornton (2010) suggests, to agree ground rules on acceptable ways to express disagreement and how to resolve conflict. It is also important, according to Hawkins (2011) for teams to move beyond tribal feuds with other teams and to focus on how their team contributes to the broader system. Specific team tools such as the Belbin Team Inventory (Belbin 2010) may be useful if the make-up of the team has not yet been determined, if team members are getting to know each other, if new members join, or if a team is experiencing problems. The Belbin Team Inventory characterises members as:

- Coordinator: organises team and team resources

- Shaper: shapes team effort and outcomes

- Plant: creative problem solver and original thinker

- Resource investigator: identifies external resources and contacts

- Monitor evaluator: provides a reality check, analyses and assesses options

- Completer finisher: focuses on completion, pays attention to fine detail

- Team worker: supports others, listens, communicates

- Implementer: makes things happen, carries out plans

- Specialists: have specialist knowledge or skills

A combination of different roles on a team is useful. A team with many plants and resource investigators but no completer finishers or implementers, may find it difficult to turn ideas into reality. However, as Belbin (2010) notes, the team inventory measures preferences for behaviour not personality. Behaviour changes over time and so too do people's preferred roles. People may actively choose to bring secondary preferences into play, when they become aware of gaps in the team as a whole. As with other tools, coach mentors make use of such tools to raise awareness by having a conversation around the results, and encouraging the team to consider whether they need or want to take any action as a result.

Applications of coaching and mentoring to innovation in SMEs

While the above discussion may apply in both large and small firms, there are some distinctive characteristics relating to innovation in SMEs. Tidd, Bessant et al. (2005) note the difference between larger SMEs which may behave similarly to larger companies, and small companies which may be more embedded in the local environment and also more likely to approach innovation incrementally. Significant differences are also noted in different sectors, e.g. a high tech firm is likely to have a higher spend on research and development than a low tech firm. SME owner managers may be totally passionate about their ideas and business and yet almost completely unaware of their impact on others, due to the lack of feedback they receive. They may need to be persuaded of the value of listening to their employees' ideas. Awareness of external sources of funding, support and technology are particularly useful for a mentor to bring to the relationship (Swap, Leonard et al. 2001).

Conclusion

It can be seen from the above that different coaching and mentoring approaches may be helpful in helping organisations become more innovative. A systems approach helps clients to understand the interactions between different elements of the organisation and how they may support innovation. A cognitive behavioural approach can be used to challenge self-limiting beliefs, unwarranted generalisations and other forms of twisted thinking. A solutions-focused approach may be applied to the organisation itself or to a problem it wishes to solve. Appreciative Inquiry, positive psychology or strengths-based approaches enable organisations to recognise and build on their in-house strengths. Furthermore, when managers adopt coaching and mentoring behaviours, they are also adopting behaviours which encourage innovation. Throughout the innovation process, the coach mentor adds value through helping people think, raising their awareness, and helping them both develop and implement ideas. Innovation leads to change, both in individual patterns of thought and in organisational routines. The next chapter focuses on coaching and mentoring for organisational change.

Useful links

The links in this chapter highlight resources to support learning about innovation.

Altshuller Institute for Triz Studies – http://www.aitriz.org/

Resources for implementing TRIZ for innovation and systematic problem solving.

De Bono – http://www.debonogroup.com/six_thinking_hats.php

Guidance for using 6 Thinking Hats and other creativity tools.

Brainstorming – http://www.brainstorming.co.uk/tutorials/creativethinkingcontents.html

Introduces creativity tools such as analogies and Scamper.

Global Innovation Network – http://www.innovationmanagement.se/

Resources for managing innovation.

Net Coach – http://www.netcoach.eu.com/index.php?id=242

Support for creativity and innovation, including an innovation audit.

References

Ahmed, P. K. and C. D. Shepherd (2010) *Innovation management: context, strategies, systems and processes*. Harlow, FT Prentice Hall.
Anonymous (2004) *Coaching and mentoring*. Harvard Business School Press.
Argyris, C. (1977) 'Double loop learning in organizations', *Harvard Business Review*, 55(5): 115–25.
Bandura, A. (1977) 'Self-efficacy: towards a unifying theory of behavioral change', *Psychological Review*, 84(2): 191–215.
Barsh, J., M. M. Capozzi and J. Davidson (2008) 'Leadership and innovation', *McKinsey Quarterly*, (1): 37–47.
Bartlett, C. A. (2005) 'Coaching the top team', in H. Morgan, P. Harkins and M. Goldsmith (eds) *The art and practice of leadership coaching*. Hoboken, NJ, John Wiley, pp. 199–202.
Belbin, R. M. (2010) *Team roles at work*. Oxford, Butterworth-Heinemann.

Bessant, J. (2003) *High-involvement innovation*. Chichester, Wiley.

Brockmann, E. N. and W. P. Anthony (2002) 'Tacit knowledge and strategic decision making', *Group & Organization Management,* 27(4): 436–55.

Burns, D. D. (1989) *The feeling good handbook*. New York, Plume/Penguin.

Cavanagh, M. J. and A. M. Grant (2010) 'The solution-focused approach to coaching', in E. Cox, T. Bachkirova and D. Clutterbuck (eds) *Complete handbook of coaching*. London, Sage, pp. 54–67.

Clutterbuck, D. and D. Megginson (2009) 'Client focused techniques', in D. Megginson and D. Clutterbuck (eds) *Further techniques for coaching and mentoring*. Oxford, Butterworth-Heinemann, pp. 129–93.

Conte, S. D. (2002) 'Business coaching and the entrepreneur: a well-suited association', *Journal of Business and Entrepreneurship*, 14(2): 123–32.

Cutler, G. (2003) 'Innovation mentoring at Whirlpool', *Research Technology Management*, 46(6): 57–8.

D'Alvano, L. and A. Hidalgo (2012) 'Innovation management techniques and development degree of innovation process in service organizations', *R&D Management*, 42(1): 60–70.

Deschamps, J.-P. (2005) 'Different leadership skills for different innovation strategies', *Strategy & Leadership*, 33(5): 31–8.

Doidge, N. (2007) *The brain that changes itself*. Viking.

Dubrin, A. J. (2010) *Leadership: research findings, practice and skills*. Mason, OH, Cengage.

Dyer, J. H., H. B. Gregersen, C. M. Christensen and M. Foster (2009) 'The innovator's DNA', *Harvard Business Review*, 87(12): 61–7.

Etzold, V. and T. Buswick (2008) 'Metaphors in strategy', *Business Strategy Series*, 9(5): 279–84.

Fitzgerald, P., S. Moss and J. Sarros (2010) *Sustainable coaching: a primer for executives and coaches*. Prahan, VIC, Tilde University Press.

Forcadell, F. J. and F. Guadamillas (2002) 'A case study on the implementation of a knowledge management strategy oriented to innovation', *Knowledge and Process Management*, 9(3): 162–71.

Gamal, D., E. T. Salah and N. Elrayyes (2011) *How to measure organization innovativeness?* Cairo, Technology Innovation and Entrepreneurship Center, Innovation Support Department.

Gill, R. (2008) 'Sustaining creativity and innovation: the role of leadership', *LT Focus*, (Summer) p.10.

Hawkins, P. (2011) *Leadership team coaching*. London, Routledge.

Hunt, J. M. and J. R. Weintraub (2007) *The coaching organization*. Thousand Oaks, Sage.

Hunt, J. M. and J. R. Weintraub (2010) *The coaching manager*. Los Angeles, Sage.

Isaksen, S. and J. Tidd (2006) *Meeting the innovation challenge*. Chichester, Wiley.

Kaplan, R. S. (2011) 'Top executives need feedback – here's how they can get it', *McKinsey Quarterly*, Spring: 1–11.

Kasser, J. E. (2009) *Active brainstorming: a systemic and systematic approach for idea generation*. Proceedings of the 19th International Symposium of the International Council on Systems Engineering, Singapore.

Klein, K. J. and J. S. Sorra (1996) 'The challenge of implementing innovation', *Academy of Management Review*, 21(4): 1055–80.

Klijn, M. and W. Tomic (2010) 'A review of creativity within organizations from a psychological perspective', *Journal of Management Development*, 29(4): 322–43.

Lee, F., A. Caza, A. Edmonton and S. Thomke (2003) 'New knowledge creation in organisations', in K. S. Cameron, J. E. Dutton and R. E. Quinn (eds) *Positive organizational scholarship*. San Francisco, Berrett-Koehler, pp. 194–204.

McCarthy, G. and J. Ahrens (2011) 'Challenges of the coaching manager', *Future of work and organisations. 25th Anzam Conference 7–9 Dec*. Auckland, New Zealand, Anzam.

McMahon, G. (2009) 'Cognitive behavioral coaching', in D. Megginson and D. Clutterbuck (eds) *Further techniques for coaching and mentoring*. Amsterdam, Butterworth-Heinemann, pp. 15–28.

Megginson, D. and D. Clutterbuck (2005) *Techniques for coaching and mentoring*. Oxford, Butterworth-Heinemann.

Mullen, C. A. and D. W. Lick (1999) *New directions in mentoring: creating a culture of synergy*. London, Falmer.

Neenan, M. and S. Palmer (2001) 'Cognitive behavioural coaching', *Stress News*, 13(3).

Nonaka, I., R. Toyama and A. Nagata (2000) 'A firm as a knowledge-creating entity: a new perspective on the theory of the firm', *Industrial and Corporate Change*, 9(1): 1–20.

Osborn, A. F. (1953) *Applied imagination*. Oxford, Scribners.

Peelle, H. E. (2006) 'Appreciative inquiry and creative problem solving in cross-functional teams', *Journal of Applied Behavioral Science*, 42: 447–67.

Pinchot, G. (2005) 'Coaching innovation leaders', in H. Morgan, P. Harkins and M. Goldsmith (eds) *The art and practice of leadership coaching*. Hoboken, John Wiley, pp. 168–72.

Prather, C. (2010) *Manager's guide to fostering innovation and creativity in teams*. Madison, McGraw-Hill.

Richard, J. T. (2003) 'Ideas on fostering creative problem solving in executive coaching', *Consulting Psychology Journal: Practice and Research*, 55(5): 249–56.

Shaw, P. and R. Linnecar (2007) *Business coaching, achieving practical results through effective engagement*. Chichester, Capstone.

Skiffington, S. and P. Zeus (2003) *Behavioral coaching: how to build sustainable personal and organizational strength*. North Ryde, NSW, McGraw-Hill.

Swap, W., D. Leonard, M. Shields and L. Abrams (2001) 'Using mentoring and storytelling to transfer knowledge in the workplace', *Journal of Management Information Systems*, 18(1): 95.

Terwiesch, C. and K. T. Ulrich (2007) 'Idea generation and the quality of the best idea', *Management Science*, 56(4): 591–605.

Thornton, C. (2010) *Group and team coaching*. Hove, Routledge.

Tidd, J., J. Bessant and K. Pavitt (2005) *Managing innovation*. Chichester, Wiley.

Wenson, J. E. (2010) 'After-coaching leadership skills and their impact on direct reports: recommendations for organizations', *Human Resource Development International*, 13(5): 607–16.

Whitaker, V. (2009) 'Offering creative choices in mentoring and coaching', in D. Megginson and D. Clutterbuck (eds) *Further techniques for coaching and mentoring*. Oxford, Butterworth-Heinemann, pp. 100–15.

White, M. A. and G. D. Bruton (2007) *The management of technology and innovation: a strategic approach*. Mason, OH, Thomson South-Western.

Whitney, D. and A. Trosten-Bloom (2010) *The power of appreciative inquiry: a practical guide to positive change*. San Francisco, CA, Berrett-Koehler.

Williams, M. H., C. J. Paulet and R. Arroyo (2006) 'The experience of Siemens in Spain', in M. Goldsmith and L. Lyons (eds) *Coaching for leadership*. San Francisco, CA, Pfeiffer, pp. 172–86.

Wycoff, J. (2003) 'The big 10 innovation killers: how to keep your innovation system alive and well', *Journal of Quality and Participation*, 26(2): 17–21, 48.

Yu, N., C. G. Collins, M. Cavanagh, K. White and G. Fairbrother (2008) 'Positive coaching with frontline managers: Enhancing their effectiveness and understanding why', *International Coaching Psychology Review*, 3(2): 110–22.

Zeus, P. and S. Skiffington (2000) *Complete guide to coaching at work*. Sydney, McGraw-Hill.

9

COACHING AND MENTORING FOR ORGANISATIONAL CHANGE

Introduction to change

It has become a cliché to suggest that the only constant is change and that the pace of change is accelerating. There are many changes in the external organisational environment, such as threats and opportunities relating to globalisation and to information communication technology. In addition, there are internal change programs, as outlined by Rock and Donde (2008) relating for example to re-structuring or cultural change. Organisations respond to competitive pressure with structural changes or pro-actively initiate changes in order to achieve their goals and out-perform the competition.

In this chapter, we look at organisational change. As organisations consist of people, applications of coaching and mentoring at the individual level discussed in Chapter 4 can also be applied at the organisational level. Coach mentors use their listening and questioning skills to help re-frame opportunities, visualise the future, and reflect on learning. Coaching managers also use their skills to help team members and employees to cope with change and help create the future.

Coaching and mentoring for organisational change

For organisations as much as for individuals, coaching and mentoring help identify gaps between where the organisation is now and where it wants to be. In fact, Lyons (2006) suggests that change management and executive coaching are 'a marriage made in heaven', which can be used as the foundation for values-based change, ensuring that change is not a top down imposition but rather a collective shift. Change can be at various levels, with the most demanding being transformational change, where the coach helps clients reconceptualise '*themselves, their roles, or their organizations*' (Dotlich 2005: 175). Coaching enables managers to '*develop behaviour that enables such change to occur*' (Deane 2001: 23).

The link between individual and organisational change is through change leaders or champions. Higgs and Rowland (2010) found that the most effective leaders of change were those who were highly self-aware, mindful and in tune with the purpose of change. They advocate providing coaching and feedback for leaders, arguing that this will have a positive effect on the implementation of change. The effectiveness of coaching in times of organisational change has been demonstrated by Grant (2013) who found that participants achieved increased goal attainment (and the goals were aligned with the organisational goals, hence both individuals and the organisation benefited) and other positive outcomes such as greater ability to deal with stress, greater job satisfaction and decreased stress and anxiety. Mentoring offers long-term support for those engaged in change leadership. A combination of coaching and mentoring may be appropriate, with mentoring continuing after the coaching engagement has concluded.

Re-structuring

Implementing strategic decisions requires change. Organisational change can take many forms and have diverse purposes, for example, growth or down-sizing, mergers or acquisitions, organisational re-design, or changes in routines, systems and procedures. For planned changes, visualisation of how the re-organisation will affect individuals is helpful in making the change real so that when it happens, people have some idea of the likely consequences for all stakeholders, how to mitigate the risks identified, and how to respond effectively. Re-building trust is a major priority after major changes. Hawkins and Smith (2006) note that while structures can be changed very quickly, culture and people are much slower to change. Shaw and Linnecar (2007) highlight the turbulence caused when the change is due to a crisis and the organisation is in the media spotlight. They argue that a coach helps those directly involved by providing time to think through the issues, as well as allowing a safe place to express emotions such as anger or disappointment. An example of how a coach mentor can help simply by listening is illustrated in Vignette 9.1.

Vignette 9.1   No time to think

'Sorry, Joe, I don't have time for a coaching session today,' said Chris.
'Okay', said Joe, 'What's happening?'
'Well, we announced the re-structure on Friday and since then I have been bombarded with media enquiries. I had to see each of the people affected and it's hard. I know their families and I know how it's going to affect them. Before we announced the re-structure, everything was so clear as to why we were doing it, but now, I just can't think straight.'
'Remind me of the reasons again', said Joe.
'Our competitors are delivering cheaper products faster than we can', said Chris, almost on autopilot. 'We added staff five years back when everyone wanted

---

our products and we kept them for the last two years, even when the demand wasn't there. We've tried to do all the right things, our people have really current skills in things like Statistical Process Control, and we're helping them find new jobs – some of them already have offers.' He was sounding more excited now and there was a note of pride in his voice. 'You know what, Joe, just that quick conversation has helped, I feel I can get back to the media now and put our company in a good light, and how this is going to save the company's future. And maybe in a few days time, we can sit down with some more of the people here and work on our future plans together.'
'Sounds good to me', said Joe. 'Just let me know when and where.'

For many managers, the most painful decision of their business life is to make a position redundant and to tell people face-to-face that they no longer have a job. Coach mentors advise at different stages of this process. In the decision phase, they help ensure that the decision makes business sense and is fair, and that the manager communicates the necessity for the decision clearly. The manager can rehearse individual communications with the coach mentor and explore possible responses. The coach mentor also helps the manager to consider how to motivate those who are still with the organisation and who may be concerned for their own future.

Coaching and mentoring also help those less immediately affected by restructuring to prioritise effectively and to avoid some of the drop in productivity associated with low morale in times of down-sizing (Bagshaw 1998). The importance of providing support not only for those leaving the organisation but also for the survivors is underscored by Gandolfi and Oster (2009). This can be done through coaching and mentoring individuals and also through using coaching and mentoring approaches to involving people in generating ideas for a sustainable organisational future.

Organisational stages of change

Just as individuals go through stages of change, so too do organisations (Carnall 2007). Carnall describes a simple model of three phases: beginnings, focusing and inclusion. Like the precontemplation, contemplation and awareness stages in the individual stages of change model described in Chapter 4, Carnall's beginnings stage consists of awareness raising, which can include diagnostic studies, feasibility studies, bench-marking with other organisations and other activities which help people to recognise the need for change and what is possible and desirable for their organisation. Harkins suggests that a coach *'gets the leaders to face up to reality, identify the challenges that exist, and build attack plans for getting beyond the barriers'* (Harkins 2005: 156). Carnall's 'focusing' stage sees the organisation move towards action, while awareness building continues. In this stage, pilot projects are conducted and support is built up in the organisation. Team coaching approaches can be used to harness the collective intelligence of the organisation and the engagement of its employees in addressing external and internal challenges. In the third stage of Carnall's model 'inclusion', the change is communicated widely and implemented, similar to the action stage of the 'stages of change' model for individuals. Although Carnall does not identify a 'maintenance' stage, he does refer to the inclusion stage as 'building and *sustaining* change' (my italics). Similar to Table 4.2 on page 61, sample questions useful at the three stages of organisational change are listed in Table 9.1.

Table 9.1   Questions for organisational change

Stage	Sample questions
Beginnings	Being honest with ourselves, how good is our company at the moment?
	How do we compare with our competitors?
	What do our customers really value? Are we doing things our customers do not value?
	How could we do things differently?
Focusing	Does everyone understand the situation we face as an organisation?
	How can we challenge our best competitor?
	Are there any low risk projects we can trial?
Action	What options do we have?
	What specifically will we do and when?
	How will we evaluate what we do?
	How will we make sure that we sustain the changes if they are effective?
	How will we recognise everyone's contribution?

Change management

Many authors, e.g. Nelissen and van Selm (2008) and Griffiths (2009), write about the fears, uncertainties and doubts which may be experienced in organisations where change is taking place. There are also many guidelines about how best to manage change, e.g. Kotter's (1995) eight step model of planned change:

1. Establish a sense of urgency

2. Form a powerful guiding coalition

3. Create a vision

4. Communicate the vision

5. Empower others to act on the vision

6. Plan for and create short-term wins

7. Consolidate improvements and produce more change

8. Institutionalise new approaches.

Dotlich (2005) classifies the common challenges people face when implementing organisational change, as systemic or technical issues, politics, power and issues relating to the organisation's values. Wissema (2000) found that in most organisations there was considerable willingness to change but that organisations did not always tap into this by listening to and involving their employees. Working with a coach mentor fosters clarity about the issues and engagement through listening to employees, sharing the vision, and working together with employees on how to make the vision reality. When managers adopt the behaviours modelled by their coach mentors, the benefits are felt not only by those with a coach mentor but are cascaded throughout the organisation.

Communication

Kotter (1995) stresses the importance of awareness of the need for change, awareness of the need for networking and of bringing people along on the change journey. One of the common reasons for failures in change management identified by Kotter is '*under-communicating the vision by a factor of 10*' (1995: 63). Researchers have found that positive responses to change are correlated with satisfaction with management communication (Nelissen and van Selm 2008). Indeed, one of the most common recommendations in the change management literature is to communicate, communicate, communicate. However, this is often interpreted as a requirement for increasing corporate communication, with managers presenting information to keep employees informed.

The other direction of communication, from employee to manager, is less frequently addressed. It is here, in the coaching manager's ability to listen and ask questions, that organisations can really benefit. Firstly people feel valued. They appreciate that their concerns are being taken seriously. Secondly, people's concerns may be valid and by hearing and considering them, the organisation may be able to implement a better change. By bringing concerns into the open, the potentially negative influence of the rumour grapevine is weakened. Lussier and Achua note that effective listening helps leaders '*to have a better understanding of the root causes of resistance*' which may lead to developing better solutions (Lussier and Achua 2010: 434). Harkins summarises the role of the change coach as '*to uncover hopes and fear, to surface hidden dialogue, and to engage in critical conversations that lead to a shared agenda, deeper commitment, and greater alignment*' (Harkins 2005: 158). Based on work by Gary Hamel, Woods (2010) suggests that resistance to change is more about a lack of engagement by people in the change process and an inability to influence what is happening, than a resistance to the change itself. The coach mentor needs to be clear on what is confidential and what can be openly shared from their discussions with individuals and teams, so that trust is built and maintained.

Organisational change and learning

Carnall (2007) argues that learning is a consequence of change. Certainly one would hope that learning takes place whenever we implement change. However, project management research indicates that the review stage is often omitted. Hence, while some specific lessons may be learned, the organisation does not take advantage of the possibilities for 'double loop learning' as described in Chapter 8. Furthermore it can also be argued that change is a consequence of learning, whether the organisation has new intelligence about its environment or an individual learns something about him or herself, it is this new learning that prompts the desire to change. Ideally then, a continuous cycle can be developed where learning leads to change which leads to further learning and so on. If the learning is shared, change is not imposed on people but is a rational choice as people understand the reason for it.

Storytelling

While narratives may help people to identify with the organisation, there is a risk of stories freezing ideas of what is good or bad in the organisation, and thus militating against change (Lapp and Carr 2008). There is a comfort in referring to old stories, especially where they relate to successful times. Geiger and Antonacopoulou (2009) warn that organisational narratives based on past success are particularly prone to contributing to inertia and blind spots as the organisation becomes unable to interpret external stimuli appropriately and to recognise new opportunities. As the authors note: '*Silencing or choosing to ignore these alternative perspectives would limit the capacity of organizations to engage in fundamental change*' (Geiger and Antonacopoulou 2009: 431). Coach mentors interrupt repeating narratives at an organisational level, challenging their relevance to the future and raising awareness of blind spots.

According to Leith (2004), large group interventions such as World Café outlined in Chapter 7, facilitate change because of the level of engagement across the organisation, the use of systems thinking, and the trust and openness adopted in these approaches. While there may be changes which cannot be re-worked to suit everyone, it is important for people to know that their input has genuinely been considered, and if their ideas are not implemented, that they understand why.

Cameron and Green (2009) note the value of reframing in change management. Skiffington and Zeus (2003) show how attaching different labels to events helps us see them differently. They suggest that coaches use this skill to help clients see changes more positively, e.g. changing from viewing change as threatening or presenting difficulties to challenging or presenting opportunities. This is not dissimilar to the tactics used by Megginson and Clutterbuck (2009) to '*change the script*'. The skill of the coach mentor lies in helping clients to frame an issue in a way that it can be addressed and helps clients recognise the resources they already possess to help solve it (Grant and Stober 2006). As illustrated in Vignette 9.2, seeing things differently can lead to change, even if there is no change in the situation or the resources available.

Vignette 9.2   The team the CEO did not trust

Maria was the CEO of a manufacturing organisation, faced with tough competition and tough down-sizing decisions. Surrounded by vested interests, Maria felt it would be helpful to talk to someone impartial, to see if her ideas were rational, feasible and fair. Her former boss suggested she talk to a mentor, Joe. Maria filled Joe in on the situation and the options she had considered so far. Joe asked about Maria's decision not to involve her own team in the discussions and decision-making. Maria explained that each of the team was too attached to their own part of the company and not taking a strategic view. They were good at their individual roles but did not look at things from the perspective of the whole company. Joe asked whether this was a new position they had adopted. Maria realised that her team had in fact never operated as a team and had never taken a strategic overview. Joe shared some of his experience working with dysfunctional teams. Seeing her team through Joe's eyes, Maria acknowledged that she did not trust them. Joe wondered out loud what the outcome might be if Maria took them into her confidence. Balancing the possible confrontations between her team members and between their teams against the possibility of more innovation and collaboration which would give the company a better basis for growth, Maria could see that the benefits outweighed the risks. There was also a huge potential benefit in the trust generated if Maria started to share information and to involve her team in decision-making. If anyone on the team proved not to be trustworthy, she would deal with that person separately. She could already feel some of the pressure lifting, knowing that the tough decisions would have solid inputs from people who understood the company and who shared her vision.

In parallel with the way coach mentors use Intentional Change Theory with individuals seeking change, so too can the principles of Appreciative Inquiry be used by coach mentors in helping organisations explore possibilities for change as shown in Table 9.2.

Table 9.2 Principles of Appreciative Inquiry (adapted from Whitney and Trosten-Bloom (2010))

Principles of Appreciative Inquiry	Application to coaching and mentoring for change
Constructionist: Reality is created through language.	Knowledge is generated through social interaction. Coach mentors foster opportunities through working with teams and through encouraging reflection by individuals on their learning.
Simultaneity: Change occurs when we ask a question.	By asking paradoxical and provocative questions, the coach mentor stimulates imagination and ideas.
Poetic: We can choose what we study.	The coach mentor helps people focus, choosing metaphors which help the organisation see itself differently, e.g. moving from a self-conception of a cork bobbing about on fast flowing water to a metaphor of a leader in a race or a chameleon changing colours.
Anticipatory: Images inspire action.	Coach mentors help people visualise the future. The anticipatory principle suggests that such visualisation helps interrupt the status quo and leads to action.

(Continued)

Table 9.2   (Continued)

Principles of Appreciative Inquiry	Application to coaching and mentoring for change
Positive: Positive questions lead to positive change.	Positive questions build on positive emotions such as hope and make change seem possible and desirable.
Wholeness: Wholeness brings out the best.	This relates well to systems coaching, understanding all the elements and how they interact, involving all stakeholders to build trust and learn from all participants.
Enactment: Acting 'as if' is self-fulfilling.	The coach mentor helps people think through consequences and rehearse new behaviour so that the client is confident and determined to implement.
Free choice: Free choice liberates power.	The coach mentor has no authority to require commitment; participants are thus treated as volunteers in line with this principle. According to Whitney and Trosten-Bloom, this 'builds enthusiasm, commitment to the organisation and fosters high performance' (2010: 71).

Solution-focused coaching can be used to explore organisational choices as it is with individuals. While data is useful in examining the root causes of problems, organisations can become so focused on data analysis that they fail to make progress toward a solution. Depending on the culture of the organisation, people may prefer a more neutral phrasing of questions than questions asking about if a miracle had happened or a magician had waved her magic wand. The principles however remain the same, a focus on the future and on taking positive steps toward it. Examples of solution-focused questions for organisations are shown in Table 9.3.

Table 9.3   Examples of solution-focused questions for organisations

Purpose of question	Example wording
Identifying possible solutions	Let's say that something amazing happens and we have solved the problem – what would it look like? What would we be doing differently? What would our customers be saying? What would our competitors think? What would be the knock-on effects for the organisation?
Strengths	What is working well at the moment? How can you tell?
	Of all the projects on the go at the moment, which are working best? What can we learn from them?
Implementation	On a scale of 1–10, if 10 is 'We have fully implemented the solution' and 1 is 'We have not yet started', where are we now? How can we move from a 3 to a 4?
	Have we ever been higher than a 3? What were we doing differently then?
	What will we do when we leave this meeting to get this started?

Context

Coach mentors need to devote time to understand the context of each person or team they work with and what is unique about each one. Mike Allen observes: '*As one's circle of mentees becomes wider, it emphasizes the importance of thinking oneself into their mind-set*' (Megginson, Clutterbuck et al. 2006: 193). The coach mentor brings positive attention to each person, valuing their contribution in a way which does not always happen in busy organisations. Leaders who adopt a coaching mentoring approach treat each team member as an individual as well as working with the team as a whole. A wide range of benefits have been reported, including improved team member performance, employee satisfaction and well-being (Grant 2010).

Culture

As Pfau (2005) points out, to change one person's behaviour can be hard enough, while to change the organisation's culture requires multiple interventions and mutually support-ing policies, practices, systems, structures, leadership and staffing, with a systems approach helping to sustain the change after the initial stimulus for change has weakened. Team coaching can be very powerful in helping transform people's anxiety about change into a source of creativity (Thornton 2010). Thornton suggests that the more anxiety there exists, the more highly structured the conversation needs to be and the more authoritative the coach needs to be. Working with all the team through the choices relating to the change helps gain commitment to the changes. Team coaching makes members aware of each other's strengths and how they can best work together to achieve the team's goals (Dubrin 2010). Kets de Vries argues strongly in favour of group coaching as '*the preferred tool for behavioural change*' (Kets de Vries 2005: 75). Group pressure means that the group supports each member in delivering on their promises. Kets de Vries lists shame, guilt and hope as some of the emotions which motivate people to change. Fear of group disapproval is very powerful, while the support and acceptance of the group provide hope and promote self-efficacy. Combining team coaching with a systems coaching approach can be used to address Kotter's (1995) recommendations to create a guiding coalition, to share the vision, to consolidate improvements and to institutionalise the changes made.

In current approaches to change management, people are informed about planned change early in the process, often before decisions have been taken about implemen-tation and how the change will affect individuals. Although well-meaning, this may result in individuals being anxious for a longer period of time than in less enlight-ened times, when individuals were often not informed until after every detail had been decided. Coach mentors may work at two levels: firstly in helping managers listen to their employees' fears, uncertainties and doubts, to visualise the future, and to commu-nicate the vision effectively; and secondly, in coaching and mentoring teams directly, in developing options for the new scenario.

Resilience

Beaudan (2001) highlights the importance of 'time-outs' from implementation, noting that people need time to 'recharge their emotional and intellectual batteries'. Other authors too have discussed the impact of 'initiative fatigue', where change keeps coming, wave after wave, so that people cannot relax into a routine. Hawkins and Smith (2006) cite the example of the UK National Health Service, where both routines and structures were changed to such an extent that the people were still trying to get used to one change when the next change arrived. Strategies used to help individuals cope with stress and burnout are important when helping people cope with organisational change, hence research into 'resilient organisations' has come to prominence in recent years, e.g. Beer (2009) and Valikangas (2010). The organisation as a whole needs to be able to cope with challenges, just as individuals do. Approaches to helping individuals build their resilience such as exploring alternative scenarios and rehearsing worst possible scenarios (Barrett 2004) can be used with organisations planning for change. St-Jean and Audet (2012) argue that mentoring helps increase entrepreneur resilience by '*helping to maintain or increase motivation when times are tough*'. Unlike a counselling or therapeutic approach, coaching and mentoring are forward-focused and help employees cope with change both by providing a channel for their questions and ideas to be heard and involving them in creating a shared vision of the future.

Conclusion

This chapter highlights approaches which coach mentors use in helping clients drive change at an organisational level and helping their clients cope with change also. Clients can reap the benefits of a coaching approach to change management, developing their employees' resilience, listening to their concerns, involving more people in deciding on how changes will best be implemented, thereby building commitment to the change. Coaching and mentoring offer a form of dialogue which ensures that people are listened to and that questions are asked which draw out people's tacit knowledge as well as their concerns. Visualisation helps people feel optimistic about future scenarios. Coaching and mentoring thus offer practical ways to implement good practice in change management.

Useful links

The links in this chapter highlight resources to support learning about organisational change.

12 Manage – http://www.12manage.com/i_co.html

Short summaries of change models and frameworks.

About.com – http://humanresources.about.com/od/managementandleadership/u/manage_people.htm

Resources for topics including coaching, mentoring, communication and change.

Businessballs – http://www.businessballs.com/changemanagement.htm

Short summaries of research related to change management.

Mind Tools – http://www.mindtools.com/pages/main/newMN_PPM.htm#Change

Change management frameworks, tools and a self-assessment of change management skills.

University of Twente – http://www.utwente.nl/cw/theorieenoverzicht/

Overview of communication theories, useful for communicating change.

References

Bagshaw, M. (1998) 'Coaching, mentoring and the sibling organization', *Industrial and Commercial Training*, 30(3): 87–9.

Barrett, F. (2004) 'Coaching for resilience', *Organization Development Journal*, 22(1): 93–6.

Beaudan, E. (2001) 'The failure of strategy – it's all in the execution', *Ivey Business Journal* (Jan–Feb): 64–8.

Beer, M. (2009) *High commitment, high performance: how to build a resilient organization for sustained advantage.* San Francisco, Jossey-Bass.

Cameron, E. and M. Green (2009) *Making sense of change management: a complete guide to the models, tools and techniques of organizational change.* London, Kogan Page.

Carnall, C. A. (2007) *Managing change in organisations.* Harlow, Prentice-Hall.

Deane, R. (2001) 'Coaching – a winning strategy', *British Journal of Administrative Management*, 25 (May–June): 22–3.

Dotlich, D. (2005) 'Creating a theory for change', in H. Morgan, P. Harkins and M. Goldsmith (eds) *The art and practice of leadership coaching.* Hoboken, NJ, Wiley, pp. 173–5.

Dubrin, A. J. (2010) *Leadership: Research findings, practice and skills.* Cengage.

Gandolfi, F. and G. Oster (2009) 'Sustaining innovation during corporate downsizing', *S.A.M. Advanced Management Journal*, 74(2): 42–53.

Geiger, D. and E. Antonacopoulou (2009) ' Narratives and organizational dynamics: exploring blind spots and organizational inertia', *Journal of Applied Behavioral Science*, 45(3): 411–36.

Grant, A. M. (2010) 'It takes time: a stages of change perspective on the adoption of workplace coaching skills', *Journal of Change Management*, 10(1): 61–77.

Grant, A. M. (2013) 'The efficacy of executive coaching in times of organisational change', *Journal of Change Management*. Available online at http://www.tandfonline.com/doi/abs/10.1080/14697017.2013.805159#.Ufw-_6N-8qQ): 1–23.

Grant, A. M. and D. R. Stober (2006) *Evidence-based coaching handbook: putting best practices to work for your clients.* Hoboken, NJ, Wiley.

Griffiths, B. (2009) 'The paradox of change: how to coach while dealing with fear and uncertainty', *Industrial and Commercial Training*, 41(2): 97–101.

Harkins, P. (2005) 'Getting the organization to click', in H. Morgan, P. Harkins and M. Goldsmith (eds) *The art and practice of leadership coaching.* Hoboken, NJ, Wiley, pp. 154–9.

Hawkins, P. and N. Smith (2006) *Coaching, mentoring and organizational consultancy: supervision and development.* Maidenhead, Open University Press.

Higgs, M. and D. Rowland (2010) 'Emperors with clothes on: the role of self-awareness in developing effective change leadership', *Journal of Change Management*, 10(4): 369–85.

Kets de Vries, M. F. (2005) 'Leadership group coaching in action: the Zen of creating high performance teams', *Academy of Management Executive*, 19(1): 61–76.

Kotter, J. P. (1995) 'Leading change: why transformation efforts fail', *Harvard Business Review*, 73(2): 59–68.

Lapp, C. A. and A. N. Carr (2008) 'Coaching can be storyselling: creating change through crises of confidence', *Journal of Organizational Change Management*, 21(5): 532–59.

Leith, M. (2004) *Leith's guide to large group intervention methods*. Martin Leith Limited. Available at http://www.largescaleinterventions.com/documents/leiths_guide_to_lgis.pdf.

Lussier, R. N. and C. F. Achua (2010) *Leadership: theory, application and skills development*. Mason, OH, Cengage.

Lyons, L. (2006) 'Coaching for change at Aventis', in M. Goldsmith and L. Lyons (eds) *Coaching for leadership*. San Francisco, Pfeiffer, pp. 163–72.

Megginson, D., D. Clutterbuck, R. Garvey, P. Stokes and R. Garret-Harris (2006) *Mentoring in action*. London, Kogan Page.

Megginson, D. and D. Clutterbuck (eds.) (2009) *Further techniques for coaching and mentoring*, Oxford, Butterworth-Heinemann.

Nelissen, P. and M. van Selm (2008) 'Surviving organizational change: how management communication helps balance mixed feelings', *Corporate Communications*, 13(3): 306–18.

Pfau, B. (2005) 'Coaching for organizational change', in H. Morgan, P. Harkins and M. Goldsmith (eds) *The art and practice of leadership coaching*. Hoboken, NJ, Wiley, pp. 186–8.

Rock, D. and R. Donde (2008) 'Driving organisational change with internal coaching programmes: part two', *Industrial and Commercial Training*, 40(2): 75–80.

Shaw, P. and R. Linnecar (2007) *Business coaching, achieving practical results through effective engagement*. Chichester, Capstone.

Skiffington, S. and P. Zeus (2003) *Behavioral coaching: how to build sustainable personal and organizational strength*. North Ryde, NSW, McGraw-Hill.

St-Jean, E. and J. Audet (2012) 'The role of mentoring in the learning development of the novice entrepreneur', *International Entrepreneurship and Management Journal*, 8(1): 119–40.

Thornton, C. (2010) *Group and team coaching*. Hove, Routledge.

Valikangas, L. (2010) *The resilient organization*. McGraw-Hill.

Whitney, D. and A. Trosten-Bloom (2010) *The power of appreciative inquiry: a practical guide to positive change*. San Francisco, CA, Berrett-Koehler.

Wissema, J. (2000) 'Fear of change? A myth!', *Journal of Change Management*, 1(1): 74–90.

Woods, D. (2010) 'Leadership coaching: strategy coaching', in J. Passmore (ed.) *Leadership coaching: working with leaders to develop elite performance*. London, Kogan Page, pp. 245–61.

10

CROSS-CULTURAL AND VIRTUAL COACHING AND MENTORING

Introduction

Coaching and mentoring are interactions with a specific client or employee. The coach mentor should always relate to the individual with whom they are working, and not see them as a representative of any particular group or stereotype. There are, however, some cross-cultural contexts in which coaching and mentoring are helpful and where research has identified some differences when compared with generic coaching and mentoring research. This chapter explores cross-cultural coaching and mentoring, and coaching and mentoring at a distance, also known as virtual coaching and mentoring.

Cross-cultural coaching and mentoring

As discussed in Chapter 3, the relationship between coach mentor and client is crucial to the success of the process. This relationship relies on communication, both verbal and non-verbal, and is deeply affected by culture. Culture can be defined as 'the collective programming of the human mind that distinguishes the members of one human group from those of another' (Hofstede, Hofstede et al. 2010). In this section, we will look at coaching and mentoring when working with people from different ethnic backgrounds, but not at organisational culture or cultures of groups such as professions or functions within an organisation. Given the diversity of today's workforce, all coach mentors should recognise the importance of diversity and this is a core competency expected by the Worldwide Association of Business Coaches.

Coaching and mentoring help clients see other people's point of view, thereby helping to realise the potential benefits of a diverse team. This is important for effective online communication, according to Salmon (2000), who also recommends other coaching and mentoring practices, such as being non-directive and asking stimulating questions, as well as frequent use of summarising, to enable people to keep track of discussions and agreements. The coaching and mentoring client needs to feel understood.

As Rosinski and Abbott (2010) point out, culture is always influential, what varies is the amount of attention we give it. Rosinski and Abbott highlight the opportunities that culture brings to the relationship, enabling an exploration of different perspectives from which new insights and solutions may be gained. In highlighting culture, it is important not to fall into the trap of believing that stereotypes apply to everyone in that culture. For example, some people in a collectivist culture are individualistic and some people in an individualist country have a collective orientation. Furthermore, many countries are now multicultural, with residents and citizens displaying some characteristics of their country of origin and some of their adopted country. The experience of ethnic minorities in organisations may be substantially different from those of the majority as they may have to deal with real or perceived discrimination.

Diversity

Coach mentors working with culturally diverse clients need to simultaneously keep in mind that each person is unique, although there are some broad cultural similarities (Webb 2010). A coach mentor with experience of working with clients from different ethnic backgrounds may recognise patterns but can never assume that those patterns apply to the individual they are working with at any given time. Brand and Coetzee (2013) report on the negative perceptions of a black coachee in a predominantly white male workplace who felt that her experience might have been different with a female black coach who understood where she was coming from. Similar perceptions were reported by Carr and Seto (2013) in Canada. However, although similarity between coach mentor and client may make rapport easier to establish, on the other hand it may also limit opportunities for growth. Vignette 10.1 shows how a coach mentor can help a client think through cross-cultural situations, recognising both their own perspective and those of others.

Vignette 10.1   Culture and age

Sonia was an ambitious young manager from India working in a logistics company in Australia. A hard worker, she had quickly been promoted to team leader. Her team mostly comprised younger people, from a variety of countries, and she found no problem in motivating them and getting the best from them. The only person she did have a problem with was Kumar, who was from the same part of India as she was. Kumar was in his late 40s and had been working at the company for over 20 years. Sonia found it difficult to be assertive with an older male from her own culture. A friend recommended Anna, a coach mentor who helped Sonia think about her sense of identity, her values and her goals. Then Anna prompted Sonia to consider specific incidents from the perspectives of different team members, including Kumar. Sonia realised how difficult it must be for Kumar to report to a young female. She decided to ask Kumar to share his expertise in team meetings. He had a gift for explaining things clearly, and she began to rely on him for training the others. Kumar blossomed. If he made a mistake, Sonia no longer gave him direct feedback about it. Instead she sought his views as to how they could change the process to lessen the likelihood of anyone making that mistake again. This led to improvements which were later adopted across the company.

Even where similar situations arise repeatedly, the coach mentor cannot assume that different clients will find the same solutions useful. One client who is frustrated at not being promoted might need training to be more assertive, another might benefit from re-framing how they see themselves in the system of their organisation, while another might have blind spots relating to the opportunities available to them. Through listening intently to the individual and their story, cross-cultural mentoring and coaching offer a powerful way to explore the opportunities for learning and growth in diversity (Zachary 2005; Moral and Abbott 2009).

Coaching has been found to help 'mental flexibility and creativity' with Wales arguing that '*understanding different views, different styles and different ethnicities engenders a more supportive environment*' (Wales 2003: 278). Successful diverse teams generate more creative solutions, according to Rosinski and Abbott (2010). Unfortunately, cultural differences can lead to conflict in organisations if not well managed. Coach mentors help individuals and teams surface implicit assumptions and agree on ways to collaborate effectively.

Cross-cultural coaching and mentoring frameworks

Rosinski's three-stage global coaching process (also applicable to mentoring) consists of:

1. *An assessment stage*, where the coach helps coachees to understand their own cultural orientation and that of others.

2. *A target-setting stage*, where coachees adopt a balanced scorecard type approach to setting targets relating to many aspects of their lives, including self, family and friends as well the organisation, the community and the world.

3. *An action stage*, where the coach helps coachees monitor their progress toward their targets, revising targets where appropriate, and reflecting on learning as they make progress.

As Rosinski and Abbott note, this process can be combined with whatever approach the coach adopts. Where one coach mentor might favour a solution-focused approach, another might adopt a positive psychology approach. Systems coaching is particularly appropriate in Confucian societies where the focus is less on the individual and more on the individual's interaction with their environment (Dreyer 2013).

An alternative cross-cultural coaching model proposed by Law, Ireland et al. (2007) challenges clients to articulate their values and cultural beliefs, to gain insights from experience, and to take culturally appropriate actions. This model emphasises the importance of cross-cultural emotional intelligence and uses 360 degree data as the basis for feedback (Passmore and Law 2009). This can also be used with mentoring. Integral coaching is a narrative coaching approach which explicitly includes culture and relationships, enabling the client to see their experience through different lenses (Armstrong 2009). Generic models like these help the coach mentor to develop their own awareness and leverage diversity with their clients.

Ontological coaching is practised by many coaches in Spain and Latin America, perhaps because this approach was developed by José Olalla (2009) in Chile and hence the materials and training were readily available in Spanish. However, ontological coaching is also popular in English-speaking countries. Coach mentors cannot assume when coaching someone from Spain or Latin America, that the best approach would be ontological coaching. Instead, coach mentors consider the individual with whom they are working and choose an approach which they are competent to use and which they think will work best with a particular individual. They then reflect on the effectiveness of their approach and may modify it with that client or with later clients.

A systems approach helps clients accommodate the multiple perspectives inherent in a cross-cultural environment (Plaister-Ten 2009). Plaister-Ten (2013) developed the cross-cultural kaleidoscope as a guide to topics to explore in the cross-cultural landscape. The model includes a focus on internal influences such as self-identity and external influences such as legal, political, economic, education, history, geography, community, spiritual, cultural norms and diversity (e.g. age and gender). These topics can help illuminate the situation in which clients find themselves and suggest useful areas to explore, but the coach mentor has to be careful to listen to the client and not jump to conclusions.

International research

Notwithstanding the caveats relating to stereotypes, there is some research relating to coaching in different cultures which may be helpful to coach mentors. The majority of research cited earlier in this book relates to coaching and mentoring in Anglo cultures such as the United Kingdom, United States or Australia, even when this is not explicitly stated in the original accounts of the research. In this section, we will highlight research relating to other parts of the world.

Link with values and practices

Instead of coaching and mentoring being seen as Western management fads, it can be helpful to frame them in the context of traditions from elsewhere in the world. Coaching and mentoring share links with Confucian and Buddhist values, such as valuing people and relationships, a focus on self-improvement, and an emphasis on reflection and practice (Wong and Leung 2007; Ng 2009). The Taoist concepts of self-knowledge and flow are also closely linked with the emphasis on raising self-awareness in coaching and mentoring. The African concept of Ubuntu, which Geber and Keane (2013) define as a relationship-centred paradigm, valuing collective responsibility, consensus and harmony, can be explored with clients in many cultures. Fiddler (1998) highlights how storytelling is used by indigenous people to share knowledge, values and reflection. Respecting cultural values, traditions and practices is important for coaching and mentoring to succeed. Fortunately many of these traditions are consistent with coaching and mentoring.

Exploring the Islamic perspective is a useful way for clients to reflect on their values and their goals according to Palmer and Arnold (2009). The authors suggest sharing Western sayings relevant to an issue and exploring whether there are similar sayings in Arabic. In discussing feedback, for example, they say there is an Arabic saying which translates roughly as 'God blesses the one who provides negative feedback'. This helps senior managers who may be offended by feedback offered by people lower than themselves in the hierarchy to see feedback as a gift to help in their own growth and development. Similar metaphors may be used in different cultures but their meaning may differ. The English phrase 'We're all in the same boat' has very different connotations to the Chinese phrase 'We are sitting in the same boat but looking in different directions' (Dreyer 2013). Metaphors and stories are also useful in mentoring in Fiji (Ruru, Sanga et al. 2013).

Coach mentors in Asia are often expected to be older, wiser, and more senior than the person they are working with (Law, Laulusa et al. 2009). It is important to establish one's credibility early in the relationship as this helps develop trust and respect (Nicholas and Twaddell 2010). Coaching in India may include spiritual guidance and holistic advice, rather than a focus purely on business (Sood 2009). Clients in Asia often expect to receive advice and solutions (Nangalia and Nangalia 2010). Mentoring may be a more appropriate choice in collectivist cultures where people are used to seeking advice from elders (Anagnos 2009; Nangalia and Nangalia 2010). Carr and Seto (2013) argue that coaches who stick rigidly to a non-directive approach may limit results for some clients, arguing instead for adjusting one's approach to create rapport and trust with different clients.

Nangalia and Nangalia found that relationship building took longer in Asia than in the West and that relationships should be strong before coaches give feedback. Ing (2010) disagrees with some of Nangalia's advice, noting that even in the early stages of a coaching relationship, coach and coachee need to agree on how they will work together and some form of partnership is thus formed. She also disagrees with the notion of coaches needing to be more directive, recommending instead that the coach help through asking questions and helping clients to discover their own solutions, rather than through telling people what to do. Furthermore, she argues that the giving of feedback helps build the relationship, and is not a subsequent stage in the process.

In many countries in Asia, as well as Brazil (Celestino and Faro 2009), and the Middle East (Palmer and Arnold 2009), feedback to managers needs to be given in such a way as not to threaten the managers' perceived status or power or affect the harmony of the group. Celestino and Faro (2009) claim that Brazilian managers often believe that success is entirely due to their own efforts. Coach mentors help these managers recognise the contribution of others. The coach mentor has to consider how best to get the feedback recipient to accept and act on the feedback they receive. Citing views of leaders in a hierarchical organisation encourages clients to take the feedback seriously, as a sign of respect to the leader. A strengths-based approach which builds on the person's strengths rather than focusing on their deficits works well in Asia (Wright 2010). In collectivist cultures, feedback is often given in private, as negative feedback in public may lead to loss of face. Positive feedback to an individual may lead to embarrassment as the individual may see the success as a group achievement.

Culture takes a long time to change but changes do happen over time. Some of these descriptions of coaching or mentoring in different countries may shift if people in those countries adopt Anglo understanding and expectations of coaching and mentoring. This has already happened in some parts of Europe, where for example, coaching in Germany was characterised in 2005 as directive, but in 2009 as *'undecided between directive and non-directive'* (Tulpa and Bresser 2009). Coaching in different countries in Europe varies, with southern European countries adopting a more directive approach, and showing a stronger preference for face-to-face interactions.

Conformity

The question of whether coach mentors should help their clients to conform or stand out from cultural norms also leads to differences of opinion. Nangalia and Nangalia (2010) suggest that clients would be reluctant to commit to actions which make them stand out, whereas Ing (2010) suggests that some clients will stand out, if their action is for the good of the group. Den Hartog (1999) suggests that leaders generally need to operate within cultural norms, but that leaders who go against these norms occasionally may be seen as charismatic. According to Gupta and Govindarajan (2002), people who act as if imprisoned by cultural stereotypes commit as costly errors as those who go against culture by accident. In other words, it is important to be aware of different cultural norms and then to decide whether to act against the norms in a specific context.

Coach mentors with expertise in diverse contexts help clients think through possible consequences, risks and benefits, enabling clients to choose wisely. Palmer and Arnold (2009) suggest that when discussing possible actions with Middle Eastern clients, it is useful to outline a Western direct or assertive approach, and ask the client about appropriate approaches in their culture. Coach mentor and client can then explore the implications of choosing different options. Rehearsing the new behaviour and considering how to respond to possible reactions can be helpful if the choice is a significant departure from the client's usual behaviour.

Group coaching

Group coaching is also increasing in Asia (Nicholas and Twaddell 2010). Coaching diverse groups helps the group understand each other better and trust each other (Legrain-Fremaux and Fox 2010). This is useful in helping multinational teams develop a shared understanding and agree ways to work together. Appreciative Inquiry helps team members recognise the positives of their diverse experience and expertise and create a new vision for the future (Tulpa and Bresser 2009).

Coaching global top teams offers additional challenges as noted by Tulpa and Woudstra (2010) who note that leaders can be overly convinced that they are right, and may be 'competitive, political, stubborn and self-serving'. Furthermore, they have a dual role in terms of functional responsibility and shared responsibility for the company performance as a whole. The top team needs to learn to work together, recognising and leveraging their diverse strengths.

Difficulties with group coaching and mentoring also arise if senior executives are unwilling to be regarded as peers of less senior people in a group. Younger executives may need to learn ways to challenge the status quo while still demonstrating the expected respect for their elders. Indirect feedback to a group can be an effective alternative to direct feedback to an individual who might otherwise lose face in the group. If asking an open question, the coach mentor needs to ensure that people feel safe and know that there is no wrong answer. In brainstorming sessions, it may be less threatening for everyone to write down their ideas individually before sharing them with the group. Before beginning a brainstorming session, coach mentors need to make sure that they are not viewed as experts who already know 'the right answer', but rather as a support for the group to help them work out the best answer.

There are also cultural aspects to goal setting. While individual goals have been shown to be motivating in individualist cultures, collective goals do not necessarily have the same impact on a collectivist culture (Robbins, Millett et al. 2011). Furthermore, the authors note that achievable and modest rather than stretching goals are more effective in high power distance cultures, where fear of failure and losing face are very strong. Goals assigned by a manager generate commitment in a high power distance culture as people are keen to satisfy their manager.

Changing environments

As noted in Chapter 2, trust is an essential element in effective coaching and mentoring relationships. Intercultural differences provide many opportunities for misunderstandings and loss of trust. Olalla defines trust as '*our assessment (judgement), based on past experience, of the likelihood we will get the results we believe we have been promised*' (Olalla 2009: 77). He suggests the use of ontological coaching to make tacit assumptions and expectations explicit so that each person knows what the other person really expects and can meet those expectations. Early stages of international mergers and acquisitions are particularly risky, as people do not yet know whether they can trust their new colleagues. Coaching and mentoring in this context can help people identify opportunities for developing relationships and trust, identify what the ideal post-merger collaboration would look like, and commit to actions to create it. Merger and acquisition coaches can help at various stages of the process (Abbott 2009) such as identifying possible cultural difficulties in the due diligence phase, making people aware of bias in their decision-making, and coaching people through change at all levels in the organisation so that cultural differences are recognised as valuable sources of innovation and future success.

Coaching is also being used in Asia to help transition to senior management. While transitions are difficult for managers everywhere, it can be particularly difficult for clients in countries such as Indonesia where there is a strong drive to preserve harmony in relationships. Coaching and mentoring help by raising the client's awareness of how to be assertive without being rude or aggressive (Heath 2010). A systems approach helps the new appointee understand their role in relation to the organisation as a whole, and helps him/her understand that it is important not to ignore poor performance by an individual or team.

Expatriates

Coaching and mentoring of expatriates is also in demand as organisations seek to increase the success rate of international assignments. Failure of expatriate assignments incurs high direct costs but also indirect costs such as lost productivity, failure to achieve strategic objectives, difficulty in attracting other managers to relocate and lost investment in training (Miser and Miser 2009). Coaching and mentoring can shorten the learning curve for an expatriate manager, whose natural tendencies may be to give direct feedback and to assume that a lack of questions means understanding or that a smile means agreement. Expatriate managers often feel frustrated at the pace of change but they need to learn that focusing on people and relationships will help get the task done. Carraher, Sullivan et al. (2008) reported that having a mentor from the expatriate's home country resulted in improvements in performance, organisational knowledge and promotability, while having a host-country mentor resulted in improvements in the same three dimensions as well as in knowledge sharing and teamwork.

Abbott and Stenig (2009) recommend a focus on cognitive, behavioural and affective issues with expatriates at all stages of their assignment. Pre-departure coaching focuses on expectations and first steps in the new location. Mentors share their experience of what they have found works in relevant countries and cultures. Post-return coaching helps managers to adjust to life back home, where their lifestyle may be less luxurious than in the offshore setting where they may have had servants and generous living allowances. It can also help managers find ways to ensure that their hard-won cross-cultural expertise is valued by the organisation and that they do not simply slide back into doing the job they used to do before their international assignment.

Some organisations offer coaching and mentoring to both expatriates and their partners before and after their assignment as well as during it, because unhappiness of a partner is often the cause of failure of expatriate assignments (Miser and Miser 2009). Pre-departure coaching and mentoring help the couple articulate their hopes and fears, think through the consequences of taking or not taking the overseas assignment, and develop realistic expectations and strategies for dealing with difficulties which can be anticipated, such as loneliness, isolation and alienation. Coaching and mentoring can help both partners during the assignment, both with work-related issues and with issues such as how to make friends and how to take advantage of opportunities which arise. On their return, coaching and mentoring can help the couple to acknowledge the growth in their personal relationships and networks, as well as the lessons learned, and to look toward the future together.

Coaching and mentoring at a distance

In today's complex organisations, coaching and mentoring cannot always take place face-to-face. While many people prefer to hold initial conversations face-to-face (Kiely 2001; Daft 2008), pressure on time and costs often lead to a combination of face-to-face and some form of distance coaching or mentoring (also known as virtual coaching and mentoring, or eCoaching and eMentoring). Managers in multinational companies have to work with people across different cultures, language, time zones and legal systems, and have to use technology for at least some of their interactions. Managers in purely domestic organisations may be responsible for teams in dispersed areas, particularly in large countries such as China, Russia or Australia. It is useful therefore to consider the impact of diverse media on the coaching and mentoring experience.

There are many benefits to virtual coaching and mentoring. eCoaching and eMentoring, particularly via an organisation's intranet, are more cost effective as well as more time effective than traditional face-to-face coaching and mentoring, according to Averweg (2010). A pilot program at BT Wholesale in the UK found that online coaching and mentoring improved productivity by 10–15% (Pollitt 2007). Whitaker (2012) describes how mentoring at a distance helps unlock potential, citing a case study of a young female entrepreneur in the Lebanon whose mentor was in the UK. Distance mentoring diminishes possible barriers, whether due to geographical distance or physical ability, and enables flexibility in timing for both parties. It also widens the pool of mentors available and provides a record of interactions (Hamilton and Scandura 2003; Headland-Wells, Gosland et al. 2006). A further advantage is that eMentoring provides a useful option for staff development in SMEs (Leppisaari and Tenhunen 2009). Zachary (2005) observes that distance mentoring can be effective for most types of mentoring and has the advantage that the relationship can continue even if one partner relocates. However, he also emphasises that expectations on both sides need to be clearly defined, including how parties will communicate, how often, and what outcomes are expected. Kacmar, McManus et al. (2012) also stress the importance of clear communication, particularly where the communication concerns negative feedback, in order to avoid a negative impact on the relationship.

Trust

Research has found that trust is the most important variable in determining the effectiveness of virtual teams (Abbott 2009). Benefits of developing trust increases team members' confidence in each other (Jarvenpaa, Knoll et al. 1998), improves problem-solving, and ability to adapt to change (Stahl and Sitkin 2005), and leads to enhanced employee satisfaction and performance (Powell, Galvin et al. 2006). According to Stahl and Sitkin (2005) and Bergiel, Bergiel et al. (2006), trust also leads to improved communication, which improves employee engagement and motivation. As noted in previous chapters, trust is vital in coaching and mentoring which in turn help to develop trust (Kayworth and Leidner 2000; Brake 2006; Dewar 2006).

Media

Telephone is the most common medium used for eCoaching and eMentoring. Mobile and landline phones are ubiquitous business tools and have the advantage of familiarity and ease of use. Telephones offer a synchronous medium, i.e. coach mentor and client respond to each other in real time. While body language is missing, tone of voice can reveal a great deal about the other person's emotions, stress levels, and levels of attentiveness. Indeed it is a useful exercise for practising coach mentors to wear a blindfold so that they can practise their skill at interpreting tone of voice and also at expressing warmth and unconditional positive regard in their own voices as they would do with facial expressions.

An increasingly popular alternative to telephone is the range of cheap or free alternatives to expensive video conferencing, such as Skype, Google Hangouts and VSee. These allow the coach mentor and client to see each other and thus bring body language as well as tone of voice back into the equation. Like telephony, they provide a synchronous medium i.e. coach mentor and client hear each other in real time. The features of different packages vary but often allow sharing of applications such as whiteboards or slides, allowing both parties to see what the other is drawing or writing. As technology is evolving rapidly, clients appreciate coach mentors who make them aware of different options for connecting online.

The lack of tone and volume makes coaching and mentoring by text more difficult, although various online conventions have arisen, such as the use of capital letters to indicate a raised voice or emoticons such as smiley faces to indicate feelings. Although lacking in the richness and immediacy of face-to-face communication, the technology also has some advantages. As an asynchronous medium, where the two parties are not online at the same time, it is not affected by time zones. Each person responds when they are next available. Coaching and mentoring by text encourages focused questions. If the coach mentor asks two questions in the same text, the client may only respond to one, so that the coach mentor quickly learns to focus each message on a single topic (McCarthy 2010). It allows both parties time to reflect before sending their next text. However, this carries a related risk that the coach mentor may follow up with a carefully crafted question, rather than be truly mindful of the person they are working with.

In addition to text media such as emails and text messages on telephones, there are also dedicated coaching applications, which prompt with relevant questions at different steps of the process and allow the coach mentor and client to share notes, goals and actions. These applications can also be used to record notes of telephone, video conferencing or face-to-face sessions. As noted in earlier chapters, the most important thing in the coaching and mentoring process is the relationship with the client. However, software can help coach mentors to focus less on technique or steps of the process and more on the human being they are working with. There is a risk that the coach mentor could use the software mechanically as they might use a model mechanically. However, if the coach mentor uses the software to widen their repertoire of questions or to record notes of coaching or mentoring sessions which they may later use for reflection or supervision, the software can be a help.

Making use of technology allows people access to the best coach mentors in the world (Zachary 2005). It enables coach mentors to offer niche services such as expatriate couples coaching and to keep in touch with clients before, during and after their overseas assignments. Managers may need to develop their coaching and mentoring skills to operate effectively at a distance. Depending on the culture, they may adopt more of a mentoring than a coaching approach. Rather than seeing technology as a barrier, technology can be seen as an enabler that facilitates interaction with people worldwide. Initially it takes time to understand what works in a particular organisation, but as leaders and team members gain experience, they learn to work effectively together. A coach mentor specialising in virtual teams shortens this learning cycle and can also flag new opportunities provided by emerging technologies.

Other challenges

In addition to the variable technology availability and bandwidth in different countries, virtual team coaching and mentoring presents an additional set of challenges, as do coaching and mentoring the team leader of a virtual team. The virtual team leader may need help, for example, in exploring options for recognition and reward for team members in different parts of the organisation, as legal systems and company practices vary. The priority of the virtual team leader may be to motivate his or her team, while the priority of the local human resources manager may be to ensure parity locally. The opportunities for learning about different practices are great, but so too is the potential for conflict. An experienced coach mentor can help, sometimes with specific knowledge about the countries in question, but more often with ways to manage conflict and to maximise the opportunities of working with a diverse team.

Virtual meetings do not have to replicate the format of face-to-face meetings (Zigurs 2003). Virtual team leaders may find it useful to have short focused virtual meetings which are less tiring for those not working in their native tongue (McCarthy 2007). Short meetings are generally easier to schedule and virtual meetings are cheaper as they do not require the travel costs or the personal cost of being away from one's family. Notification of issues for discussion before meetings allows team members to take soundings locally before making a commitment in a meeting.

As with face-to-face teams, it is useful for the virtual coach mentor to work with individuals as well as the team as a whole. Coach mentors can also work in collaboration, with one team coach mentor working virtually with the team as a whole, and individual coach mentors working locally with each team member. Peer coaching and mentoring where team members coach and mentor each other, and do not rely solely on the team leader or coach mentor to support them, are also effective online (Vaughan Frazee 2008; Leppisaari and Tenhunen 2009).

Conclusion

Coaching and mentoring are used in a wide array of contexts worldwide. The basic principles remain the same. We help people by listening to them respectfully, help them develop their self-awareness and awareness of options through our questioning, help people set goals that matter to them, and give them constructive feedback to help them develop and grow.

Coaching and mentoring people with different cultural backgrounds forces coach mentors to articulate their own beliefs and principles, for example in regard to how directive or non-directive they should be. Workshops can be helpful to explain how the process will work, so that clients have realistic expectations.

Coaching and mentoring are often conducted via technology rather than face-to-face these days. While eCoaching may be difficult, it also offers benefits for both organisations and individuals such as tightly focused conversations and easy access to world-class coach mentors.

Useful links

The links in this chapter highlight resources to support learning about cross-cultural and virtual coaching and mentoring.

American Speech-Language-Hearing Association – http://www.asha.org/students/gatheringplace/tiperel.htm

Tips on virtual mentoring.

Centre for International Business Coaching – http://www.internationalbusiness-coaching.com/

Geoff Abbott's site with case studies of executive coaching with expatriate clients.

Cultural Orientation Framework – http://www.philrosinski.com/cof/

Philippe Rosinski's cultural orientation framework for use in coaching.

Google Hangouts – http://www.google.com/+/learnmore/hangouts/

Allows free video conferencing for up to ten people on computer or phones. Use with Google Drive to collaborate on shared documents.

Geert Hofstede – http://geert-hofstede.com/national-culture.html

Explains Hofstede's cultural dimensions and allows instant comparisons between three countries at a time on each dimension.

Michel Moral – http://www.michel-moral.com/INTERCULTURAL_COACHING-English

Discussion of intercultural and other coaching topics.

Skype – http://www.skype.com/en/features/

Allows free video and voice calls between up to 25 people on computer or phones. Add-ons available for translating messages.

Startwright – http://www.startwright.com/virtual.htm

Links to resources for virtual teams.

Thiagi – http://www.thiagi.com/freebies-and-goodies.html

Free training games and other resources including quotations on diversity and inclusion.

Fons Trompenaars – http://www2.thtconsulting.com/resources/articles/

Articles explaining Trompenaars' intercultural dimensions and dilemmas.

VSee – http://vsee.com/features

Group video conferencing with screen share and drag and drop file transfer. Free and paid versions available. Number of users limited by bandwidth and CPU – 6–7 quoted.

World Values Survey – http://www.worldvaluessurvey.org/index_findings

Maps and groups values held in countries around the world.

Worldwide Association of Business Coaches – http://www.wabccoaches.com/includes/popups/competencies.html

Competencies for business coaches include respect for and knowledge of multicultural issues and diversity.

References

Abbott, G. (2009) 'Executive coaching through cross-border mergers and acquisitions', in M. Moral and G. Abbott (eds) *Routledge Companion to International Business Coaching*. Abingdon, Routledge, pp. 299–317.

Abbott, G. and B. W. Stenig (2009) 'Coaching expatriate executives', in M. Moral and G. Abbott (eds) *Routledge Companion to International Business Coaching*. Abingdon, Routledge, pp. 181–202.

Anagnos, J. (2009) 'Coaching in Australasia', in J. Passmore (ed.) *Diversity in Coaching*. London, Association for Coaching, pp. 57–71.

Armstrong, H. (2009) 'Integral coaching', in M. Moral and G. Abbott (eds) *The Routledge companion to international business coaching*. Abingdon, Routledge, pp. 34–44.

Averweg, U. R. (2010) 'Enabling role of an intranet to augment e-coaching', *Industrial and Commercial Training*, 42(1): 47–52.

Bergiel, B.J., Bergiel, E.B. and Balsmeier, P.W. (2006) 'The reality of virtual teams', *Competition Forum*, 4(2): 427–32.

Brake, T. (2006)' Leading global virtual teams', *Industrial and Commercial Training*, 38(3): 116–21.

Brand, H. and M. Coetzee (2013) 'An explorative study of the experiences of the coach and coachee during executive coaching', *Journal of Social Science*, 34(3): 247–56.

Carr, C. and L. Seto (2013) 'An action research study on coaches' cultural awareness in the public sector', *International Journal of Evidence-Based Coaching and Mentoring*, 11(2): 94–111.

Carraher, S. M., S. E. Sullivan and M. M. Crocitto (2008) 'Mentoring across global boundaries: an empirical examination of home- and host-country mentors on expatriate career outcomes', *Journal of International Business Studies*, 39: 1310–26.

Celestino, S. and I. Faro (2009) 'Coaching in Brazil', in J. Passmore (ed.) *Diversity in coaching*. London, Association for Coaching, pp. 87–95.

Daft, R. (2008) *The leadership experience*. Mason, OH, Thomson.

den Hartog, D. N. (1999) 'Culture specific and cross culturally generalizable implicit leadership theories', *Leadership Quarterly*, 10(2): 219–56.

Dewar, T. (2006) 'Virtual teams-virtually impossible?', *Performance Improvement*, 45(5): 22–5.

Dreyer, P. (2013) 'Coaching in Japan – eine Einfuehrung', in R. Franke and J. Milner (eds) *Interkulturelles Coaching*. Bonn, Managerseminare, pp. 17–38.

Fiddler, M. (1998) Storytelling by first nation users in an online computer environment – a literature review. Available at http://kihs.knet.ca/pn/documents/margaret-iterature-review.pdf.

Geber, H. and M. Keane (2013) 'Extending the worldview of coaching research and practice in Southern Africa: the concept of Ubuntu', *International Journal of Evidence-Based Coaching and Mentoring*, 11(2): 8–18.

Gupta, V. and V. Govindarajan (2002) 'Cultivating a global mindset', *Academy of Management Executive*, 16(1): 116–26.

Hamilton, B. A. and T. Scandura (2003) 'E-Mentoring: implications for organizational learning and development in a wired world', *Organization Dynamics*, 31(4): 388–402

Headland-Wells, J., J. Gosland and J. Craig (2006) 'Beyond the organisation: the design and management of E-mentoring systems', *International Journal of Information Management*, 26: 372–85.

Heath, D. (2010) 'Coaching through 360°', in D. Wright, A. Leong, K. E. Webb and S. Chia (eds) *Coaching in Asia: the first decade*. Singapore, Candid Creation, pp. 97–111.

Hofstede, G. and G. J. Hofstede (2010) *Cultures and organizations: software of the mind*. New York, McGraw-Hill.

Ing, L. (2010) 'Honouring who, what and where you are', in D. Wright, A. Leong, K. E. Webb and S. Chia (eds) *Coaching in Asia: the first decade*. Singapore, Candid Creation Publishing, pp. 33–48.

Jarvenpaa, S., L. K. Knoll and D. E. Leidner (1998) 'Is anybody out there? Antecedents of trust in global virtual teams', *Journal of Management Information Systems*, 14(4): 29.

Kacmar, C. J., D. J. McManus and A. Young (2012) 'Telementoring in global organizations: computer mediated communication technologies and mentoring networks', *International Journal of Applied Science and Technology*, 2(1): 1–11.

Kayworth, T. R. and D. E. Leidner (2000) 'The global virtual manager: a prescription for success', *European Management Journal*, 18(2): 183–94.

Kiely, L. S. (2001) 'Overcoming time and distance: international virtual executive teams', in W. H. Mobley and M. W. McCall (eds) *Advances in global leadership*, Vol. 2. Stamford, CT, JAI Press, pp. 185–216.

Law, H., S. Ireland and Z. Hussain (2007) *The psychology of coaching, mentoring and learning*. Hoboken, NJ, Wiley.

Law, H., L. Laulusa and G. Cheng (2009) 'When Far East meets west: seeking cultural synthesis through coaching', in M. Moral and G. Abbott (eds) *Routledge companion to international business coaching*. Abingdon, Routledge, pp. 241–55.

Legrain-Fremaux, E. and M. Fox (2010) 'Leadership coaching: inspiration from Asia', in D. Wright, A. Leong, K. E. Webb and S. Chia (eds) *Coaching in Asia: the first decade*. Singapore, Candid Creation, pp. 49–59.

Leppisaari, I. and M.-L. Tenhunen (2009) 'Searching for ementoring practices for SME staff development', *Service Business*, 3(2): 189–207.

McCarthy, G. (2007) 'Toolkit for managing virtual teams', *The Human Factor*, 2(1): 26–9.

McCarthy, G. (2010) *Virtual teams, eLearning and developing coaches*. 4th Australian Conference on Evidence-Based Coaching. Sydney.

Miser, A. L. and M. F. Miser (2009) 'Couples coaching for expatriate couples', in M. Moral and G. Abbott (eds) *Routledge companion to international business coaching*. Abingdon, Routledge, pp. 203–17.

Moral, M. and G. Abbott (eds) (2009) *Routledge companion to international business coaching*. Abingdon, Routledge.

Nangalia, L. and A. Nangalia (2010) 'The coach in Asian society: impact of social hierarchy on the coaching relationship', *International Journal of Evidence-Based Coaching and Mentoring*, 8(2): 51–66.

Ng, C. (2009) 'Coaching in China', in J. Passmore (ed.) *Diversity in coaching*. London, Routledge, pp. 96–109.

Nicholas, J. and K. Twaddell (2010) 'Group executive coaching in Asia: same same but different', in D. Wright, A. Leong, K. E. Webb and S. Chia (eds) *Coaching in Asia: the first decade*. Singapore, Candid Creation Publishing: 3–19.

Olalla, J. (2009) 'Ontological coaching: intercultural coaching and trust', in M. Moral and G. Abbott (eds) *Routledge companion to international business coaching*. Abingdon, Routledge, pp. 75–83.

Palmer, S. and V. J. Arnold (2009) 'Coaching in the Middle East', in J. Passmore (ed.) *Diversity in coaching*. London, Association for Coaching, pp. 110–26.

Passmore, J. and H. Law (2009) 'Cross-cultural and diversity coaching', in J. Passmore (ed.) *Diversity in coaching*. London, Association for Coaching, pp. 4–16.

Plaister-Ten, J. (2009) 'Towards greater cultural understanding in coaching', *International Journal of Evidence-Based Coaching and Mentoring* (Special Issue 3): 64–81.

Plaister-Ten, J. (2013) 'Raising culturally-derived awareness and building culturally-appropriate responsibility: The development of the Cross-Cultural Kaleidoscope', *International Journal of Evidence-Based Coaching and Mentoring*, 11(2): 54–69.

Pollitt, D. (2007) 'BT Wholesale pilots online coaching and mentoring: individual productivity improvements of up to 15 percent seem feasible', *Human Resource Management International Digest*, 15(7): 20–22.

Powell, A., J. Galvin and G. Piccoli (2006) 'Antecedents to team member commitment from near and far', *Information Technology & People*, 19(4): 299.

Robbins, S. R., T. Judge, B. Millett and M. Boyle (2011) *Organisational behaviour*. Frenchs Forest, NSW, Pearson.

Rosinski, P. and G. Abbott (2010)' Intercultural coaching', in J. Passmore (ed.) *Excellence in coaching: the industry guide*. London, Association for Coaching, pp. 175–88.

Ruru, D., K. Sanga, K. Walker and R. Edwin (2013) 'Adapting mentorship across the professions: a Fijian view', *International Journal of Evidence-Based Coaching and Mentoring*, 11(2): 70–93.

Salmon, G. (2000) *e-moderating – the key to teaching and learning online*. London, Kogan Page.

Sood, Y. (2009) 'Coaching in India', in J. Passmore (ed.) *Diversity in coaching*. London, Routledge, pp. 127–33.

Stahl, G. and Sitkin, S. (2005) *Trust in Mergers & Acquisitions: Managing Culture and Human Resources*. Palo Alto, CA, Stanford Business Press.

Tulpa, K. and F. Bresser (2009) 'Coaching in Europe', in J. Passmore (ed.) *Diversity in coaching*. London, Association for Coaching, pp. 19–40.

Tulpa, K. and G. Woudstra (2010) 'Coaching the global top team', in J. Passmore (ed.) *Leadership coaching: working with leaders to develop elite performance*. London, Association for Coaching, Kogan Page, pp. 263–84.

Vaughan Frazee, R. (2008) *E-coaching in organizaitons: a study of features, practices and determinants of use*. San Diego, University of San Diego. PhD.

Wales, S. (2003) 'Why coaching?', *Journal of Change Management*, 3(3): 275–82.

Webb, K. E. (2010) 'Cross-cultural coaching', in D. Wright, A. Leong, K. E. Webb and S. Chia (eds) *Coaching in Asia: the first decade*. Singapore, Candid Creation, pp. 20–32.

Whitaker, C. (2012) 'Cross-cultural mentoring: the United Kingdom and Lebanon', *Developing Successful Diversity Mentoring Programmes: An International Casebook*: 209.

Wong, E. and L. Leung (2007) *The power of Ren: China's coaching phenomenon*. Singapore, Wiley.

Wright, D. (2010) 'Facilitating inspired change through strengths-based coaching conversations', in D. Wright, A. Leong, K. E. Webb and S. Chia (eds) *Coaching in Asia: the first decade*. Singapore, Candid Creation, pp. 79–96.

Zachary, L. J. (2005) *Creating a mentoring culture*. San Francisco, CA, Jossey-Bass.

Zigurs, I. (2003) 'Leadership in virtual teams: oxymoron or opportunity', *Organizational Dynamics*, 31(4): 339–51.

11

ETHICAL ISSUES IN COACHING AND MENTORING

Introduction

In the unregulated world of coaching and mentoring, it is of paramount importance that each coach mentor upholds high standards of professional and ethical conduct. This is in the interest of clients, the sponsoring organisation and the coach mentors themselves. Coaching and mentoring are powerful interventions, where '*well-meaning but poorly trained and inexperienced coaches may do more harm than good*' (Bluckert 2006). Professional coaching and mentoring organisations such as the European Mentoring and Coaching Council and the International Coach Federation have codes of conduct to which members must adhere. Clients can contact these associations if they have a complaint and non-compliant coach mentors could have their membership revoked. Unfortunately many clients do not know of the existence of such associations nor how to contact them. Furthermore, their coach mentor may or may not be a member.

Some forms of misconduct could make the coach mentor liable for prosecution, for example, misrepresenting the coach mentor's expertise could lead to a charge under trade descriptions legislation. Brennan and Wildflower (2010) observe that coaches can be tempted to promise unrealistic outcomes, in an effort to win a contract. No qualifications or registration are required for coaches or mentors and some unethical practitioners tarnish the reputation of the process itself (Peltier 2010). If a client is dissatisfied, they may simply choose not to work with that coach mentor again. As in other instances of poor customer experiences, they are also likely to share their dissatisfaction with others, not only dissatisfaction with the individual coach mentor, but with their experience of coaching or mentoring.

It is sometimes the case that what people have experienced is neither coaching nor mentoring, although it has been described to the client as such. Negative word of mouth has a wide impact on people's respect for the process. Ethical practice in coaching and mentoring, according to Hawkins and Smith, is '*to balance the appropriate needs of multiple clients, with due regard and fairness to all parties and the delicate threads and web of relationships between them*' (Hawkins and Smith 2006: 248).

In this chapter, we look at ethical issues in coaching and mentoring and some of the guidance that currently exists in terms of codes of conduct, professional standards and ethical decision-making guidelines.

Capability

Coach mentors are generally people who like to help. However, this desire to help must be tempered with an honest assessment of one's own capability. Where coach mentors lack appropriate expertise, the responsible and ethical thing to do is to refer the person to an appropriately qualified person. In addition to the risk of doing harm to the client, coach mentors may be sued for malpractice if they offer a service which they are not qualified to provide, or if in the view of the individual client or the organisation, they have not provided the service for which they were contracted. Hannafey and Vitulano (2012) define the relationship as an agency relation in which the coach has a clear duty to serve the interests of another, and one in which high levels of trust and confidentiality are required. Contracts provide some level of protection in defining expectations and responsibilities on all sides of the coaching process and may include an arbitration clause specifying how disputes will be resolved (Rostron 2009).

Mental health

Mental health issues are more often acknowledged these days than in the past. Nevertheless some people believe there is still a stigma attached and do not share a diagnosis of mental illness as often as they might a physical illness. It has been estimated that the rate of mental ill-health is at least as high among those coming to coaching as in the general population (Buckley 2010). A study at the University of Sydney found that between 25% and 50% of those seeking coaching had clinical levels of anxiety, depression or stress (Grant 2009) while a study at the University of Wollongong found that 86% of coaches interviewed had seen clients with mental health issues (McGowan 2010). Mental health and personality issues may in fact be more prevalent among coaching clients than in the general population, because executives often suffer from stress and also because narcissism is more common among executives than among the general population (Kearney 2010). The rate of ill-health may also be higher where coaching and mentoring are regarded as more socially acceptable services than counselling or therapy, resulting in some people being referred to a coach mentor, when in fact they first need to address underlying personal issues with a counsellor, therapist or psychologist.

The coach mentor therefore has a responsibility to be aware of how to recognise signs of mental ill-health and refer where appropriate to a qualified professional. Many coaches have a network of professionals with similar philosophies, e.g. psychologists who use a strengths-based approach, to whom they can refer clients. If the coach mentor is a trained psychologist and believes themselves qualified to provide the relevant service, they should re-negotiate their contract, if it specifies that an organisation is paying for coaching, when the client really needs counselling or therapy. In other words, the coach mentor must be honest about the service they are providing.

Regardless of whether or not they have psychological training, all coach mentors need to be able to recognise possible signs of mental ill-health. Buckley (2010) summarises the key signals as unexpected changes over time in appearance, behaviour (e.g. becoming nervous/repetitive/lethargic), mood (overly optimistic or pessimistic) and whether the client is present, experiencing the world rationally or seeming preoccupied. None of these signals mean that there is a mental health issue, but suggest that the coach mentor may need to explore with the client whether they are aware of and can give insight into these changes. The coach mentor may also want to understand whether the change is confined to a particular sphere of activity or pervasive, and whether it is a long-term issue or a response to a recent event. In extreme cases, where a client appears to be contemplating self-harm or of harming others, then the coach mentor must contact the appropriate health professionals. This duty of care over-rides any considerations of confidentiality. If it is not an extreme case, the coach mentor has time to reflect. Options include referral to a qualified professional, delay if the problem is temporary and the client may benefit from coaching or mentoring at a later stage, or continuing, if the client is receiving help with a specific issue, and has the resilience and self-awareness to separate the focus of coaching from the problem issue, and also if the coach mentor believes they can help and not be negatively affected themselves.

Obeying the law

If the issue relates to potential criminal charges, e.g. the client has admitted to fraud, the coach mentor may fail to convince him/her to admit their wrong-doing to the company. If the coach mentor decides not to report it, the coach mentor should resign, as he/she cannot act in the best interest of the company which is paying for their services. This may not be enough to provide protection if the client is prosecuted and it transpires that the coach mentor knew of his/her wrong-doing but did not report it. Courts may require coach mentors to give evidence, regardless of any confidentiality clause in their contract. Rostron (2009) suggests that it is wise for the coach mentor to have indemnity insurance in case such issues arise.

A contract may also specify that if information relating to drug or alcohol abuse comes to light, then the coach mentor must disclose it to the organisation. Individual clients should be made aware of such clauses at the outset so that they understand the consequences of any admissions they make to the coach mentor. Leimon, Moscovici et al. give an example of a confidentiality clause which coach mentors could include: '*While recognising the need for discretion and confidentiality, all parties agree to take into account all aspects relating to the law and duty of care*' (Leimon, Moscovici et al. 2005: 168). Agreeing up front what can be disclosed is important if the coach mentor wishes to use some of the outcomes as evidence of the effectiveness of the process. Without the agreement of the person being coached or mentored, no information should be disclosed other than that required by law.

While it is useful to have a contract which makes client expectations explicit, even if there is no such contract, the coach mentor is still bound not to share proprietary information from one company with another. Regardless of ethical issues in such cases, if the coach mentor were identified as the source of information leaking to a competitor, this would ruin their reputation in the industry. Coach mentors may share generic ideas about best practices, trends and opportunities for improvement that they have gleaned from their work in the industry but without identifying any specifics (Govindarajan 2005). Legislation relating to insider trading also applies if the coach mentor buys or sells shares based on information which they have obtained in the course of their work with a company, and which is not publicly available.

The coach mentor should also disclose potential conflicts of interest in advance e.g. if tendering for work with a competitor, or if the coach mentor had a close relative in the organisation issuing the tender. In the latter case, the relative would have a duty to disclose the conflict within their organisation and should not be involved in the selection decision.

In addition to ethical coaching and mentoring practice, the external coach mentor also needs to understand the need for ethics and corporate governance in their own organisation and in their clients. Legal requirements for governance vary according to the size of the organisation and the country of operation. It is up to each coach mentor to be familiar with the relevant requirements wherever they operate. Relevant laws include those relating to data protection, taxation and occupational health and safety. If offering a service in other countries, e.g. an online coaching service for expatriates, it is important to spell out in advance which laws will take priority, e.g. the country where the coach mentor is based, the country where the expatriate is based, or the country where the head office is located. While obeying the law is not enough to ensure one is behaving ethically, obeying the law is necessary in order to be a good citizen – and sometimes, in order to keep out of jail. For example, in Australia, directors can be prosecuted if they knowingly trade while insolvent. An unwary coach mentor directing his/her own company might hold the optimistic view that its difficulties are temporary and carry on trading. In such a scenario, he/she would be liable for prosecution and possible jail sentences. Membership of a professional association, business chamber or other group which includes updates on relevant legislation, helps sole traders and small businesses (most coach mentors are small businesses) to keep up-to-date.

Loyalty and confidentiality

Coaching and mentoring in a business context usually involves at least three parties: coach mentor, client and a representative of the organisation. There may in fact be more than one organisational representative, as there may be some involvement of the sponsor or champion for coaching and mentoring, as well as the person who selects and organises coaching and mentoring, usually a HR or Learning and Development person, and sometimes the client's manager as well. The coaching or mentoring contract is usually with the organisation, not the individual client. Unlike a life coach, the business coach mentor owes loyalty to multiple stakeholders, and must integrate the business requirements with their duty of care for individual clients (Rostron 2009). They must also adhere to the laws of the countries in which they operate.

Because of this, confidentiality is a vexed question for many coach mentors. They are sometimes conflicted when the client reveals something, which the company would be interested in knowing. Ideally the coach mentor agrees boundaries of confidentiality with both client and company representatives before or at the start of any contract. For example, coach mentors working with a number of people in the same organisation might agree to report back on general issues or opportunities for improvement to the company, and would ensure each client were aware of this.

If, however, an issue arises during coaching or mentoring which had not been anticipated, the coach mentor has to decide what to do in the light of their own code of conduct and what they regard as the best interest of both client and organisation. In keeping with the philosophy of encouraging people to take responsibility for their own actions, coach mentors can encourage individual clients to talk to the company. If the client declines to do so, coach mentors must decide what to do, based on their own code of conduct and principles. Vignette 11.1 shows the issues which can emerge if confidentiality is breached and trust is lost.

Vignette 11.1   A breach of trust

For the tenth time that Friday, Nina wondered what she should do. Three of her coaching clients, all in the same company, had each told her that Eddie, one of the other managers, was bullying his team members. None of them had agreed to talk to HR in their company about it and none of them would talk to Eddie directly. 'I wouldn't risk having him target me', as one of them had put it. Surely she could not ignore it, now that she knew about it. And she had heard it from three different people, so it wasn't just a piece of idle gossip. She picked up her phone and dialled the HR Manager.

'Hello Frank', she said, 'it's Nina. Frank, you know I don't reveal anything about the content of individual coaching sessions …'

'Yes', he said.

'Well, I am hearing that there is some behaviour going on that might need to be addressed. Obviously I can't say who told me but ...'

'I see', said Frank. 'Can you be a bit more specific about the behaviour you're talking about?'

'Well for example, one of the managers calls his team members offensive nicknames and yells at them when they make a mistake.'

'Ah, I see', said Frank. 'I think I know who you're talking about now and I could guess who told you those things. Don't worry, I'll have a word with Eddie, I'm seeing him this evening informally so I'll just bring it up quietly.'

At lunch-time on Monday, Nina came out of a coaching session and found numerous voice mails. It soon became obvious that Eddie had gone in on Monday morning and raged at his colleagues, Nina's clients. They in turn were horrified that she had breached their trust when they had specifically said they did not want to talk to HR or to Eddie. Why hadn't she told them what she was going to do? Didn't she know that Frank and Eddie went drinking together every week? Next she got a call from Frank, informing her that all three of her clients had decided not to continue with coaching. He was sorry, he said, as he had been hoping to expand the use of coaching within the company, but now word had got out that anything you said would get back to the company, no one wanted anything to do with a coach.

It all seemed so unfair to Nina. She hadn't passed on any of the other information that had been shared with her. But the issue of bullying had seemed like something the company should know about and do something about. But then she hadn't known that Frank and Eddie were drinking buddies. Maybe she should have asked a bit more about why her clients hadn't wanted to go to HR. And maybe she should have respected her clients' decision not to go to HR. She wondered what issues might arise with her other clients and if there was anything she could do to foresee them or prevent them becoming problems if they did arise. She wished she had someone to think through the options and consequences with. Maybe she should find herself a coach mentor?

It is not unusual for a client to change employer after they have been coached or mentored. It may be the first time since they left school or university that they have reflected on their own direction and where they want to be. They may now recognise different skills, see new opportunities and realise that they want to do something else. In fact, some coach mentors make a point of highlighting this risk to the company at the contracting stage. If a client is considering leaving the company, it is best if he/she tells the company rather than reveal to the coach mentor that the work that is being paid for by the organisation will benefit another organisation.

Questions of loyalty may arise if the coach mentor is working with a team leader and his/her team. The team leader might ask the coach mentor to focus on outcomes impacting on his or her key performance indicators and ultimately bonus payments, whereas the coach mentor may have contracted to work on more general team issues such as effective ways of working together, creativity tools and techniques, or structured problem-solving. While any of these may indirectly lead to improvements in the relevant key performance indicators, the coach mentor needs to be careful to address the scope of their contract or re-negotiate where appropriate.

Extending contracts

An ethical issue arises when a contract comes to an end but the individual client wishes it to continue. The coach mentor must be guided by what is in the client's best interest, which is not necessarily what the client wants. Sometimes it will be in the client's best interest to transfer to a new coach mentor. As mentioned in Chapter 3, there may be a sense of grief and mourning when the relationship comes to an end. However, this can be alleviated by planning for a good ending, as Cox (2010) recommends. Mentoring relationships tend to be of longer duration, but here too it is wise to review the relationship periodically together with the mentee's goals or dreams, and decide whether a different or an additional mentor would be of benefit.

Sometimes the client needs training, rather than coaching or mentoring, and the coach mentor should recognise this. The coach mentor needs to be honest about what they are offering and provide what they have been contracted to provide, re-negotiating where necessary so that they deliver what they have promised.

Multiple roles

An issue which regularly arises for coaching managers, and also for HR (human resource) managers who act as internal coaches, is the interaction between their different roles. When HR managers and other managers offer coaching and mentoring, the trust engendered in coaching and mentoring conversations may encourage people to disclose more than they might otherwise do to a manager. The coaching manager must be careful not to encourage confidences which the employee would later regret. Any confidences given to an internal or external coach mentor must be maintained. As Brennan and Wildflower note, '*With the privilege of coaching comes great responsibility to maintain client confidentiality*' (Brennan and Wildflower 2010: 374).

The coaching manager may switch between coaching, mentoring, and directing a number of times in a single conversation, sometimes listening and prompting with open questions, sometimes offering more advice, and sometimes being directive. Hicks and McCracken (2011) recommend that the coaching manager explicitly signal their change of role, so that people understand the role the manager is playing at all times.

External coaches may also switch, sometimes offering advice in consultancy mode and sometimes providing training. Their multiple roles may include that of accountant, financial adviser or lawyer. The coach mentor can usefully share some of their knowledge and experience and help clients to make use of it in their own context. In other words, the coach mentor does not provide a ready-made solution to the client's issue, but information which the client can adapt to address their own situation. Peltier (2010) identifies a difference between therapeutic roles and coaching in the area of social functions. Whereas mental health clinicians would not have dinner or play golf with clients, coaches may be expected to attend social functions organised by the sponsoring organisations. Not to attend, according to Peltier, might suggest that the coach is unsupportive of the organisation, whereas attending would allow the coach to network with other members of the organisation and observe their client in a work setting. He warns, however, that the coach should behave professionally at the function, as it is not a purely social occasion.

Many HR managers are already used to working through confidentiality issues and, in particular, balancing the interest of the individual employee with the interest of the employer. HR managers also have access to a range of confidential information in their HR role, which may or may not be useful to their coaching role. Some assessment information may provide insights or give an indication of the prevalence of particular patterns of behaviour. However, it might also lead a coaching HR manager to make assumptions about the employee's current beliefs and behaviour. As Vignette 11.2 suggests, it may be more useful for coaching HR managers to work directly with employees, without their view being coloured by the information in HR files.

Vignette 11.2   A question of priorities

'Come on in, Peter', said Mark. 'How are things going?'

'Hi Mark, not bad', said Peter.

'And have you made progress on the actions we agreed in our last coaching session?'

'Well, not a lot, really. You know we're really busy with the new contract, so that's where I've had to focus. It's not that those other things aren't important, it's just that obviously the day-to-day business has to take priority.'

'Mmm', said Mark. It wasn't the first time Peter had made similar sorts of excuses. Mark was beginning to wonder if the same pattern played out in other parts of Peter's job. He felt a bit unsure as to whether the issue was that Peter always procrastinated, or whether he did some things promptly. Maybe he should have looked at Peter's HR file, there would be a psychometric profile and some other assessments in there, which might give him some short cuts about how to handle the conversation. But maybe instead of asking him about the file, he could ask him about the issue. 'Of course, I understand that, Peter. I know you have a passion for quality and customer service. Tell me a bit about how you divide up your time between the day-to-day and the longer-term priorities.'

'Divide up my time? You sound like Tom. When he does my performance review, he's always saying that I should set aside some time for the company goals. He just doesn't understand. I think he just wants to get his bonus paid, it's not about the goals at all.'

'Let's think about the goals for a minute', said Mark. 'If we did achieve them somehow, would that have any impact?'

'Oh sure', said Peter. 'They're all good ideas, and they would be good for the customers too, they're things like shortening lead times and zero defects. It's just that we don't have time to work on them.'

'Let's imagine we did have time to work on them, what difference would that make?'

'Well, the customers would be happy so they'd probably order more from us themselves and recommend us to other people.'

'And how about your job, would that change in any way?'

'I suppose so', said Peter. 'If our quality really was, maybe not zero defects, but a lot better first time round than it is now, I wouldn't be spending as much time checking, or apologising to customers and organising replacements or refunds.'

'What would you be doing?' asked Mark.

'I'd be looking for ways to make us even better, and talking to customers about other things they might appreciate but maybe hadn't talked about. I'd be getting our people together to look for new ideas, not just problem-solving.' He looked into the distance as if he could see a different place.

'That sounds fantastic, and well worth getting to', said Mark.

'You know you're right', said Peter. 'I hadn't really thought about it like that, the goals and the stuff we talked about, they all just sounded like extra things I had to do, and now I can see that they are the things that are really going to let me do what I think is important, which is improve things for the customers.'

'So how do you think you might find some time to work on them?'

'To start with, I'm going to do a half hour on Tuesdays and Thursdays, just after lunch. I know if I say I'll do an hour, it won't happen, it will seem too long, but I

(Continued)

(Continued)

can fit in half an hour. I'll put it in my diary. And I'm going to call that half hour "Customer Focus" to remind myself what it's all about.'

'Sounds great', said Mark. 'Let's say we catch up again in two weeks time, and you can tell me how it's going.'

'Good idea', said Peter. 'It's good to have a deadline to make sure I make a start.'

As Peter left, Mark felt a surge of optimism. It seemed like Peter really was going to try something different. And it hadn't required Mark to make use of any of the HR information. It would be interesting to see if Peter's new behaviour was noticed by his manager. But Mark didn't feel he needed to put his HR hat on to address that. As Peter started making progress, they could talk about ways for Peter to get Tom involved. He was beginning to see how he could be an internal coach without blurring the lines with his HR responsibilities.

A contract for internal coaching and mentoring managers, where both parties agree their mutual expectations in advance, including what may or may not be disclosed without prior discussion, can reduce the uncertainties in the process for all parties.

Sometimes things go wrong in a coaching or mentoring relationship. Zachary (2005) introduces the notion of a safety net, where people are helped to recover from a breakdown in the process, rather than abandoned to find their own way. The safety net aims both to prevent things going wrong and to alleviate any harm caused if things do go wrong. Safety nets include proper preparation for both coach mentor and client with understanding of mutual expectations, a confidentiality agreement, appropriate feedback mechanisms for organisation and individual client, and on-going support for both coach mentor and client.

Ethical guidance

Guidance on ethical practice is available from many national and international professional coaching and mentoring associations. Brennan and Wildflower identify five common themes across the codes of conduct of several associations:

- Do no harm: do not cause needless injury or harm to others.
- Duty of care: act in ways that promote the welfare of other people.
- Know your limits: competence and practice within your scope.
- Respect the interests of the client.
- Respect the law.

(Brennan and Wildflower 2010: 370).

De Jong reviews a broad range of ethical theory and concludes that the following principles form a firm platform for ethical decision-making in coaching:

- Beneficence: helping the client, acting in the client's best interest, promoting the client's well-being.

- Non-malfeasance: do no harm.

- Fidelity: being faithful and truthful, keeping our commitments, honouring trust placed in us.

- Autonomy: respect for the client's right and ability to self-govern.

- Justice: being fair and impartial.

- Self-respect: developing one's self-awareness and acting in accordance with the above principles.

(de Jong 2010: 208)

In addition to the generic guidelines such as those provided by professional associations, it is useful for individual coach mentors to define their own code of conduct or their own guidelines for applying the generic codes. For example, internal coach mentors and coaching managers may choose to align a generic coaching or mentoring code with their organisation's code of conduct and values, and to have implementation guidelines that reflect organisational policy and procedures. External coach mentors may also find it useful to amend a generic code in a way that makes sense for the contexts in which they usually operate. Coaching and mentoring contracts can refer to the code of conduct, rather than attempting to address all possible scenarios in the contract itself. However, such guidelines should not be seen as rules to follow rigidly. Instead they are aids to our own decisions as to what is right or wrong in a particular situation.

Team coaching is not normally addressed specifically in professional association guidelines and yet there are specific ethical issues to address. Hawkins (2011) identifies a number of principles for team coaches, including being there to serve the team rather than individual or factional interests; to facilitate collective not individual performance, functioning and dynamics; and to facilitate more effective and direct communication within the team and between the team and its stakeholders. Confidentiality is again of prime importance in developing and maintaining trust. Coach mentors may receive information from individual team members and from the team leader which is at odds with what is said in team meetings. To share such information publicly would risk damaging relationships within the team and with the coach mentor. Instead the coach mentor has to understand why different information emerges and create opportunities which enable people to share safely within team meetings.

Just as rehearsal helps coaching and mentoring clients to prepare for a situation, so too it can help a coach mentor to think through possible scenarios or ethical dilemmas and decide how they might react. Duffy and Passmore (2010) suggest a six-point process which coaches can follow, as shown in Figure 11.1.

According to Duffy and Passmore (2010), Step 1 is where the coach mentor hones their awareness of ethical issues through the professional association of which they are members, and links the organisation's guidance to their personal values and beliefs.

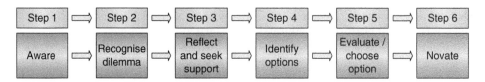

Figure 11.1   Ethical decision-making, adapted from Duffy and Passmore (2010)

Without such awareness, coach mentors may unwittingly behave unethically. In Step 2, coach mentors recognise that they are facing a dilemma. In Step 3, coach mentors take time to reflect and seek support and advice, whether from peers or supervisors. In Step 4, coach mentors develop a series of possible solutions to the issue. In Step 5, coach mentors compare the possible solutions with their personal or professional code, consider the consequences, risks and benefits, and again may discuss with peers or supervisors before selecting an option for action. In Step 6, coach mentors novate, i.e. incorporate the new approach in their journal and practice. Duffy and Passmore advocate the sharing of such dilemmas in a confidential way with one's own network and with professional bodies, so that others may learn from the experience.

Connor and Pokora (2012) add some helpful practical points, noting that if we hear something distressing, we may start listening more to our inner voice than to the client. In such cases, they advise that coaches and mentors should take time to reflect, to check what they have heard, to review the resources available, and seek support where possible. If the issue is genuinely troubling and the coach mentor has high levels of empathy, he/she may experience a form of vicarious trauma (Couley 2011). Previous research is mixed in relation to the positive or negative impact of de-briefing or supervision in relation to vicarious trauma. What is certain, however, is that coach mentors may need some form of help and may themselves suffer from stress or mental health related issues. Organisations may be liable if an issue is foreseeable and they do nothing to support their employees, in this case internal coach mentors.

Supervision

Supervision is identified as a source of guidance and support by both Duffy and Passmore (2010) and by Connor and Pokora (2012). Supervision helps people hone their ethical decision-making skills as well as helping them think through specific questions such as whether to continue coaching someone with mental health issues as mentioned above. Clients should be informed in advance that the coach mentor will discuss issues with their supervisor in confidence without identifying them (Connor and Pokora 2012). Increasingly clients expect that coach mentors will have a supervisor, as this demonstrates an investment by the coach mentor in their own development and growth. Supervision also provides emotional support (Bluckert 2006; Moyes 2009). Vignette 11.3 highlights a discussion on extending contracts, where the coaching supervisor helps the coach articulate the options and choose the one they believe best for the client as well as identify options for their own business development.

Vignette 11.3   Referrals

Anna arrived at her supervision session with Toni, looking somewhat distracted. She had been thinking for days about what she should do about the request from John to extend his coaching contract with her. Toni asked her what was bothering her about the request.

'Well, partly it's because I'm not sure whether I'm the best coach for him now that he has been promoted. I mean, I know I helped him gain confidence and articulate his goals, but now I'm not sure what we would work on.'

'Okay,' said Toni, 'and what else bothers you about it?'

'Well, his organisation pays well and on time, so I wonder if maybe the reason I'm thinking about saying yes is more about me than about his needs.'

'Mm,' said Toni, 'let's say you weren't coaching John, can you think of someone else who would be good coaching him?'

'Oh definitely', said Anna. 'Maria would be perfect with him, she would challenge him more than I do and help him really develop at his new level. I've been so used to helping him gain confidence to get to this level, I'm not sure I could challenge him in the same way.'

'So summing up,' said Toni, 'you think someone else would be better for John's new stage but you don't want to lose the income, is that it?'

'Sounds terrible when you put it like that', said Anna, looking embarrassed.

'It's the tension between the duty of care and the commercial aspect of your job', said Toni. 'Let's say you did refer John to Maria, how might that work for you?'

'Well I wouldn't want anything like a referral fee, I would only refer him because I think it's the best for him. But ...'

'Go on', said Toni with an encouraging smile.

'Maybe Maria and I can work together like this more often, I'm better at getting clients to the transition stage and she's better with helping clients once they have been promoted, so maybe we can refer work to each other and even do joint tenders, that way we'll both benefit and so will our clients.'

And as she left her supervision session, she knew she had made the right decision. It would be John's choice whether to work with Maria or not, but she felt she could explain clearly to him why she thought it would help him more than continuing to work with her. She felt glad that there was no direct monetary gain for her in the decision and yet she could see that she could develop a sustainable coaching practice with Maria, if they both played to their strengths.

Forms of supervision vary. The classic clinical model is one-to-one, either face-to-face or by telephone/video conference. However, peer-coaching, similar in many ways to an action learning group, is also popular, but its effectiveness varies. A hybrid with one coach supervisor for a group of coaches is also popular. Duffy and Passmore (2010) suggest that supervisors are most useful for novices, whereas peer networks or reciprocal coaching may be more relevant for experienced practitioners. Online supervision is also common – the UK is one of the few countries to have courses in coaching supervision. Coaches in other countries such as Australia can find it difficult to find qualified coaching supervisors (Whyte 2013).

A coach may choose one of several different advisors to help in their reflection and development, including their accreditation as a coach with a professional body which requires a specific number of hours of coaching supervision or as a way of demonstrating to clients that the coach mentor is a responsible practitioner. While it is possible to reflect on one's own, and this is good practice, *only* to reflect on one's own may increase the risk of not identifying one's own blind spots or self-limiting beliefs. A supervisor enhances our ability to reflect (Connor and Pokora 2012).

A coach may like to have a coach of their own or a mentor or a coach supervisor, each offering support in different areas as illustrated in Table 11.1.

Of course a coach mentor may wish to achieve many of the purposes in Table 11.1 and hence may want an advisor who can adopt different roles as needed. Gray (2010) advocates an integrated role where the supervisor also acts as mentor. A clinically trained supervisor may be well placed to provide supervision in relation to the process and the ethical issues which arise. However, if clinically trained supervisors have limited understanding of business issues, they will be less able to help the coach mentor think through options for coaching for strategy, systems implications or legislative requirements in relation to the coach mentor's business. In fact, as Whyte's *Research Bulletin* (2013) argues, supervision is not the only way for coaches to think through issues. Reading, education and self-reflection can be used in combination with supervision or as alternatives to supervision. While supervision is long established in psychology, therapy and counselling, there is no consensus as yet about whether this model of supervision is appropriate for business coaching. Different models may also be appropriate in different cultures. Moral (2011) for example, describes how systemic reflection is used in group supervision in France.

While the question of the appropriate form of supervision for external coach mentors is being widely debated, there is less discussion of the need for supervision or support for internal coaching managers or HR managers who offer coaching and mentoring. A recent study conducted by Driessen (2013) found that HR managers experience a variety of ethical dilemmas related to trust, unclear boundaries, lack of organisational protocols and unclear agendas. Her participants would welcome more

Table 11.1   Focus of supervision

Focus of support	Role
I want someone who will help me think through what I want to achieve and how I want to develop my business.	Coach
I want advice on how to grow my business, how to price my services and how to cope with self-doubt.	Mentor
I want someone to help me identify where I can improve my practice and help me think through ethical issues.	Coaching supervisor
Achieve accreditation.	Coach supervisor
Meet organisational client requirements.	Coach supervisor

training and support. However, general managers often do not reflect on their practice and may feel less of a need for support. Peer-support networks may be an acceptable alternative to encourage reflection and improvement. Maxwell (2011) concludes that different models of supervision may be appropriate for internal coaches, e.g. an action learning set rather than a model based on clinical practice.

Just as a coach mentor helps a client think through issues and make choices, an experienced supervisor asks questions which prompt the coach mentor to think through issues from multiple perspectives, exploring angles which the coach mentor may not have considered, and make informed choices. Supervisors have their own ethical decisions to consider including their duty of care to their client, the coach mentor, the need for confidentiality, and when and where an issue might over-ride the need for confidentiality, e.g. if a client is contemplating self-harm. Passmore (2009) suggests that supervisors should be available for emergency consultations if the need arises. However, for the vast majority of coach mentors in business, this is an unlikely scenario. Coaching psychologists may be more likely to need such a service than coach mentors in general.

If a coach mentor is to share any information from their coaching and mentoring with a coach, coach supervisor, mentor or group of peer supervisors, this must be clearly stated from the outset. If the organisation has specified that its coaches must have a supervisor, then the presumption is that some anonymous information will be shared in supervision. A confidentiality agreement may form part of the coaching contract, stating for example that only the issue will be discussed, but no specifying features that could identify either the individual client or their organisation. If a particularly sensitive issue arises, the coach mentor may wish to check if the client is still happy for the information to be shared in supervision, explaining how this will be of benefit. This extra check will reinforce the trust between coach mentor and client. After all, circumstances change and the particular issue involved may not have been foreseen when the confidentiality agreement was drafted. Therefore even if a general agreement is in place, the coach mentor should not take the individual client's agreement about a particular issue for granted.

Supervisors can also help the coach mentor identify needs for professional development and explore opportunities for growth as discussed next.

Professional development

As a young industry with relatively few qualifications available, many coaches are self-taught or have only attended a short training program. Mentors generally receive limited if any training by the organisation in which they mentor. Being self-taught demonstrates the person's interest and desire to do a good job but it often lacks a systematic framework. Short training programs equip people with skills but often teach a single proprietary model which may not be appropriate for the clients or context in which the coach mentor is operating. The effectiveness of such short training programs is variable. Coach mentors can be misled into believing that there is only one way to coach or mentor, and that they need to get through all the steps of the model taught if they are to be 'proper coaches'. Unpublished masters research papers (Baker-Finch 2011; Charker 2012) suggest that such courses do equip coaches or coaching managers with relevant skills such as active listening and open questions, however, without on-going support and development in their organisation, coaching managers may lack the confidence to apply their skills on a daily basis. Grant (2010) found that it took about six months of support after a training course for managers to adopt a coaching style as their normal mode of behaviour.

Fortunately the number of higher education courses is increasing, particularly in Europe and Australia, and these provide the opportunity both for a deeper under-standing of theory and for developing a range of skills. These courses vary hugely depending on whether they focus more or less on psychology, more or less on organi-sations, whether they include both coaching and mentoring or only one or the other, whether they teach a specific model or a range of models, and whether they are more influenced by theories such as adult learning or leadership. Coach mentors therefore need to research thoroughly before selecting a course which will best suit them and the context in which they operate. All courses should help develop the coach mentor's ethical capacity using scenarios and real world dilemmas (Hawkins and Smith 2006; Passmore 2009; Duffy and Passmore 2010). Peer supervision is sometimes offered as part of coaching and mentoring training programs and can be very helpful in iden-tifying options for resolving ethical dilemmas. However, where all peers are students, it is wise to have an experienced mentor or supervisor on hand to provide guidance on subtle dilemmas.

In addition to education and training, coach mentors can gain from accreditation with a recognised body. Such organisations exist in many parts of the world, such as Europe, South Africa, Australia, New Zealand, as well as global organisations such as the International Coach Federation. These organisations have created codes of conduct for their members, as well as providing many useful resources. In addition to these organisa-tions, collaboration between coaching professionals, clients, and coaching academics has led to the development of guidelines for Coaching in Organizations (SAI 2011) which contains a wealth of relevant information.

Conclusion

Ethical issues arise in many guises. Some such as confidentiality and dual/multiple roles are relatively common, hence the coach mentor can consider them in advance and have some idea of how they may respond. Others will arise unexpectedly. In this case, it is useful for the coach mentor to have an ethical framework in mind and sources of guidance, whether in a supervisor or a professional association, to help them make ethical decisions. If the client is at risk of self-harm or harming others, the coach mentor's duty of care over-rides any agreement on confidentiality. In less life-threatening situations, the coach mentor seeks solutions which are both in the individual client's interest and the organisation's interest. If the two interests collide, the coach mentor attempts to persuade the client to take responsibility for address-ing directly with the organisation. At all times, the coach mentor must act in accord-ance with their own values, with the law, and with the code of conduct of their professional association and the code of conduct of the organisations in which they work. There are common elements to many such codes of conduct so that conflict between them is rare. These codes help coach mentors to select appropriate options for resolving ethical dilemmas in their practice, with the over-riding consideration to act in the client's best interest.

However, what sometimes happens is that the code of conduct espoused by an organisation is not actually adhered to in real life. Coach mentors may therefore be faced with a situation where they are uncomfortable with what a client is doing. Although the practice identified may not be illegal, if the coach mentor is uncomfortable ethically, he/she should raise the issue for discussion. If the client is unwilling to change, the coach mentor should terminate the relationship. To continue would risk damage to their reputation and to the reputation of the coaching and mentoring process. Whether or not the coach mentor becomes a whistle-blower depends on the severity of the practice and the coach mentor's own views of right and wrong. On the positive side, coach mentors with a reputation for ethical professional practice enhance both their own reputation and the reputation of coaching and mentoring.

Useful links

The links in this chapter highlight resources to support learning about ethics in coaching and mentoring.

Association for Coaching – http://www.associationforcoaching.com/pages/about/code-ethics-good-practice

Code of ethics and good practice.

Association of Coaching Supervisors – http://www.associationofcoachingsupervisors.com/

Forum for coaching supervisors.

Association for Professional Executive Coaching and Supervision – http://www.apecs.org/coachingEthicalGuidelines.asp

Ethical guidelines.

European Mentoring and Coaching Council – http://www.emccouncil.org/

Code of ethics.

International Coach Federation – http://www.coachfederation.org/about/landing.cfm?ItemNumber=854&navItemNumber=634

Code of ethics.

St James Ethics Centre – http://www.ethics.org.au/content/ethical-decision-making

Guide to ethical decision-making.

Worldwide Association of Business Coaching – http://www.wabccoaches.com/includes/popups/code_of_ethics_2nd_edition_december_17_2007.html

Code of business coaching ethics and integrity.

References

Baker-Finch, S. (2011) 'Does training in coaching skills develop coaching managers?' Master of Business Coaching Unpublished Research Report. Sydney, Sydney Business School, University of Wollongong.

Bluckert, P. (2006) *Psychological dimensions of executive coaching*. Maidenhead, Open University Press.

Brennan, D. and L. Wildflower (2010) 'Ethics in coaching', in E. Cox, T. Bachkirova and D. Clutterbuck (eds) *Complete handbook of coaching*. London, Sage, pp. 369–80.

Buckley, M. (2010) 'Coaching and mental health', in E. Cox, T. Bachkirova and D. Clutterbuck (eds) *The complete handbook of coaching*. London, Sage, pp. 394–404.

Charker, P. (2012) 'Does a two day coaching skills workshop equip a manager with the competencies to coach?' Master of Business Coaching Unpublished Research Report. Sydney, Sydney Business School, University of Wollongong.

Connor, J. and J. Pokora (2012) *Coaching and mentoring at work*. Maidenhead, Open University Press.

Couley, A. (2011) *Perceived psychological distress of coach practitioners in Australia*. Sydney Business School. Sydney, University of Wollongong. Master of Business Coaching.

Cox, E. (2010) 'Last things first: ending well in the coaching relationship', in S. Palmer and A. McDowall (eds) *The coaching relationship*. Hove, Routledge, pp. 159–81.

de Jong, A. (2010) 'Coaching ethics: integrity in the moment of choice', in J. Passmore (ed.) *Excellence in coaching: the industry guide*. London, Association for Coaching, pp. 204–14.

Driessen, D. (2013) 'Can HR practitioners deliver coaching?' Master of Business Coaching Unpublished Research Report. Sydney, Sydney Business School, University of Wollongong.

Duffy, M. and J. Passmore (2010) 'Ethics in coaching: an ethical decision making framework for coaching psychologists', *International Coaching Psychology Review*, 5(2): 140–51.

Govindarajan, V. (2005) 'Coaching for strategic thinking capability, strategy coaching', in H. Morgan, P. Harkins and M. Goldsmith (eds) *The art and practice of leadership coaching*. Hoboken, NJ, Wiley, pp.196–9.

Grant, A. M. (2009) 'Coach or couch', *Harvard Business Review* (Jan.): 97.

Grant, A. M. (2010) 'It takes time: a stages of change perspective on the adoption of workplace coaching skills', *Journal of Change Management*, 10(1): 61–77.

Gray, D. E. (2010) 'Towards the lifelong skills and business development of coaches: a integrated model of supervision and mentoring', *Coaching: An International Journal of Theory, Research and Practice*, 3(1): 60–72.

Hannafey, F. T. and L. A. Vitulano (2012) 'Ethics and executive coaching: an agency theory approach', *Journal of Business Ethics*: 1–5.

Hawkins, P. (2011) *Leadership team coaching*. London, Routledge.

Hawkins, P. and N. Smith (2006) *Coaching, mentoring and organizational consultancy: supervision and development*. Maidenhead, Open University Press.

Hicks, R. and J. McCracken (2011) 'Coaching as a Leadership Style', *Physician Executive*, 37(5): 70–2.

Kearney, K. S. (2010) 'Grappling with the gods: reflection for coaches of the narcissistic leader', *International Journal of Evidence-Based Coaching and Mentoring*, 8(1): 1–13.

Leimon, A., F. Moscovici and G. McMahon (2005) *Essential business coaching*. Hove, Routledge.

Maxwell, A. (2011) 'Supervising the internal coach: still flying under the radar?' 1st International Conference in Coaching Supervision. Oxford, Oxford Brookes.

McGowan, C. (2010) 'Do business coaches think they need counselling skills?' Master of Business Coaching Unpublished Research Report. Sydney, Sydney Business School, University of Wollongong.

Moral, M. (2011) 'A French model of supervision: supervising a "several to several" coaching journey', in T. Bachkirova, P. Jackson and D. Clutterbuck (eds) *Coaching and mentoring supervision: theory and practice*. Maidenhead, Open University Press, pp. 67–77.

Moyes, B. (2009) 'Literature review of coaching supervision', *International Coaching Psychology Review*, 4(2): 162–73.

Passmore, J. (2009) 'Coaching ethics: making ethical decisions–novices and experts', *The Coaching Psychologist*, 5(1): 6–10.

Peltier, B. (2010) *The psychology of executive coaching: theory and application*. New York, Routledge.

Rostron, S. S. (2009) *Business coaching international*. London, Karnac.

SAI (2011) *Coaching in Organizations Handbook*. SAI Global. HB332-2011.

Whyte (2013) 'What is coaching supervision and why is it important?' *Research Bulletin*, Whyte & Co. 11.

Zachary, L. J. (2005) *Creating a mentoring culture*. San Francisco, CA, Jossey-Bass.

12

SUCCESS IN COACHING AND MENTORING

Introduction

Given the huge investment of time, personal commitment and expense in coaching and mentoring, it would be useful to understand what success looks like. Of course, the answer to this question will vary from one individual to another and from one organisation to another. Nevertheless, previous research identifies a number of critical success factors which will be discussed in this chapter.

There are several ways to evaluate the effectiveness of the coaching and mentoring process. These vary from evaluation sheets similar to those used for training (so-called 'happy sheets') to pre- and post-psychological measurements, and attempts to measure the return on investment, considering impact at the organisational level. These approaches will be discussed below.

The chapter concludes with a discussion of emerging and continuing trends in coaching and mentoring.

Critical success factors

In both coaching (Bluckert 2005) and mentoring (Garvey 2010), the relationship (including trust) is identified as central to the process. Blackman (2006) explored success factors from the coachee's perspectives, and identified factors relating to the coach (e.g. maintains confidentiality, communicates clearly, is able to see things from my point of view), factors relating to the coachee (e.g. self-efficacy, commitment, motivation), as well as organisational support and aspects relating to the coaching process (e.g. relates personal goals to organisational goals and focuses on my success rather than on my failings). Given the importance of the relationship, a good selection process and well-defined selection criteria are essential to the success of the coaching or mentoring process.

Garvey (2010) stresses the centrality of the mentoring relationship in facilitating learning. Bluckert (2005) suggests that the relationship is '*not just a critical success factor but* the *critical success factor in coaching*'. Furthermore, Bluckert stresses the importance of the client's trust in the integrity and competence of the coach. Blackman (2006) identified a further set of characteristics such as confidentiality, shared values and a similar personality.

The value of experience in the same industry may initially be a plus, helping establish credibility and rapport with the client, as well as suggesting areas to explore together (Gray et al. 2011). Grant (2005) on the other hand suggests that coaches facilitate a process, and do not require specific knowledge of the sector. In contrast, Clutterbuck and Megginson criticise the idea that coaches do not need contextual knowledge of the client's world as '*one of the most pernicious myths about coaching*' (Clutterbuck and Megginson 2011: 306), warning that a complete lack of knowledge may lead to both unethical and ineffective practice. In their discussion of ethical issues in executive coaching, Hannafey and Vitulano (2012) suggest that executive coaches may not always understand the complex business environments or market pressures challenging their clients. Standards Australia's guidelines on *Coaching in Organizations* (SAI 2011) suggest a range of questions which an organisation might like to ask prospective coaches including questions relating to their experience both in coaching and in the industry. Providing the coach mentor helps the client to come up with appropriate solutions for their current context, the coach mentor's prior knowledge will be an asset and not a hindrance.

The specific purpose of coaching or mentoring also needs to be taken into account. Some coach mentors specialise in leadership coaching, group coaching or transitions coaching (SAI 2011). An organisation may hire coach mentors with expertise in specific areas such as mentoring for diversity or coaching expatriate couples prior to, during or after an overseas posting.

Contracting process

Tenders for coaching contracts have become more sophisticated over the last few years, requiring coaches to articulate their methodology, explain exactly what they propose to do and what outcomes may be expected. Some self-taught coaches have found this development challenging, having survived in the past based on word of mouth recommendations and a more informal approach. However the development has been positive in developing a shared understanding between coach mentor and the sponsoring organisation.

For large organisations, issuing a coaching contract is often a multi-stage process, with companies first replying to a tender and the replies and recommendations then checked against the desired criteria. Shortlisted companies are invited to present and/or do live coaching demonstrations. Large companies may establish a panel of preferred providers, thus shortening the process for future contracts (SAI 2011). The final stage is between individual coach and client. Sometimes HR may be present at the first meeting between the two, but more commonly the coach and client meet to see if there is a good fit, and inform HR of the outcome.

Unlike in life coaching, the selection process for an external business coach is likely to involve at least three parties, the organisational contact who signs the contract (often a HR manager but sometimes a procurement manager), the coach and the client. The coaching champion or sponsor may also be involved, particularly if they have strong views on the approaches they believe will work best in their organisation. Procurement managers are often less au fait with coaching than HR managers, which may lengthen the time it takes for coaches to explain their proposals, particularly if it is the first coaching contract which the organisation has negotiated. Procurement managers may focus on reducing the price of the contract, seeking to get the best proposal for the lowest price but perhaps with less understanding of how to assess coaching proposals than for other services. Coaches need to be aware of trends in the marketplace as well as developments in coaching and mentoring research in order to remain competitive in their offerings.

Where an organisation employs internal coaches, the process is shorter. Typically an employee registers an interest in being coached or is encouraged to seek coaching. A match is suggested by the person responsible for the panel of internal coaches, where possible ensuring that the two people are not in the same department. The coach and internal client then meet to see if the match works. Employees of a coaching manager on the other hand do not have any choice. It is therefore critically important that coaching managers have a relationship of trust with their employees, to give coaching the best chance of success.

The choice of mentor may be more or less informal. Some organisations assign a mentor to every new employee, as well as to employees starting a new role or employees seen as having good prospects for development. In other organisations, employees may themselves seek a mentor, either within their own organisation or externally. Again it is usual for the mentor and mentee to meet, in order to ensure a good fit. Mentors are usually chosen because they are seen as people with an interest in developing others. Mentors may or may not have received mentoring training. In fact, Garvey claims that mentoring requires '*only minimum training and some on-going support*' (Garvey 2010: 350). Some mentors are keen to 'give something back', although there is a risk that they may see 'giving something back' as giving advice, and their advice may be based on out-dated knowledge. However, Garvey notes that experienced mentors do not give gratuitous advice. On the other hand, if the mentor shares experience which helps the client to identify options or to think through issues, then this '*establishes rapport, empathy credibility, and additionally, accelerates learning*' (Garvey 2010: 346). Other important criteria are the mentor's ability to listen and ask questions of the mentee, and to guide the mentee in identifying learning opportunities.

Defining effectiveness

The message to those selecting coaches and mentors is the ancient one of 'Caveat emptor', buyer beware. If organisations articulate what they require, it is more likely that they will find coach mentors who meet their requirements.

While some common success factors may be identified, others are, if not unique, at least more valued by some clients than others. This is because the coaching and mentoring process is not a pre-defined interaction, which will be successful if all listed steps are followed. Instead success relies heavily on the quality of the relationship, the rapport between coach mentor and client, and the emotional intelligence of both. Different coach mentors may be effective with the same client at different times because the client's needs change over time and in different contexts.

One way to assess effectiveness is to use the critical success factors identified above and evaluate the extent to which the recommended factors for success such as trust and willingness to be coached are present. This may be combined with an evaluation of the competence of the coach mentor. If these inputs are strong, then the coaching and mentoring process should lead to positive outcomes. In fact, de Haan and Duckworth (2013) argue that we can assume that coaching is effective, therefore the most useful focus at this stage of the development of the profession is on the 'active ingredients', e.g. the coaching relationship, the coach and client personalities, and the coach technique.

Some of these criteria are, however, difficult to assess. For example, how should the effectiveness of the relationship be measured? Blackman's research (2006) found that clients valued coaches who were similar to them, had similar values and goals, were the same gender and age, and had a similar personality. However, such similarity may not always be the best platform for a coaching or mentoring relationship, as differences may give rise to more opportunities for exploration and challenge (Megginson and Clutterbuck 2006) or offer as many possibilities for learning (Wycherley and Cox 2008). Previous research cited by Gray and Goregaokar (2010) has found that women may prefer a male mentor because males may be perceived as having more power in the organisation and thus have a greater ability to help the mentee's career. The authors did not, however, find the same preference for a male external coach.

Wycherley and Cox (2008) note that similarities in terms of gender, culture or other aspects of diversity may make it quicker to achieve rapport. They argue, however, that coaches should be able to establish rapport with any client. Furthermore, the research supporting several of the criteria is mixed, according to Wycherley and Cox, for example in relation to personality matching or chemistry, gender or experience in similar size organisations. Garvey, Stokes et al. (2009) suggest that a balance is needed between similarity and difference: similarity to foster rapport and difference to add value. Rather than focusing on the inputs as suggested by de Haan and Duckworth, increasingly we are seeing an interest in some form of outcome measurement and this is the next topic in this chapter.

Return on investment and evaluation

Clutterbuck (2009) suggests that many current measurements of coaching are 'naïve and prone to giving false positives'. Happy sheets (customer satisfaction ratings) and client testimonials are often used (McGurk 2011). In Kirkpatrick and Kirkpatrick's (2006) training evaluation terms, this is Level 1, the client's reaction. Given the importance of the relationship between coach mentor and client, some assessment of the client's response is important (Ely, Boyce et al. 2010). However, as most clients have a positive relationship with their coach mentor, they may be reluctant to give negative feedback. The feedback they do give may be useful for the coach mentor's ego or marketing purposes but is of little use in identifying the true benefits to the organisation (which may only be apparent several months or even years later if the individual client's behavioural change is sustained). Nor is it of use to the coach mentor seeking to identify areas for improvement. As the Australian *Coaching in Organizations Handbook* (SAI 2011) points out, the purpose of the measurement should inform the choice of measurement.

Before and after measurements are more often undertaken by researchers than organisations, particularly by coaching researchers with psychological training. Using validated tools, the coach mentor can use improvements in such measures to prove they have had an impact. Unfortunately, unless the selected tools happen to match exactly what the organisation was hoping coaching would achieve, such measurements are only indicators of change at the individual level. They do not indicate whether any organisational improvements follow from the individual changes. Furthermore, the after measurements are often undertaken on completion of coaching and do not prove whether the change will be maintained.

In addition to using validated tools, some researchers design specific questionnaires for their before and after measurements. Evers, Brouwers et al. (2006) for example compared the outcome expectations and self-efficacy beliefs of a group of managers before and after they received coaching with those of a group who did not receive coaching. The group who received coaching showed improvements in self-efficacy relating to goal setting compared with their results before coaching. Spence (2007) also showed an increase in goal attainment using the Goal Attainment Scaling tool. However Garvey, Stokes et al. (2009) warn that goals are not always in the interests of the client, but may instead aid the coach in confining discussions to topics acceptable to the sponsors or topics which the coach feels competent to address. Put another way, while goal attainment may seem to demonstrate the coach's effectiveness, this is only true if setting goals is actually the right thing for the client at that time and if appropriate goals are chosen.

Evaluations of coaching and mentoring rarely focus on what has been learned (Kirkpatricks' Level 2 (2006)) although this is possible, as Ely, Boyce et al. (2010) point out, suggesting that the two most relevant outcomes to assess are improvements in self-awareness and in cognitive flexibility. An increase in self-awareness may be demonstrated if the gap between the client's self-assessment and the assessment of other people who have completed a 360° assessment for the client before coaching is less than the gap between the self-assessment and the assessment of others after coaching. Questions relating to cognitive flexibility, ability to cope with change, and to respond quickly, can be incorporated in 360° surveys. A manager who has previously had issues relating to on-time completion of projects and who is coached or mentored on ways to improve this, may be able to demonstrate changes in behaviours (Kirkpatricks' Level 3) and in results (Kirkpatricks' Level 4), e.g. on-time completion. The results may lag behind the changes in behaviours as team members may take time to see the change as genuine and respond to the change. Organisational support to sustain the change in behaviour is important, even if initial results do not show a benefit. It is also possible for the conclusion of a coaching engagement to show positive results but for these to fade over time. Again organisational support is vital (Grant 2010). Measurements should be taken periodically, to ensure that the outcome has time to show in results and that the change is sustained.

Apart from the issue of when to take before and after measurements, using before and after measurements can be problematic for other reasons. Depending on how they are defined, they may make it more difficult to change focus during the process. If, for example, the initial focus and hence the before measurement was on how the client communicated with his/her team, the coaching or mentoring process might be confined to that, even if it emerged, in early conversations, that the client first needed to understand their own values and goals and their alignment with organisational values and goals. The measurements in this case may be useful to the coach mentor and to the organisation, but may not be in the client's best interest. To adopt an ethical stance of doing no harm, the coach mentor would have to negotiate a change in focus that would benefit both the individual client and organisation, even if on this occasion, it meant not having a pair of matched before and after measurements. Measurements may also be affected by attention paid to the process. For example, a discussion with a client and their line manager before coaching may make the manager more interested in supporting the client and more likely to observe changes in the client's behaviour. Whether or not there is any difference in the actual outcomes, the manager may give higher scores when evaluating the effectiveness of coaching. Of course, there may be an actual difference because of the line manager's support. On the other hand, if the coach's interest in measurement is for marketing purposes, then an increase in scores may be all they seek.

Many organisations claim to use an outcomes-based assessment of organisational impact. Kirkpatrick uses the terms Return on Expectations (ROE), rather than Return on Investment (ROI), for Level 4 (Kirkpatrick and Kirkpatrick 2009). Taylor (2011) uses the term Impact on Business as an alternative. As numerous benefits have been identified for coaching and mentoring, organisations sometimes cite these benefits to justify their investment, with a seemingly straightforward calculation comparing the amount of money invested with the monetary value of the outcomes achieved. However, published calculations for return on investment in coaching are often exaggerated, with a return of 6:1 commonly quoted (Leimon, Moscovici et al. 2005) and some greater than 7:1 (Parker-Wilkins 2006). These calculations often include all improvements in the organisation, e.g. improved retention saves money not only in terms of direct recruitment costs but also saving on the costs of training new people, lower productivity while new people are developing their skills, and possible losses in customer service or reputation, while the new people are developing their relationships with customers and colleagues. However, as Levenson (2009) warns, reducing staff turnover is only a good thing if the people who stay are more valuable to the organisation than the people who would replace them if they left.

Furthermore, such calculations usually ignore other changes taking place at the same time, although organisations are not controlled laboratories where only one factor is changed at a time. Simultaneous change initiatives may each claim the credit for all improvements identified, although there is no proof that, for example, the coaching initiative is solely responsible for any of the improvements. Coaching and mentoring may contribute but they may not be the only initiative to contribute (Levenson 2009). Some approaches attempt to allow for this by asking the managers to estimate how much of the improvements is due to coaching and for their level of confidence in their estimate (Fogleman 2006). ROI calculations are usually based on the perceptions of the managers involved, and not always validated by other sources. As De Meuse, Guangrong et al. (2009) point out, retrospective interviews are subjective. Managers keen for coaching or mentoring to continue, may consciously or unconsciously exaggerate positive effects. De Meuse et al. found that the positive effects identified in the studies they reviewed were reported as higher by individuals who had been coached than by other respondents, indicating a positive bias.

Rather than relying on a generic formula, organisations can define their expectations in introducing coaching or mentoring and then define specific measures to assess whether their expectations have in fact been met. For example, an organisation with a strong focus on innovation may decide that its primary interest in introducing coaching and mentoring is to increase the number of ideas put forward by employees. This would be relatively straightforward to measure, although there might be some debate about what qualifies as 'new', e.g. does an improvement to an existing idea qualify? Another alternative to a purely financial approach is the Well-Being and Engagement Framework proposed by Grant (2012) as a way of determining how effective a coaching engagement has been. Other organisations might adopt a balanced scorecard approach (Leedham 2005) considering such factors as the coach mentor's skills and attributes, improvements in employees' confidence and motivation as well as their skills and behaviours, and ultimately looking at improvements in individual performance and business results. Feldman and Lankau however argue that coaching may be '*too many causal links away from financial results to demonstrate direct and significant relationships*' (2005: 843). Nevertheless, De Meuse et al. (2009) support the idea of evaluating the coaching process at various stages as different measures may be appropriate for each one, e.g. the evaluation of the coach's skills will be different from the evaluation of employees' confidence. Eby et al. (2008) suggest that mentoring in the workplace is most likely to have a positive impact on interpersonal relationships, job satisfaction and helping behaviours, each of which can be measured.

Articulating the organisation's expectations helps develop a shared understanding and gives a clear signal as to what the organisation is expecting to gain from coaching and mentoring. Agreeing the timing of the measurements creates a realistic sense of what may be observed when. For example, increases in self-awareness are often cited as outcomes of coaching and mentoring. Is that sufficient for the organisation, or will the organisation only be satisfied if the increase in self-awareness leads to changes in behaviour which result in improved performance against the organisation's metrics such as improved performance by the individual client in communicating with their team or improved ratings of the individual client in 360° surveys or employee engagement surveys? Levenson (2009) argues that organisations first need to define which leadership behaviours will lead to improved business outcomes and then measure improvements in those behaviours, some of which can be attributed to the coaching process.

The same approach can be used in calculating the return on introducing a coaching culture. If the organisation is expecting to see benefits in terms of employee engagement and evaluation of managers by employees, then these can be measured before the introduction of a coaching culture and on an on-going basis thereafter, to ensure that the benefits are realised and sustained. Coaching may be seen as a stand-alone intervention or as a support for other change or development initiatives, which also generate improvements in individual effectiveness and organisational development (Wales 2003).

Measuring the benefits of mentoring is less commonly undertaken than measurements of coaching effectiveness (Clutterbuck 2009; EFMD 2009). This may be because mentoring is often offered on a voluntary basis or by someone within the same organisation, with perhaps only limited investment in training and support. Hence there is less need to demonstrate return on investment than for coaching provided by external coaches. However, a similar approach could be adopted to calculate the return on investment in mentoring, if the organisation is clear on what it expects from mentoring. Such a review may also highlight a need for further investment if the organisation is to obtain the benefits anticipated. The form and purpose of mentoring dictate the measurement used. Underhill (2006) reviewed the outcomes of over two decades of mentoring research, and found that mentoring had a positive impact on the career outcomes of those mentored. Interestingly her study found that informal mentoring had more positive outcomes than formal, possibly because in informal mentoring partnerships, the relationship is often stronger than in programs where mentors are assigned.

In implementing a coaching or mentoring culture, organisations may use a combination of internal and external coaches and mentors, as well as providing training and other support. Organisations are advised to be clear on their expectations from the outset so that they can measure the effectiveness of whichever approach they adopt and do so at the right time. The coaching and mentoring culture self-assessments described in Chapter 6 could be adapted by organisations so that they articulate their own ideal scenario and interim steps towards achieving it and then repeat the audit over time to check whether progress is being made. This exercise in collectively visualising how an ideal coaching and mentoring culture would look, feel and behave, is powerful in its own right.

It is also important to include measures during the coaching and mentoring process to allow the coach mentor and client to amend or adapt the process as necessary. If measures are only taken after completion of the coaching and mentoring process, no improvements can be made to that particular engagement. As Garvey, Stokes et al. (2009) point out, not all possible challenges can be anticipated, but having a development-focused evaluation allows the process to address those which do arise.

It is not necessary to measure every benefit. For example, Niemes (2002) found that coaching improved engagement and, as previous research had demonstrated that engagement improved productivity, he concluded that coaching improved productivity. The benefits of the measurements need to be weighed against the cost of undertaking the measurements. Just because we can measure something does not mean we should. A useful question to ask is: 'How will this measurement add value and for whom?' Some form of measurement is useful, but whether the measurement is organised by the coach mentor, the individual client or the sponsoring organisation, the purpose of measurement should be clear and communicated to all stakeholders.

As organisations mature in their selection and implementation of a variety of learning and development alternatives, various combinations may be used to good effect. Coaching has been shown to improve the implementation of what has been learned in training when the trainees are back in the workplace. Olivero, Bane et al. (1997) for example found that training combined with coaching resulted in productivity increases almost four times higher than those achieved by training alone. Thach (2002) found that combining 360° feedback with coaching resulted in an increase in leadership effectiveness as assessed by peers and self-reports. A future development of evaluation may therefore be to evaluate the combination of learning and development approaches used in particular contexts, rather than to evaluate each approach separately.

It is a truism that training budgets are among the first to suffer in difficult financial times. If coaching and mentoring are to be seen as an investment rather than a cost, they need to demonstrate that they benefit the organisation in some meaningful way. This may be different in every organisation and at different levels of organisations. Measurement may be needed at the individual, team and organisational levels.

Different data may be required for different individuals as the purpose of coaching and mentoring may vary and hence its effectiveness may be measured in different ways. As Garvey, Stokes et al. (2009) point out, coaching and mentoring are one-to-one relationships and hence ideally suited to ideographic measures, i.e. measures which capture what is unique to a particular individual and context. The data should be used not simply to demonstrate effectiveness but to generate new insights for the coach mentor and the client. The data may also help identify areas for improvement, particularly if data can be compared with data in the literature or with formal or informal benchmarking with other organisations. Defining the benefits expected, and when and how to measure them, are important aspects of implementing coaching and mentoring in any organisation.

Future of coaching and mentoring

While there are still voices querying whether coaching is merely the latest management fad, the consensus appears to be that both coaching and mentoring are here to stay (Peltier 2010). A number of topics discussed elsewhere in this book are considered now in the light of current debate and likely future scenarios.

Developing standards

While both coaching and mentoring are seen as services, coaching is often identified as an emerging industry whose practitioners are developing professional standards. Neither coaching nor mentoring are regulated by legislation, so while the situation may no longer be the 'wild west' described by Sherman and Freas (2004), it is still very much the case of 'buyer beware'.

Professional associations such as the International Coach Federation, the European Mentoring and Coaching Council and the Association for Coaching are collaborating in the Global Coaching and Mentoring Alliance to develop the credibility and professionalism of coaching and mentoring. Member associations identify competencies and define codes of ethics. As might be expected, their requirements are only binding on their members. Their guidelines, however, may be used by anyone. Common elements include skills relating to the coaching process such as listening and questioning, skills relating to relationship and account management, self-management and professional development, and skills relating to planning and evaluating the process itself.

There are international standards for mentoring, though as Clutterbuck (2009) notes, these have so far not been widely adopted. The International Mentoring Association defines a set of standards for accreditation of mentoring programs, which focuses on six key areas: design of the program, roles and responsibilities, mentor selection and assignment, mentor professional development, formative assessment, and program evaluation. While it does not dictate the forms of evaluation to be used, it expects there to be evidence of such evaluation.

Standards Australia has developed guidelines for coaching in organisations (SAI 2011) which cover a wide range of topics, including competencies, ethics and coaching contracts. While many practitioners and purchasers of coaching in large organisations in

Australia are aware of the guidelines, so far there is little evidence of clients in small or medium enterprises using the guidelines. This may change if more coaches refer to the guidelines in their publicity materials and tenders.

Educating clients about the nature of coaching and mentoring is an important part of future developments as is the education of the coaches and mentors themselves. If all parties are aware of relevant standards and codes, the standards and codes are more likely to be implemented.

Internal coaching and mentoring

Increased awareness of the power of coaching and mentoring combined with pressure on budgets is leading to an increase in internal coach mentors and coaching managers. People who have been coached and mentored themselves often adopt coaching and mentoring practices. Whether or not organisations have a formal mentoring program, mentoring will exist, according to Garvey (2010) because people like to 'give something back' or in some way influence or leave their mark. Organisations which have not formally implemented a coaching program may also find that their managers are already adopting a coaching style (Apthorpe 2011). This may be because a coaching style is effective across generations while a more traditional hierarchical style is not effective with Generation Y employees. Hence a coaching style allows managers to adopt the same style with everyone. However, some managers become stressed because they would like to be in coaching mode at all times, whereas their role sometimes requires them to mentor or direct. Hicks and McCracken (2010) identify the three roles of the leader as coach, mentor and teacher. They advise leaders to physically indicate when they are switching roles so that the employee is not confused about which role the leader is adopting. There is a need for more guidance as to when to choose which approach and the effectiveness of different approaches in different contexts.

Team coaching and mentoring

Team coaching is increasing in popularity, perhaps due to a lack of understanding in organisations about the nature of team coaching and an assumption that it might lower the cost of bringing an external coach into the organisation. Team coaching is different from team facilitation, where facilitators focus more on the process while team coaches focus on helping the team as a whole define and/or align their goals and agree how to achieve them. They may or may not be involved in follow up and feedback. Another option is for the team leader to have a mentor and the team to have a team coach. Again it comes back to the purpose of coaching and mentoring and choosing the right people to help achieve it.

In group mentoring, the mentor ensures that everyone can participate, asks thought-provoking questions, provides feedback, shares personal experience and acts as a sounding board (Zachary 2005). The power of the group lies in the diverse perspectives available, both in terms of the questions asked and the experience and feedback shared. As well as working with the group as a whole, team coaches work with individual team members to address issues which impact on team performance. Confidentiality is at least, if not more, important than in coaching individuals. The team coach must avoid revealing in team meetings information which was shared in confidence.

Another reason for the rise in popularity of team coaching is where individuals have found coaching useful for themselves personally and would like to replicate the success with their team. The team leader's coach observes the leader in action and shares their observations with the team leader. The team leader may initially assume that their coach would be an excellent choice to coach the team as a whole. However, individual coaches may not have the expertise to work with a group. While team coaching qualifications are available at a limited number of universities, many team coaches are self-taught, combining what they have learned about coaching in general with what they know about team leadership and group dynamics. This is an area where far more research is needed to underpin effective team coaching practices.

Cross-cultural coaching

Multinationals are increasingly seeking coach mentors with intercultural competence, an understanding of the global corporation, and the ability to coach and mentor at a distance, possibly in collaboration with other coach mentors, who have local expertise and specific areas of competence. Coaching and mentoring are being embraced more and more in Asia and other regions, leading to an initial demand for coach mentors with cross-cultural experience. Over time, as local coaches in these regions are trained and develop their own expertise, the demand for coaches from other countries may lessen. However, multinationals often want a common approach to the initiatives they put in place so coach mentors who collaborate internationally are likely to continue to be in demand. Many purely domestic organisations also have multicultural workforces, with a requirement for coach mentors to be able to work with people with different worldviews and help others to work effectively together, whether on new product development, process improvement or functional and cross-functional teams. The willingness of the coach mentor to see the individual and not the stereotype underpins this developing area.

Specialisation

Specialisation is likely to increase among coach mentors who charge for their services. While new coach mentors may be tempted to accept every offer of work that comes their way, this can lead to ethical issues if coach mentors take on work outside their professional competence. As an alternative, many coach mentors are choosing to specialise in applications such as careers coaching, transitions and outplacement or team coaching and mentoring, cross-cultural and expatriate coaching and mentoring. This is to avoid the situation described in Taylor where *'being all things to all people dilutes effectiveness and impacts on personal branding'* (2011: 11). Instead, coach mentors develop specific services which they offer to the market, referring other requests to people with expertise in those areas. In talking about expertise here, we do not mean content expertise, e.g. expertise in financial planning, but rather coaching and mentoring expertise in areas such as cross-cultural or team coaching, or expertise in a particular sector e.g. working with not-for-profit organisations or particular industry sectors. The Australian *Coaching in Organizations Handbook* (SAI 2011) advocates that no payment should be made for referrals. Instead a decision to refer is taken if it is in the best interest of the client.

Supervision

Supervision has been a hot topic in coaching for some years now. The demand seems highest from coaching psychologists and psychotherapists who see coaching as a powerful intervention with the potential to do harm, which can be reduced by supervision by an experienced practitioner, who can explore issues with the novice as the issues arise, helping the novice identify alternatives and develop an ethical decision-making framework. Supervision is a safe place for *'co-creative and generative thinking where new learning is forged for clients, coach and supervisor, and for the profession'* (Hawkins 2010: 392).

Mentors, coaching managers and coaches from a non-clinical background may see less need for supervision. After all, managers and consultants are not supervised by an external supervisor, only by their own manager, while mentors often receive no supervision, requiring only limited training and some on-going support (Garvey 2010). Support may be offered in the form of a periodic get-together of mentors, in effect a form of peer supervision. An experienced mentor may be available in these meetings or by telephone/video conference for times when the new mentor needs to discuss issues that arise. This seems to be generally recognised as a good thing and there is less of the debate found in the coaching literature about what constitutes good practice in supervision. A manager's approach to coaching may use approaches such as solution-focused questions and not delve into underlying personality issues. Nevertheless managers could benefit from reflecting on their practice with another practitioner and receiving support from that person.

There are a number of questions around supervision. One is to clearly define its purpose. Is it to protect the client or to help the coach's development, or both? Is it to protect the purchaser of coaching services by giving them some reassurance that the coach takes their own development seriously and has advice available in case of difficulty? Is supervision only required when the coach is newly qualified or is on-going supervision required?

The topic of supervision is being debated by professional mentoring and coaching organisations around the world. The European Mentoring and Coaching Council require all members to have on-going supervision, without defining the form and frequency of supervision (EMCC 2010). The International Coach Federation has defined an interim position, recommending but not currently mandating supervision. The Worldwide Association of Business Coaches includes supervision in professional development but does not define requirements further. The Association for Coaching requires three months of supervision for foundation executive coaches, six months for executive coaches, and nine months for master executive coaches. The Australian New Zealand Institute of Coaching (ANZI Coaching) requires on-going supervision for coaches to maintain their accreditation statues, varying from ten hours per year for associate coaches, six hours per year for professional coaches and one hour per year for master coaches. ANZI and the Association for Coaching offer regular supervision sessions to their members. There is also the Association of Coaching Supervisors which seeks to support coaching supervisors. While the form and frequency may not be agreed, there is an apparent consensus that supervision is 'a good thing'. Nonetheless there is little research to demonstrate its effectiveness and that a novice coach becomes a better coach as a result, apart from a small number of surveys of perceptions of coaches (Connor and Pokora 2012). Nor is there proof that clients benefit from their coach being supervised. There is a clear benefit to the coach supervisor who is paid for their service, thus providing an additional income strand, but other benefits remain to be proven.

Just as coaching is specific to the participants and context involved, so too with coaching supervision – in other words a common format may not be applicable to everyone. Professional associations, in their genuine desire to raise standards in coaching and mentoring, may restrict through their accreditation processes the forms of supervision which the coach mentor may choose and the criteria for judging whether a supervisor is acceptable or not. Similarly, purchasers of coaching and mentoring services may not have considered the options available. For pragmatic reasons, coach mentors will comply with the requirements of professional associations and of purchasers. There are limited possibilities for training in coaching supervision, with the UK currently offering more options than elsewhere. Coach supervisors tend to be self-taught. Hawkins (2010) advocates action learning as the most effective way to learn to be a supervisor, with the trainee supervisor working with a coach, and with a shadow supervisor who gives feedback to the trainee supervisor. In addition, the trainee supervisor receives supervision on their coaching from an experienced supervisor. This is another area where more research is needed to explore the effectiveness of different options.

Conclusion

This book has explored coaching and mentoring in business, bringing together a diverse range of research and practical examples. Each chapter could be developed into a book in its own right as coaches, mentors and their clients see the benefits of adopting these approaches to support individual and organisational objectives. Those interested in following up any of the topics in more detail can read the original research from which the book has drawn its evidence and continue to keep up-to-date as more research is published every year. Coaching is influenced by many disciplines including adult learning, leadership, management, and psychology, and relevant research is published in an equally broad range of journals and databases. Keeping up-to-date is thus an increasingly challenging task but one which specialisation and membership of professional associations can help address.

As noted in this chapter, there is a need for more research in many areas relating to coaching and mentoring. This research should not be conducted solely by academics. It is the collaboration of academics and practitioners in rigorous ethical research which will provide the foundation for evidence-based coaching and mentoring. In this way, coaching and mentoring will strengthen their reputation as ethical and credible offerings which will enhance the experience and the achievements of individuals, teams and organisations.

Useful links

The links in this chapter highlight resources to support learning about standards, evaluation and supervision.

Australian New Zealand Institute of Coaching – http://www.anzicoaching.com/furtherinfo/how-do-i-maintain-my-accredited-status/

Defines requirements for supervision for different levels of accreditation.

Association for Coaching – http://www.associationforcoaching.com/pages/accreditation/ac-coach-accreditation

Accreditation requires reflective statement, supervision log and reference from coaching supervisor.

David Clutterbuck – http://www.davidclutterbuckpartnership.com/articles-blogs/

Includes blog on evaluating mentoring.

Coaching and Mentoring Network – http://www.coachingnetwork.org.uk/resource-centre/articles/ViewArticle.asp?artId=80

Summarises measures which can be used to evaluate coaching effectiveness at individual, team and organisational level.

European Mentoring and Coaching Council – http://www.emccouncil.org/eu/en/15

Includes template for reflection and professional development log.

International Coach Federation – http://www.coachfederation.org/credential/landing.cfm?ItemNumber=2212&navItemNumber=2241

Includes duties of a coaching supervisor and guidelines for selecting a supervisor.

Mentoring Association – http://mentoring-association.org/standards/

Guidelines for mentoring programs.

Worldwide Association of Business Coaches – http://www.wabccoaches.com/

Guidelines for supervision in professional development.

References

Apthorpe, L. (2011) *Can coaching behaviours exist naturally within an organisation?* Master of Business Coaching Unpublished Research Report. Sydney, Sydney Business School, University of Wollongong.

Blackman, A. (2006) 'Factors that contribute to the effectiveness of business coaching: the coachees perspective', *The Business Review*, Cambridge, 5(1): 98.

Bluckert, P. (2005) 'Critical factors in executive coaching – the coaching relationship', *Industrial and Commercial Training*, 37(6/7): 336–40.

Clutterbuck, D. (2009) 'The use of internal resources for coaching and mentoring', *Global Focus: The EFMD Business Magazine*, 3 (Special Supplement: The role of corporate coaching in business): 3–6.

Clutterbuck, D. and D. Megginson (2011) 'Coaching maturity: an emerging concept', in L. Wildflower and D. Brennan (eds) *The handbook of knowledge-based coaching*. San Francisco, CA, Jossey-Bass.

Connor, J. and J. Pokora (2012) *Coaching and mentoring at work*. Maidenhead, Open University Press.

de Haan, E. and A. Duckworth (2013) 'Signalling a new trend in executive coaching outcome research', *International Coaching Psychology Review*, 8(1): 6–19.

De Meuse, K. P., D. Guangrong and R. J. Lee (2009) 'Evaluating the effectiveness of executive coaching: beyond ROI?', *Coaching: An International Journal of Theory, Research and Practice*, 2(2): 117–34.

Eby, L. T., T. D. Allen, S. C. Evans, T. Ng and D. DuBois (2008) 'Does mentoring matter? A multidisciplinary meta-analysis comparing mentored and non-mentored individuals', *Journal of Vocational Behavior*, 72(2): 254–67.

EFMD (2009) *The use of internal resources for coaching and mentoring in European companies.* Brussels, EFMD.

Ely, K., L. A. Boyce, J. K. Nelson, S. J. Zaccoro, G. Hernez-Broome and W. Whyman (2010) 'Evaluating leadership coaching: a review and integrated framework', *The Leadership Quarterly*, 21(4): 585–99.

EMCC (2010) 'EMCC Guidelines on Supervision', European Mentoring and Coaching Council. Retrieved 15 January 2012.

Evers, W. J. G., A. Brouwers and W. Tomic (2006) 'A quasi-experimental study on management coaching effectiveness', *Consulting Psychology Journal: Practice & Research*, (Summer): 176–82.

Feldman, D. C. and M. J. Lankau (2005) 'Executive coaching: a review and agenda for future research', *Journal of Management*, 31(6): 829–48.

Fogleman, J. A. (2006) *An analysis of business coaching evaluation methodologies.* University College, Denver, University of Denver. Master of Professional Studies.

Garvey, B. (2010) 'Mentoring in a coaching world', in E. Cox, T. Bachkirova and D. Clutterbuck (eds) *Complete handbook of coaching.* London, Sage, pp. 341–54.

Garvey, B., P. Stokes, et al. (2009) *Coaching and mentoring theory and practice.* London, Sage Publications Ltd.

Grant, A. M. (2005) 'What is evidence-based executive, workplace and life coaching?', in A. M. Grant, M. Cavanagh and T. Kemp (eds) *Evidence-based coaching Vol. 1: Theory, Research and Practice from the Behavioural Sciences.* Bowen Hills, QLD, Australian Academic Press. 1, pp. 1–12.

Grant, A. M. (2010) 'It takes time: a stages of change perspective on the adoption of workplace coaching skills', *Journal of Change Management*, 10(1): 61–77.

Grant, A. M. (2012) 'ROI is a poor measure of coaching success: towards a more holistic approach using a well-being and engagement framework', *Coaching: An International Journal of Theory, Research and Practice*, 5(2): 74–85.

Gray, D. E. and Goregaokar, H. (2010) 'Choosing an executive coach: The influence of gender on the coach-coachee matching process', *Management Learning*, 41(5): 525–544.

Gray, D. E., Ekiknci, Y. and Goregaokar, H. (2011) 'A five-dimensional model of attributes: Some precursors of executive coach selection', *International Journal of Selection and Assessment*, 19: 415–28.

Hannafey, F. T. and Vitulano, L. A. (2012) 'Ethics and executive coaching: An agency theory approach', *Journal of Business Ethics*, 115(3): 559–603.

Hawkins, P. (2010) 'Coaching supervision', in E. Cox, T. Bachkirova and D. Clutterbuck (eds) *Complete handbook of coaching.* London, Sage, pp. 381–93.

Hicks, R. P. and J. P. McCracken (2010) 'Three hats of a leader: coaching, mentoring and teaching', *Physician Executive*, 36(6): 68–70.

Kirkpatrick, D. L. and J. D. Kirkpatrick (2006) *Evaluating training programs: the four levels.* San Francisco, CA, Berrett-Koehler.

Kirkpatrick, D. L. and W. K. Kirkpatrick (2009) *The Kirkpatrick 4 levels: A fresh look after 50 years 1959–2009*, Kirkpatrick.

Leedham, M. (2005) 'The coaching scorecard: a holistic approach to evaluating the benefits of business coaching', *International Journal of Evidence-Based Coaching and Mentoring*, 3(2): 30–44.

Leimon, A., F. Moscovici and G. McMahon (2005) *Essential business coaching*, Hove, Routledge.

Levenson, A. (2009) 'Measuring and maximizing the business impact of executive coaching', *Consulting Psychology Journal: Practice & Research*, 61(2): 103–21.

McGurk, J. (2011) 'Real-world coaching evaluation', *Training Journal*: 70–4.

Megginson, D. and Clutterbuck, D. (2006) 'Creating a coaching culture', *Industrial and Commercial Training*, 38(5): 232–37.

Niemes, J. (2002) 'Discovering the value of executive coaching as a business transformation tool', *Journal of Organizational Excellence*, 21(4): 61–9.

Olivero, G., K. D. Bane and R. E. Kopelman (1997) 'Executive coaching as a transfer of training tool: effects on productivity in a public agency', *Public Personnel Management*, 26(4): 461–9.

Parker-Wilkins, V. (2006) 'Business impact of executive coaching: demonstrating monetary value', *Industrial and Commercial Training*, 38(3): 122–7.

Peltier, B. (2010) *The psychology of executive coaching: theory and application*. New York, Routledge.

SAI (2011) *Coaching in Organizations Handbook*, SAI Global. HB332-2011.

Sherman, S. and A. Freas (2004) 'The Wild West of executive coaching', *Harvard Business Review*, 82(11): 82–9.

Spence, G. (2007) 'GAS powered coaching: Goal Attainment Scaling and its use in coaching research and practice', *International Coaching Psychology Review*, 2(2): 155–67.

Taylor, M. (2011) *The influence of transformative coaching on leadership behaviour, leadership style, individual and team engagement*. University of Stellenbosch Business School. Stellenbosch, University of Stellenbosch. Master of Philosophy (Management Coaching).

Thach, E. C. (2002) 'The impact of executive coaching and 360° feedback on leadership effectiveness', *Leadership & Organization Development Journal*, 23(4): 205–14.

Underhill, C. M. (2006) 'The effectiveness of mentoring programs in corporate settings: a meta-analytical review of the literature', *Journal of Vocational Behavior*, 68: 292–307.

Wales, S. (2003) 'Why coaching?', *Journal of Change Management*, 3(3): 275–82.

Wycherley, I. M. and Cox, E. (2008) 'Factors in the selection and matching of executive coaches in organisations', *Coaching: An International Journal of Theory, Research and Practice*, 1(1): 39–53.

Zachary, L. J. (2005) *Creating a mentoring culture*. San Francisco, CA, Jossey-Bass.

INDEX

Note: the letter 'f' after a page number refers to a figure; the letter 't' refers to a table; the letter 'v' refers to a vignette.